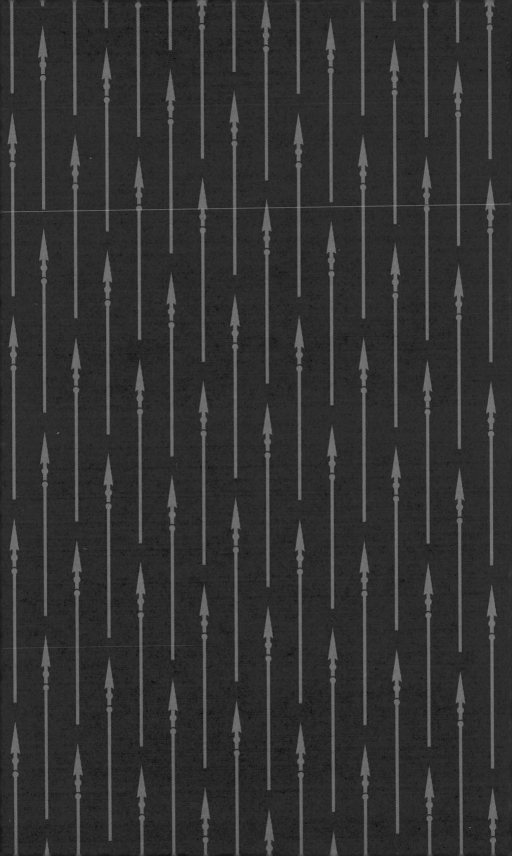

BECOMING
ELISABETH
ELLIOT

BECOMING
ELISABETH ELLIOT

ELLEN VAUGHN

B&H
PUBLISHING
NASHVILLE, TENNESSEE

Published by B&H Publishing Group
Nashville, Tennessee

Dewey Decimal Classification: B
Subject Heading: ELLIOT, ELISABETH / MISSIONARIES /
WOMEN AUTHORS

5 6 7 8 9 10 • 25 24 23 22 21

In honor of Mincaye,
whose memory makes me smile,
whose life represents the reality of Christ's transforming power,
and the hope that God's love and forgiveness
will flow to every unreached people group on the planet

soli Deo Gloria

Mincaye with Ellen Vaughn,
Amazon jungle, July 2019

Contents

Part Three: Being

Foreword

I was lying in a hotel bed late at night, paralyzed with crumpled sheets half-covering my useless limbs. It felt strange to welcome my heroine of the faith into the room. As she approached my bed, her Bible pressed to her chest, Elisabeth Elliot's commanding demeanor softened with her smile. I was twenty-six years old and seasoned by a decade of quadriplegia, but still, I was awestruck.

We were both speaking at the same conference, and after my talk, Elisabeth had asked to meet with me. She wanted to hear more. She had said, "Is it all that extraordinary for others to see the 'stamp of Christ' on your life? If we feel it is, what shall we then say of the state of Christendom?"

I'm not all that extraordinary, I thought as Elisabeth smoothed her skirt and sat on the bed opposite me. But her comment did cut to the heart of things . . . and that's what I admired about her. I loved her matter-of-fact way of living by daily dying for Christ. It was a no-nonsense way of looking at things. Just pull-yourself-up by the grace of God, hoist your cross on your shoulder, and follow your Savior down the bloodstained path to Calvary. And don't complain about it.

I was first introduced to Elisabeth Elliot in 1965 when, in high school, I read her book *Through Gates of Splendor*. I was mesmerized by the haunting photo of the twenty-nine-year-old jungle missionary holding her baby and staring out a window through a cloud of grief. Her husband of less than three years had just been savagely speared to death by the very Stone-Age people he had tried to reach for Christ. What drove her to remain on the mission field, and then to bring the gospel to the very people who had murdered Jim and his colleagues? Was Jesus worth it?

I had a chance to ask myself the same question right after high school graduation, when a broken neck landed me in those dark valleys Elisabeth wrote about. Sitting in my wheelchair and turning pages with the eraser-tip end of a pencil, I worked my way through her second book, *Shadow of the Almighty*. In this woman, I knew I'd get the unvarnished truth about God and suffering. I wanted to know if Jesus was worth it. True to form, her writings did not skate the surface. I discovered that she unflinchingly believed her Savior to be ecstasy beyond compare. And after reading more of her books, I heard the Spirit of Jesus whisper in my heart, "Be like her."

So now, to have a private audience with my role model was an incredible treasure. In that hotel room, we talked of many things, but landed on the shared satisfaction that neither of us felt all that extraordinary. We were simply followers of Christ who had plumbed the depths of His joy by tasting His afflictions. Those afflictions had cut deep gashes in our hearts through which grace and joy had poured in, stretching and filling our souls with an abundance of our Lord. That night, we relished the loveliness of Jesus, convinced that He was more than worth it.

The hour drew late. Elisabeth was to speak at the conference the next morning, so she stood and gathered her things. But before she left, she turned and said with her chin high, "Suffering is never for nothing, Joni."

It's a different era now. Many young people I know don't recognize the name of Elisabeth Elliot. They live in an egalitarian culture where everyone's story is extraordinary, whether it has the stamp of Christ or not. The leaders they look up to lack heroic qualities. Courage is rare. Good character, rarer. Moral purity feels arcane. Suffering should be mitigated at all costs. And if it cannot be avoided, it must be drugged, divorced, escaped from, or prayed away.

The timing of this book couldn't be better. We may not know it, but in an age of antiheroes, our souls crave an authentic witness. We long to see a follower of Christ square off against sin and stand firm against the winds of adversity; one whose ironclad character cannot be dismantled. We want to see someone in whom living for Christ and dying for Him is indistinguishable. We crave a visceral story that has meat on it. A story that rises above the average. That soars and inspires.

Becoming Elisabeth Elliot is that story. And no one can tell it better than my old friend Ellen Vaughn. She excels in writing a biography—her meticulous research skills are coupled with an ability to write that is utterly matchless. The first time I read the book you hold in your hands, it blew me away, a little like the house that flew apart when scientists first tested the atomic bomb. I was in awe of her masterly way with words, her intellect; here was a woman—though very different in personality from my hero—who wrote and thought like Elisabeth Elliot.

On the following pages, you will come to know the most remarkable Christian woman of the last century—what shaped her convictions, forged her faith, and honed an unyielding passion to win souls for Christ. To those who knew her well, she was Betty. To the world, she was Elisabeth, a captain and not a private in the army of God; a soldier among a gallery of heroes, all of them content to leave home and country in order to waste their lives in jungles and caves for the sake of gaining souls for the heavenly kingdom.

That is the husky stuff of which Elisabeth Elliot was made. This book is the story of how she became that way; Ellen's second volume will continue with the rest of her story. But what you'll read here shows clearly Elisabeth's *ordinariness*, how she was subject to the same temptations and distractions that plague us all, and what she embraced, through Christ, to become *extraordinary.*

Forty-five years have passed since my encounter with Elisabeth in that hotel room. After living long with paralysis, chronic pain, and cancer, I still gravitate to her example. At night, I often focus my faith by rereading her classic works. Tonight, in fact, my caregiver will sit cross-legged on the opposite bed and read aloud from *Shadow of the Almighty.* When the book is closed and I am turned in my bed, the lights out, her words will shimmer in my heart.

As you read Ellen's story of Elisabeth's early years, I hope you'll breathe in a fresh sense of God's grace and utter reality in a weak and distracted world. I hope you'll be convinced that the same grace which sustained a young Betty Elliot to become a captain in God's army will in fact whisper to your soul, "Be like her."

Joni Eareckson Tada
Joni and Friends International Disability Center
2020

PART ONE

Beginning

CHAPTER 1

Death in the Afternoon

It was April 11, 1948, in Wheaton, Illinois, thirty miles west of Chicago. Jim Elliot was a junior at Wheaton College, a star wrestler, Greek major, poet, and jokester. He and three friends—another Jim, Walt, and Hobey—laughed and kidded one another as they piled into Hobey's 1946 Nash, a classic mid-century American car with big rounded bumpers and a three-speed manual transmission. They were headed to a local hospital to visit patients and tell any who cared to hear about Christ.

The Nash arrived at the President Street train crossing near Wheaton's campus. The Chicago and North Western Railway served area commuters, as well as hauling tons of produce from the west through Chicago, the gateway to the east.

The signal lights flashed; the boys could see that the heavy freight train was at least a block and a half away. Like twenty-year-olds every-where, they went for it. The train watchman ran out of his shack at the crossing and down onto the tracks, yelling and waving them back. Hobey jolted to a stop in the middle of the tracks to avoid hitting him.

Trying to get off the tracks, Hobey panicked and stalled the Nash. He could not get the clutch to engage. Jim, Walt, and Jim threw open their doors, leapt out, and rolled to safety, yelling for their friend to follow. Hobey tried to start the car again.

As the watchman and the boys screamed, there was the added shriek of metal on metal as the freight train's engineer tried desperately to brake. In the last second before impact, Hobey threw open his car door and jumped clear.

The enormous freight train hit the Nash on the right rear fender, spinning the sturdy car so fast that it hit again on the left front fender, crushing it like a soda can. Instead of sudden death on a Sunday afternoon, their blood blotting the railroad tracks, the boys were merely "spun and sobered," as Jim Elliot wrote to his parents later.

It was a "narrow escape," he said. "The details are fairly accurate in the papers, but newspapermen know nothing about the ministering spirits sent by the Maker of the universe" to protect His people.

"It sobered me considerably to think that the Lord kept me from harm in this," Jim concluded. *"Certainly He has a work that He wants me in somewhere."*[1]

JANUARY 5, 1956

Missionary Jim Elliot, now twenty-eight, stands ankle deep in the Curaray River, somewhere in the mysterious green rainforest of eastern Ecuador. He has found the work for which God saved his life on those Wheaton train tracks eight years earlier.

Clad only in his underwear because of the heat, phrasebook in one hand, he's shouting out expressions of friendship and good cheer, the equivalent of "we come in peace." The four missionaries with him— Nate, Ed, Pete, and Roger—laugh as Jim bellows his heart out to the unresponsive jungle, slapping at a million gnats as he does so.

Jim preaching to the jungle, January 1956

This extreme camping trip is the culmination of years of prayers, hopes, and planning. Each of these missionaries, already working with other indigenous tribes, has developed an unlikely attraction to an unreached people group known as the Aucas, or *naked savages*, who had lived in Stone Age isolation for generations, killing all outsiders who attempted to enter their territory.

The tribe would later be known by their actual name, the Waodani,[2] or *the People*. "Auca," used many years ago in Ecuador, is now understood as an offensive term.*

These five young missionaries believe that the violent Waodani story can change. For years, they've dreamed of introducing the love of Jesus to the tribe. They've made their benign intentions known for the past thirteen weeks, using an ingenious bucket-drop system to send gifts from pilot Nate Saint's low-flying airplane down to a small Waodani settlement deep in the jungle. The Waodani soon responded enthusiastically, sending their own gifts—smoked monkey tail, pottery, a parrot—back up to the airplane, via the bucket.

Now, with their overtures of friendship established and reciprocated, the missionaries believe the time has come to meet in person.

They've established a campsite near the Waodani settlement, and christened it "Palm Beach." They've built a tree house so they can sleep in safety. They communicate with their wives back at the mission stations by radio (using code since the channel is shared by other missionaries in the area). Due to the sensational reputation of the violent tribe, their mission to the Waodani is top secret. For now.

"Biti miti punimupa!" Jim shouts cheerfully, his broad shoulders and back to his friends, his face set toward the jungle. *I like you; I want to be your friend.* *"Biti winki pungi amupa!"* *We want to see you!*

---

*I've chosen to call the tribe "Waodani" throughout this book, both in my own writing and in my quotes of others' words from the time period when that slur was routinely—and innocently—used. If I were a historian, anthropologist, or linguist, I might not have come to this decision. Missionaries, journalists, laypeople, and everyone else used "Auca" routinely in the 1950s and '60s. The 1956 outreach to the tribe, for example, was historically known as "Operation Auca." Calling it "Operation Waodani" would be an anachronism. But it is hard, with a twenty-first-century mind-set, to read a racial, ethnic, disability-related, or any other slur and not recoil with negativity toward those who uttered it. If the missionaries or journalists I've quoted in this book who used "Auca" long ago had meant it as an insult, I would in fact have retained its use, in order to be faithful to their original *intent*. But they used it without prejudice and most often, in the missionaries' cases, with great love.

What Jim does not know is that the Waodani are a kinship-based society that has no corresponding word in their unique language for "friend." His phrases are corrupted, taught to him by a native Waodani speaker who'd fled the tribe years earlier. Living among the Quichua people, she'd forgotten much of her mother tongue, and had unintentionally mixed in phonetics that would not be intelligible to the Waodani.

So there is no response from the jungle. But Jim and the other guys have a sense that the Waodani—who are masters of concealment—are watching them.

About forty miles northwest of Jim Elliot's heartfelt orations, his young wife sits at her wooden desk in Shandia, the missions station where she and Jim work with a community of Quichua Indians. Elisabeth Elliot is tall, slender, and blue-eyed, with light brown hair, dimples, and a distinctive gap between her front teeth. Her face is full of intelligence and curiosity. She is in the right place, as there are many curiosities in the jungle.

Elisabeth has taken advantage of her ten-month-old daughter's naptime to write in her small black journal. She uses a fountain pen, her fluid prose flowing in bright teal ink on the smooth white pages.

"Jim is gone to the Waodani now," she writes. "My heart longs and yearns for him. I sensed a great gulf between us in this last month, and longed to bridge it somehow . . . I can hardly restrain myself from pouring out my love for him, telling him how I love him and live for him."[3]

But she's excited about the Waodani project, sharing the same desire as her husband and fellow missionaries that this people group have the chance to hear the gospel. She had argued that she and baby Valerie should be the ones to go with Jim, reasoning that the tribe would be far less likely to attack a family unit than they would a group of five men.

Uncharacteristically, this was an argument that she lost.

So now she waits, a woman at home.

FRIDAY, JANUARY 6, 1956

Back at Palm Beach, Jim and company were preparing for another long day of communing with insects and preaching to the trees when two women silently stepped out of the jungle on the opposite side of the river from the camp. They were naked, with the distinctive stretched earlobes and waist-strings of the Waodani.

Jim Elliot plunged into the river, took their hands, and ushered them across. Nate, Ed, Roger, and Pete welcomed them with much nodding, smiling, and vigorous cheerful pantomimes. Seeing that the reception was welcoming, a Waodani man emerged from the foliage as well.

The rest of the day passed in a friendly clash of cultures. The tribespeople had no idea what the North Americans were saying, and vice versa. But the visitors peered at the men's cameras, magazines, airplane, and gear, tried some insect repellent, ate a hamburger, and drank some lemonade. The man even went for a spin with Nate in his plane; as they skimmed over the Waodani village, he leaned far out from the Piper, shouting and waving at his astonished tribesmen below.

Later in the afternoon, the young woman got up and abruptly headed into the jungle. The man followed her. The older woman stayed with the missionaries, chatting away. She slept by the campfire that night when the missionaries climbed up into their tree house, thirty-five feet off the ground.

Buzzing with excitement, the missionaries could hardly sleep. It was the first friendly contact with this untouched, violent tribe. They prayed it would be the beginning of a great new frontier for the gospel.

SUNDAY, JANUARY 8, 1956

At her home in Shandia, Elisabeth Elliot bathed little Valerie and tidied up. She prayed for Jim, Nate, Ed, Pete, and Roger.

Back at Palm Beach, the long, hot day before had passed without a follow-up visit from the Waodani. But on this Sunday morning, January 8, when Nate Saint flew out over the jungle canopy, he spotted a group of naked people fording the river, moving in the direction of Palm Beach.

He buzzed back to the camp. "This is it," he shouted to Jim, Pete, Ed, and Roger when he landed. "They're on their way!"

Nate radioed his wife with an update at 12:30 p.m. He told her of spotting the group of Waodani. "Pray for us," he said. "This is the day! Will contact you next at 4:30."

The event that some say galvanized the Christian mission movement for the second half of the twentieth century took less than fifteen minutes. Days later, the search and recovery party found the carnage. When they fished Nate's bloody body out of the Curaray River, his watch had stopped at 3:12 p.m.

CHAPTER 2

Discovering the Story

When Jim Elliot and his fellow missionaries took their last breaths on that January day so long ago, no one knew they were gone except for the people who'd killed them. Elisabeth Elliot and the other wives continued their usual duties, teaching classes, manning the radio, taking care of small children. They prayed earnestly for their men, not knowing that they had already passed beyond the realm of needing prayers.

It wasn't until five days after the attack that the wives knew for sure that all their husbands were dead. The rest of the world learned right along with them. Even in that time long before the internet, headlines and radio reports about the missing Americans had already flashed around the globe, with thousands praying for the men to be found safe.

Back then missionaries weren't just an anachronistic oddity tolerated on the fringes of culture. *Life* magazine, one of the premier mainstream media vehicles of the day, rushed its best photojournalist to Ecuador to cover the story. He joined the recovery party along with the U.S. and Ecuadorian army troops, missionaries, and Quichua Indians who trekked into the jungle, guns cocked, to search for the missing men. The searchers—and the wives waiting back at the mission station—hoped against hope that some of the men had survived. But then, one by one, the missionaries' bodies were found in the river, the spears that killed them still embedded in what was left of their flesh. They were identifiable only by their wedding rings, watches, and tattered clothing.

"Go ye into all the world," *Life* magazine reported, quoting from the King James Version of the Bible. "Five do, and die."[1]

Some months later, mainstream New York publisher Harper & Brothers commissioned recently widowed Elisabeth Elliot to write an account of the men's story. She did so, improbably, in about six weeks in a Manhattan hotel room. With anxious editors breathing down her neck, she skillfully wove together the missionaries' journals and other writings against the backdrop of their growing conviction that God wanted them to make contact with a tribe known for its history of killing all outsiders. The story of the men's plans, their families, and the quickening pace of the journey toward the result readers already knew—the speared bodies floating in the river—made for a dramatic, unforgettable read. Filled with powerful black-and-white photographs, *Through Gates of Splendor* shot to the top of the bestseller lists, and is still known as one of the seminal Christian books of the twentieth century.

Elisabeth Elliot may have been a missionary, a linguist, a wife, and a mother, but *Through Gates of Splendor* revealed that she was something else as well: a powerful writer. Her prose was skillful, unsentimental, muscular. Her observations rang true. And her clear-eyed portrayal of a set of individuals absolutely sold out to obey God, no matter what, captured the imagination of a generation.

Elisabeth would go on to write dozens of books over the course of her life. She spoke at conferences, retreats, and seminars all over the world—300 days a year—all while hosting a long-running radio show. The *New York Times* called her a "tenacious missionary in the face of tragedy." She challenged, infuriated, awakened, and emboldened readers and listeners for decades.

All this started in the 1950s, a time when women wore starched dresses, bobby pins, and pearls. Jungle missionaries were no exception.

After the deaths, Elisabeth, tall and tidy in her shirtwaist dress, returned to work among the Quichua Indians, where she and her husband Jim had planted a church. Elisabeth taught classes, did medical work, and worked on Bible translation with the local believers, now led by an indigenous pastor Jim had discipled. Her daughter Valerie, ten months old when her dad was killed, was now a toddler. While working with the Quichuas, Elisabeth prayed some unlikely prayers. One of them went something like this: "Lord, if you want me to do something—anything—about the Waodani, I'm available."

One sunny day in 1957, two Waodani women walked out of their tribal lands and into a remote Quichua village. Several Quichua men trekked to where Elisabeth was staying, anxious to let her know of this extraordinary development. Elisabeth left her daughter Valerie with a friend, hurriedly packed her carrying net with supplies, and walked six hours to the settlement where the Waodani had appeared. She brought the two Waodani women back to live with her. Over several months, she began to learn their language. Slowly. The two native women became anxious to return to their tribe. They eventually invited Elisabeth and her fellow missionary, Rachel Saint (sister of Nate Saint), to come live with them among the Waodani.

Most of us would have wanted hard assurances that contact between the violent tribe and the North American "foreigners" would go better than it had in January 1956. There were none.

After much prayer and many feverish pages of journal exposition, Elisabeth Elliot believed that God was in fact directing her to live with the tribe. So she trekked deeper into the jungle with her tiny blond sprite of a daughter . . . to meet the very people who had killed her husband and friends.

When Elisabeth and Rachel went to dwell among them, many of the Waodani—and most of the men who had speared the missionaries—saw a new way to live. They saw that Elisabeth and Rachel did not want vengeance for the deaths of their loved ones. They saw that forgiveness was the way out of the endless cycle of dark violence that had terrorized their tribe. Many stopped spearing; they decided to follow Jesus, who was speared for their sins, and to walk on God's trail.

I was not yet on the planet in January 1956, but I grew up, like Elisabeth, in a Christian family that constantly hosted missionaries from faraway lands. I grew up hungry for exotic cultures. I loved how the Holy Spirit relentlessly drew people to Jesus regardless of their context or background. I was curious: how did these stories unfold, *really*?

I read some of Elisabeth Elliot's books as a teenager, but I didn't think I could adhere to the disciplines she upheld. As a young professional, I heard her speak at Prison Fellowship, where I worked at the time, and at my church in the Washington, D.C. area. She was articulate and intellectually rigorous, tall, imposing, and severe. No fluff. I admired her greatly, but I wasn't sure I liked her much. Little did I know that I'd one day become her biographer, and I'd discover not only the roots of her rigorous self-discipline, but also her playfulness, her ardent love of nature, her passion, and both her exquisite sense of irony and her deep, essential humor. I still admire her, but now I like her a lot.

Why is it important to tell her story now?

Readers who already esteem Elisabeth Elliot will perhaps discover here a deeper, more complex, and yet more relatable role model—a term she despised, preferring "visible example"—than they realized. Those who have dismissed her for the "traditionalism" of some of her views, or those who loathed her books on womanhood, will perhaps find someone with whom they still disagree, but whose authentic spiritual pursuit they can admire.

And what of all those who have never heard of her? On a cold and blustery day, I wandered through the campus of Wheaton College, once Mecca for all things evangelical, and alma mater for many of the Christian leaders of the twentieth century, including Jim and Elisabeth Elliot. I stood near the student housing at Saint and Elliot apartments, sipping a latte.

"Excuse me," I'd call out to students passing by. "I'm conducting a survey." Eager to help, they'd pause for a moment.

"Do you know who Elisabeth Elliot is?"

The response was almost always the same.

"Oh, gosh, no, sorry! What year is she?"

I'd follow up, "Well, how about Jim Elliot?" (I didn't mention that we were standing in front of a building named for him.) A few students nodded, perhaps thinking of the huge mural in their student center that depicts Wheaton grads like Jim who went on to do heroic things for Christ and His kingdom.

"Oh, yeah, the guy who got speared, right?"

After Elisabeth's death in 2015, I visited her home on the rocky, north shore of Boston. There was a long object lying along the length of a heating duct near the floor.

I asked if I could pick it up.

A spear, one of many, that killed Jim Elliot.

My heart beat faster. The smooth wood, the heft of the eight-foot shaft, the sharp, slender, notched tip . . . it was a sacramental moment, handling this physical object that spoke to me of a spiritual transaction in the heavenlies that I could not begin to understand.

I knew, standing in Elisabeth Elliot's home, with her favorite books, her piano, her teacups, and the wild ocean she loved just beyond the picture window, that those long-ago deaths in the jungle were just *part* of her story. For Elisabeth, as for all of us, the most dramatic chapters may well be less significant than the daily faithfulness that traces the brave trajectory of a human life radically submitted to Christ.

I wanted to introduce this gutsy woman of faith to a generation that does not know her. Was she perfect? By no means. Was she committed to living her life flat-out for Christ, holding nothing back? Yes. She was curious, intellectually honest, and unafraid. Not just about living with naked people who could kill her while she slept, but unafraid that the quest for Truth might lead her to an inconvenient conclusion.

Not to say too much on the overworked subject of generational stereotypes, but it's been said that many—not all—Baby Boomers are tribal, in the sense that we tend to find our "group" and stick with it. Particularly in the Christian subculture, many of us grew up being told who was doctrinally pure and who wasn't. Who had been born again, and who had not. Once a brand was approved for the evangelical tribe, all was well. The bestseller lists in evangelical publishing's heyday were dominated by white men (and a few white women) whose books could have contained just about anything. As long as the approved name was on the cover, sales were assured.

Elisabeth Elliot was one of those names. But she actually has more in common with Millennials and the generations that follow than she does with the Baby Boomers who first bought her books.

In contrast to the Boomers, younger believers are generally more skeptical. They're not looking for a seal of approval from some authority figure, or the imprimatur of a certain brand. They evaluate material on its merits, regardless of where it comes from, and then make their choice.

Elisabeth Elliot was that type of thinker. She spoke the truth as she believed God gave her discernment to see it, fully willing to anger either conservatives or progressives. She didn't play to her base. She traveled to the Middle East and wrote what she saw there, not what she was supposed to see. She saw the cultures of indigenous peoples in the Amazonian jungle with a remarkably "modern" eye, always seeking to distinguish between what was gospel truth and what was cultural overlay. She chafed at triumphalism or hyped sentimentality in missionary stories. She tried to report what was true, even if people didn't want to hear the unadorned version.

She was far from perfect. She made plenty of mistakes, some private, as well as some that were subject to public scrutiny because of her role as a well-known author and speaker. She mourned over her gaffes and errors but didn't fall into the trap of tiresome self-focus.

Alas, she would mourn in her journal, *I am ridiculous; God help me!* And then she would move on, like the apostle Paul, who mourned over the wretched man that he was but didn't stay there. For Paul it was all about Christ. The same was true for Elisabeth Elliot.

She was equally at home in an erudite New York exhibit opening as she was in a jungle hut surrounded by naked Indians, which is to say that she felt like an outsider in either place. She was most comfortable in her own home, and though she was a prolific author, she would far rather wash up the tea-cups and dust the parlor than sit at her desk and write. She loved a world that still had proper parlors and china cups and mourned its passing.

She reveled in both long-dead mystical writers and cutting-edge novelists. She celebrated the great heights of the classics, reading Plato or Sophocles in the original Greek; she loved the patois of conversations overheard in an airport. A skillful mimic, she could replicate accents, cadences, word usage, and speech patterns of everyone from British royalty to New York cab drivers.

Yet in the weakening years of her once-strong life, she lost language altogether, retreating into the silence of her particular experience of dementia.

She was a person who accepted that the Lord gives and the Lord takes away with equanimity. From the formation of her complex personality, she did not give much sway to feelings. Some thought this meant she did not have any. Her journals reveal otherwise. She was host to wild, passionate, sometimes untrammeled emotions. But regardless, her actions emerged not from the ebb and flow of her passions, but from what she believed to be God's will. As a college co-ed it was, *Love this man . . . but wait five years for him to make up his mind to marry you. As a new widow, Go into the jungle and live with the tribal people who killed your husband and his colleagues. And take your tiny daughter with you.*

Her life played out against backdrops as various and exotic as a palm-leaf hut in the Amazonian jungle (long before it was considered chic by eco-travelers) to cocktail parties in Manhattan. She was as fascinated by a naked jungle woman playfully wearing a pet monkey on her head as she was intrigued by a socialite cuddling a Yorkie and sipping champagne. Her story conveys all the discipline and patient suffering for which she is well-known in the often-repeated stories about the violent death of her first husband. But her most noble accomplishment was not weathering that excoriating loss. It was practicing—through both the high dramas and the low, dull days that constitute any human life—the daily self-death required for one's soul to flourish.

It is this theme of death that gives the narrative arc of her life. This is not particularly cheerful, but if there was one empowering, paradoxical element within Elisabeth Elliot that defined her core, it was a healthy willingness to die. Again and again, if God so willed, always believing in His promise that real, robust, exhilarating life comes out of every death.

We may or may not agree with her convictions about gender roles. We might or might not cozy up to her sometimes chilly personality. Some might chafe at Jim Elliot's obtuse decisions in the course of their courtship. But in all of this, we can still admire—and learn from—the steely core of this remarkable woman. She really did see dying to self, and taking up her cross to follow Jesus—at all costs—as a biblical mandate to be obeyed. Period.

That's why her biography reflects the life and deaths, plural, of Elisabeth Elliot. Her presupposition—that we are to die to self, and it is only in dying that we actually find real life—informed her views about life choices, time management, risk avoidance, public opinion

. . . everything. This is why she was radical. This is why her life continues to be relevant today. We might disagree with some of her conclusions, but if we believe the Bible, it's hard to disagree with her core motivation.

It was a long life, with too many chapters to appreciably digest in one book. One doubts that Elisabeth intentionally lived her experiences to align with a biographer's organizational needs, but her early decades of dramatic love and loss, her countercultural choices, and her compelling spiritual journey as a human being create a first story that stands alone.

So this book tells the colorful tale of how Elisabeth Elliot came to be, through her adventures in the jungles of Ecuador. The next volume will tell the rest of the story: her later years of travel and writing, her powerful voice in the Christian marketplace of ideas, her willingness to face controversy, her unlikely mid-life marriage whose passion and joy astonished her, a devastating loss, her surprising and long-lasting third marriage, her world-wide appeal as a speaker, her strong public persona and vulnerable private trials, and then her devastating journey through the one thing she feared the most, the loss of her extraordinary mental capacity.

Elisabeth knew the challenges a biographer faces. In her little-known story of the founder of the Latin America Mission, a complex man named Kenneth Strachan, Elisabeth wrote,

> It is an awesome burden which the biographer takes up. Whatever he does will be a judgment—upon the subject most obviously, upon the biographer himself, and upon any who were associated with the subject.[2]

She told those inviting her to write Strachan's story that "unless I was given complete freedom to write about him *as I saw him*" she couldn't consider it.

This freedom was granted to her, as it has been granted in my own less articulate efforts to write about Elisabeth Elliot.

The process of writing a biography, of course, is much more than being granted permission to do so as you see fit, particularly with a story that is well known by some and completely unknown to others. Some will disagree with what I omit about Elisabeth Elliot; others will not be happy with what I include. The earnest biographer is doomed.

But in this, I take my marching orders from Elisabeth. Regarding the Strachan biography, she said,

> And so I began—trying to *discover*, not to construct, the truth about this man. The careless—apparently, at times, haphazard—shape of the life unfolded itself before my eyes

through his own writings and the testimony of those who knew him. . . . Again and again I found myself tempted to ask what my readers would want this man to be, or what I wanted him to be, or what he himself thought he was—and I had to ignore all such questions in favor of the one relevant consideration: Is this true? Is this how it really was? And of course this is the question that any writer, of any kind of literature, has to be asking all the time.[3]

Elisabeth concluded, "I have tried to lay bare the facts of the case, answering the question, *Is this what he was?* with as much truthfulness, sympathy, and clarity, as I possess."[4]

In my efforts to lay bare the facts of Elisabeth Elliot's case, I've been helped immeasurably by so many who knew her well. I've also been guided by her own voice: the free-flowing, steady, articulate hand that filled journals decade after decade of her long life, chronicling daily happenings, of course, but more surely recording the inner person shaped and honed by the God who chronicles all events. They convey a person I wish the public had known more deeply.

These journals have never been published. They are passionate, hilarious, sensual, brilliant, mundane, witty, self-deprecating, sensitive, complicated, and always . . . well, almost always . . . utterly committed and submitted to doing God's will, no matter how high the cost. For Elisabeth, the central question was not, "How does this make me feel?" but simply, "Is this true?" If so, then the next question was, "What do I need to do about it to obey God?" *Boom.*

The journals I've relied on—and the observations of others—fill out a biographical picture of Elisabeth Elliot. A biography, particularly a narrative biography like this one, isn't a series of photographs, which capture moments in time. It is more like a portrait, which captures enduring, recognizable truth about a human being. This biographer has sought the truth about a fellow pilgrim on life's journey, one who has gone before us, and tried to paint a verbal portrait of Elisabeth Elliot in both her glories and her humanity. It's not a hagiography, an "exposé," or an analysis of her theological or social views. It's a *story*: one I've tried to tell with as much truthfulness, sympathy, clarity—and charity—as I possess.

PART TWO

Becoming

CHAPTER 3

G. M. T.

"The incarnation took all that properly belongs to our humanity and delivered it back to us, redeemed. All of our inclinations and appetites and capacities and yearnings are purified and gathered up and glorified by Christ. He did not come to thin out human life; He came to set it free. All the dancing and feasting and processing and singing and building and sculpting and baking and merrymaking that belong to us, and that were stolen away into the service of false gods, are returned to us in the gospel."
—Thomas Howard

*F*rom Elisabeth's birth on December 21, 1926, in Brussels, Belgium, her mother Katharine Howard carefully chronicled her daughter's development in a hardback, light blue baby book. Its thick, cream-colored pages, decorated with intricate calligraphy and marked with precise, fountain pen notes, tracked Baby Elisabeth's progress. The photo pasted into one of the first pages shows Katharine—twenty-seven years old—propped in a brass bed against a backdrop of striped wallpaper. Her glossy, dark hair fell in a thick braid past her waist; she tenderly held a plump, rosy-lipped baby who appeared to be contemplating the nature of the universe.

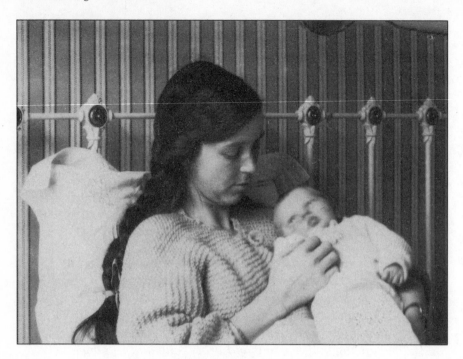

Elisabeth Howard, seven days old, December 1926

The pages go on to record walks in the park with big brother Philip, and photos with family—baby swathed in layers of ruffles and flounces, grandfather swathed in layers of tweeds, and grandma with a luxuriant bun, a broach, and sensible lace-up boots. The book's pages hold locks of fine baby hair, still glinting gold. Elisabeth's first words were at nine months, she walked at a year, and by sixteen months she had "a large vocabulary," her mother wrote proudly. It was a hint of things to come.

Katharine and her husband, Philip Eugene Howard Jr., were missionaries in Brussels with the Belgian Gospel Mission. Founded after the First World War, the Mission had combined humanitarian aid with evangelism among Belgian soldiers who'd returned home from the hideous battlefields of the Great War. It went on to found a new Protestant outreach to get the Bible into Belgian laypeople's hands. (Belgium was 99 percent Catholic at the time, and ordinary people just didn't have Bibles.)

Philip and Katharine taught Sunday school, held tent evangelism meetings, and befriended their neighbors. Their home was a fifth-floor walk-up with no plumbing; they carried fresh water up the narrow flights of stairs each day, and later carried the slop water down. Katharine had come from a home where her parents employed cooks, a butler, and a maid. She had not spent much time in the kitchen until her marriage and subsequent "honeymoon" getting started in ministry in Brussels. Philip, from humbler means, knew how to cook two things: coffee and oatmeal.

One day Katharine went to the marketplace to get her groceries for the week. A stall glistened with gorgeous pieces of salmon on ice, and Katharine suddenly remembered how delicious salmon had been at home. In her hesitant French she asked the fishmonger how much, and she agreed. He packaged it up, and by the time that she discovered she had misunderstood, and the cost was her entire week's grocery budget, she was too embarrassed to cancel the sale. Katharine and Philip dined on their sumptuous salmon that night . . . and ate almost nothing else for the rest of the week.

By the time baby Elisabeth arrived, Katharine was more acclimated to both French and her new domestic life; having already had her first child, Phil. The days passed quickly, and her baby girl—always known as "Betty" or "Bets"—grew strong.

Just a few months after Betty was born, the Howards returned to their home in the United States in response to a family need at the *Sunday School Times*. Philip's Uncle Charley was the editor; Philip would become associate editor. The *Times* was a non-denominational weekly periodical full of news stories, inspirational writing, and editorials. It was the only magazine of its kind at the time, and a recognized influence among Protestants around the world.

The family lived in a duplex in a crowded neighborhood in Philadelphia for eight or nine years until they moved to a rambling three-story home in Moorestown, New Jersey. Philip took the train to his office in Philadelphia each day, a tall, lean figure who arrived at the train platform precisely on time, his leather briefcase full of articles he had neatly edited the night before.

Life at home ran as punctually as the train schedule. Thirteen months after Betty's birth, brother David arrived, then Virginia, Thomas, and James. Each morning Philip and Katharine arose before dawn to read their Bibles. Children who were able dressed themselves and appeared promptly at the breakfast table at one minute to 7 a.m. Punctuality ruled; to be late was to rob people of their most precious possession, their time.

After the morning meal, family devotions commenced in the parlor, where no stray toast crumbs might mar the proceedings. There was a hymn—all the verses—with either Philip or Katharine playing the piano, Bible reading, a devotional selection from Charles Spurgeon or Jonathan Edwards, and then prayers on one's knees, ending with the Lord's Prayer. (Evening devotions, after supper, followed the same structure.)

Later in life, Betty recalled this strict regimen with admiration. Even on "the most exciting day of the year when we went to New Hampshire for our vacation, and left at five o'clock in the morning, we didn't skip family devotions. Christmas morning, we didn't open presents until prayers were done. We grew up with the understanding that the Scriptures were top priority."[1]

At night, the younger children were tucked into their beds with individual prayers and more Bible reading, then the tireless Katharine Howard would sing them the hymn that Betty would later sing to her own daughter, Valerie, when she'd tuck her into her little pallet in their jungle hut:

> *Jesus tender Shepherd hear me*
> *Bless Thy little lamb tonight*
> *Through the darkness*
> *Be Thou near me*
> *Keep me safe 'til morning light.*

Though the Howard household, with six children, was a busy place, it was never chaotic. Every room was kept in perfect order. Objects were lovingly placed on bookcases or tables with an artistic sense of intentionality. Rooms were swept, clothes put away, dishes cleaned, windows washed, curtains dusted, and shoes shined. If you wanted a rubber band, you could go to the one spot in the one drawer in the entire house that was designated for rubber bands, and there they were, neatly looped and ready for duty. Philip Howard's desk was always clear, with only a clean white pad of paper resting on its glossy surface, and two perfectly sharpened pencils stationed nearby—everything placed at perfect right angles. Betty embraced this passion for order with life-long enthusiasm, but as a child, after dutifully dusting her father's home office, she'd put the pad or the pencils back ever so slightly crooked . . . just for the fun of seeing her dad right them as soon as he came back to his desk that evening.

If the children ever complained about the rigorous standards of neatness and discipline, they were reminded that such rules were necessary for G. M. T., or "Good Missionary Training." Four of the six Howards did in fact become missionaries, and the other two became a writer and university professor, and a pastor.

The Howard home, however, was much more than an OCD training camp. All the children remembered laughing until they cried when their father would tell stories about colorful characters from their church. (Like the elderly Sunday school teacher whose poorly-fitting

false teeth clacked while she opined about Jehoshaphat and other biblical characters.) They'd howl when their mother—who had a habit of
using ALL CAPS in her oral and written speech in order to dramati-
cally emphasize certain points—would tell stories from her privileged
childhood.

Though it was a thoroughly Victorian home in its sensibilities,
Tom Howard said years later, "there was no humbug, no pompous-
ness." Mostly, he remembered, "screaming with laughter."[2]

The children knew they were loved, even without a lot of cuddling
and embracing. Betty wrote that it had not been easy for her mother
to learn to physically express her love for her children. She had not
received hugs or kisses from her own father, nor her stepmother after
her mother died when she was twelve.

When Tom Howard, Betty's younger brother, was in his eighties,
we looked together at an old photograph. It was of Tom, then about
twenty-one, when he surprised his beloved sister Betty in Ecuador
after Jim was killed. The black and white photo shows Tom, who'd
just emerged from a tiny airplane, standing with a barefoot Betty in
the jungle grass. Her mouth is wide open in a huge, shocked, delighted
smile, and Tom is grinning, too. But neither brother nor sister is reaching out to embrace the other. Instead, they are awkwardly holding
onto one another's forearms, like junior sailors learning a basic rescue
technique.

"Ah," said Tom, smiling at the memory. "That's classic. Howards
don't hug."[3]

Tom Howard visiting Betty Elliot, July 1958

Philip Howard, their father, was an amateur ornithologist. He'd lost an eye due to a teen-age indiscretion with a firecracker, but he'd trained himself to be more observant with one eye than most people are with two. He would stop on a path in the woods and listen, utterly attentive in the stillness, and recognize various birdcalls, or the subtle sound of the wind in the trees, the rustle of the leaves that heralded a bird high on a branch, and then he'd spot a Blue-winged Warbler no one else could have found. He taught his children to observe. After guests departed, he'd ask them what color socks one of the men was wearing, or what the jeweled pin looked like that was perched on Mrs. McDoogle's chest. Philip's children developed the habit of both the naturalist and the writer to truly *see*, to clearly perceive their surroundings and be able to describe them with exquisite precision.

Philip named the Moorestown family home "Birdsong." He had a distinct birdcall for each of his six children and his wife. Betty's was the wood pewee. (It seems fitting that many years later, when she lived among the Waodani people, they called her *"Gikari,"* or "Woodpecker.")

"Birdsong" 1954

When Philip would arrive home from work, he'd whistle a chicka-dee call. From the kitchen, his chickadee Katharine would respond with her own version of the sound. Philip created a family newspaper called, of course, *Chirps from Birdsong*, and invited his kids to contribute poems, stories, news items, or cartoons. Betty's first published works appeared in this distinguished periodical.

Betty came from a long line of writers. In addition to his work in the *Sunday School Times*, her father Philip Howard Jr.'s essays were compiled into books. His father, Philip Howard Sr., wrote a variety of books and hymns, and had two brothers-in-law who were both authors. Samuel Scoville—a newspaper columnist and author of adventure tomes for boys with titles like *Boy Scouts in the Wilderness*—and great-uncle Charles Gallaudet Trumbull—with a theological book called *The Life That Wins*, an exploration of "victorious Christian living" that sold millions of copies, as well as *Taking Men Alive: Studies in the Principles and Practice of Individual Soul Winning*. Betty's great-grandfather, Henry Clay Trumbull, was the patriarch of this illustrious group. He was a tall man with a black felt slouch hat, a sociable smile, and a grizzled beard that hung down to the middle of his chest. Born in 1830, he came to faith in Christ in his early twenties and was ordained in 1852. During the Civil War, he became chaplain of the 10th Connecticut Regiment, stationed in North Carolina. He was captured by the Confederates at the Battle of Ft. Wagner and held in a southern prison for several months. After the war he became editor for the *Sunday School Times*, wrote thirty-three books, and lectured at Yale University. He was married to Alice Gallaudet, daughter of the celebrated founder of the American School for the Deaf. He was close friends with Dwight L. Moody, appeared on platforms with Ulysses S. Grant, and traveled to Egypt and Palestine to explore ancient cultures and biblical archeological sites.

Henry Trumbull's sister was a formidable woman named Annie Trumbull Slosson, author of sixteen short books with titles like *Fishin' Jimmy* and *Puzzled Souls*, best described as New England dialect stories with an inspirational point. These first appeared in magazines like *The Atlantic Monthly* and *Harper's Bazaar*. Annie was also a dedicated amateur entomologist, fascinated by the study of insects. In 1892, she helped to found the New York Entomological Society, becoming its first female member.

Given this industrious literary heritage, it's no surprise that the Howard home was filled with bookcases. Philip Howard was a stickler for proper English, and he read out loud to the children men of majestic prose like Charles Spurgeon and Matthew Henry. Yet literary greats like Shakespeare, Dickens, the Brontë sisters, and Tolstoy were absent from the Howard shelves. Philip and Katharine didn't spend time on great classic literature, music, or painting. They focused on theology, hymns, and flannel-boards.

A huge, unabridged dictionary rested in a place of honor next to the dining room table. As the family discussed observations from their day, the latest theological issues in the *Sunday School Times*, highlights from the children's lessons, birds, insects, nature, and other topics, the children were expected to look up words they didn't know. Their vocabularies grew accordingly.

Moorestown was founded by Quakers, and the speech of many of the Howards' neighbors and friends flowed with Quaker "thees" and "thous." Since the hymns and Bible readings that marked the Howard family's days were also full of King James Version speech, it's no surprise that Betty's journals address God as "Thee" and her verb forms used structures like "Thou wouldst" for the duration of her long life.

In Philadelphia the Howards attended a Reformed Episcopal Church. Betty loved the high church liturgy. In Moorestown, they went to a Presbyterian church, and then joined a small denomination called Bible Protestant. The Howards weren't picky about denominational affiliation; they just wanted a church that faithfully exposited the Bible. Betty "received Jesus as her Savior" when she was four or five, and made a further commitment of her life to Christ's service when she was about twelve.

Both sets of grandparents lived nearby. Katharine's parents resided in a grand home in Germantown, Pennsylvania, and invited the Howards for dinner every other Sunday. It was a formal affair with a maid in a white uniform; the children were made to understand that the sooner they all disappeared into the backyard after lunch, the better. Betty did not remember ever hearing her maternal grandfather address a remark to any of the kids. She called him the Grandfather Who Never Smiled.

By contrast, the Howard grandparents were warm, loving, open, and thrilled to see the children whenever they could come. Betty's father would joke about the disparity between his humble home of origin and his wife's. Ah, yes, he'd say, "While your mother was eating rare roast beef, I was eating [scrambled] eggs, fried smelts, and jelly." Though the Howards weren't swimming in financial resources, they did have a rich intellectual and spiritual heritage. Philip went to the University of Pennsylvania and earned his Phi Beta Kappa key. Meanwhile, at seventeen, Katharine—who did not go to college—was tooling around town in a sporty red Buick roadster, attired in a fetching beaver hat and a raccoon coat, all gifts from her father.

Home life was performance-driven and yet secure. As Betty grew, she was shy with strangers—though this was usually interpreted as standoffishness. She was always tall for her age. As an adult she'd often recall an incident in an elegant hotel lobby in Atlantic City when a little girl raced across the grand room to ask Betty how old she was . . . and then raced back, shrieking, "Granny, Granny, that great big girl over there is only seven years old!" As the years went by, Betty's self-image was not helped when she'd visit her father's office in Philadelphia.

"My, how you've grown," all the nice office ladies would say. "Soon you'll be just like your father!"

Philip Howard was 6'3".

According to Betty's brother Dave (her junior by thirteen months) she channeled her frustration by using her height to his disadvantage, cornering him against the wall, growling, "You're so . . . SMALL!"

By age eleven, Betty had begun her lifelong habit of confiding her private thoughts to paper. Her first journal was a small, black, hardbound book, "a page a day for 1938." Written in ALL CAPS at the top of the first page, a penciled warning: "THIS DIARY IS ABSOLUTELY PRIVATE TO ALL BOYS. WOMEN, GIRLS, AND MEN CAN READ IT."

The privileged pages that follow dutifully note each day's weather, and are filled with accounts of snowball fights, hide-and-seek, hop-scotch, kick the can, music lessons, and school projects. For Easter Sunday 1938, Betty stiffly reported that she wore her new suede shoes and blue straw hat, white gloves, and a blue suit "adorned with synthetic cherries." In another entry, she sounds more like a kid again: "Guess what! We went to see *Snow White and the Seven Dwarfs*! I have never seen such a swell movie. It was in full color, too. It was really peachy."

A few months beyond that, she internalized an event that was far more severe than a Disney matinee. Or, as she put it after she became an adult, "I got a glimpse of what discipleship may entail."

CHAPTER 4

At Any Cost

"If I die here in Glasgow, I shall be eaten by worms; if I
can but live and die serving the Lord Jesus, it will make
no difference to me whether I am eaten by cannibals or by
worms; for in the Great Day my resurrection body will arise
as fair as yours in the likeness of our risen Redeemer."
—John Gibson Paton

*B*ecause of Philip Howard's work at the *Sunday School Times*, visiting missionaries who were in the U.S. on furlough would often dine at the Howards'. Betty sat spellbound at the dinner table, listening to Mr. L. L. Legters tell of his years in Mexico translating the Bible for tribal people. And Miss Helen Yost, a "delightful redhead" who worked alone for decades with Native Americans in Arizona. Betty loved Sir Alexander Clark, knighted for his work in Africa by Queen Elizabeth, telling of his less-than-distinguished flight up a tree when he was charged by an enormous Cape buffalo. Their family's guestbook listed visitors from forty-two different countries. Their stories captured her imagination, merging with the accounts she'd read of Mary Slessor, and David Livingstone, working for the Lord in deepest Africa. When Betty thought of the possibility of being a missionary herself, the picture in her mind was always of a thatched hut; a hut, somewhere in the wilds of Africa.

One missionary who visited the Howard family in the early 1930s was Betty Scott. She was in her mid-twenties, with creamy light skin, shiny dark hair, and an owlish pair of round, black spectacles. The Howards knew her father—a seasoned missionary named Charles Earnest Scott. Betty Scott had grown up in China and returned to the States at age seventeen to attend Moody Bible Institute. She'd fallen in love with a fellow student named John Stam . . . but returned to the mission field without him, as he had more schooling to complete and she didn't yet know if God was leading them to marriage. She started working in China in 1931, full of promise, resolution, passion, and commitment.

The following year, John sailed for China as well, and he and Betty were married in October 1933. They lived in Anhui, a small, mountainous province in eastern China, working with poor villagers, helping them and telling them about Jesus. The Stams were apolitical, of course, but in the autumn of 1934, they were swept up in one of the many partisan convulsions of China's difficult history. It was called The Long March, a massive military retreat of the Red Army of the Communist Party as they managed a fifty-six-hundred-mile escape from the consolidated forces of the Chinese Nationalist Party. The Long March facilitated Mao Zedong's rise to power, with his eventual bloody takeover of all of China.

Communist soldiers swarmed through the Stams' village, arresting John and Betty. They plundered their possessions, including cash the missionaries had gathered for poverty relief. They told the Stams they would ransom them for the equivalent of $20,000 and forced them—carrying their three-month-old daughter, Helen Priscilla—to march twelve miles to another town, where they stopped for the night in the home of a local merchant who had fled.

The next morning, before the soldiers forced them from the house, Betty hid baby Helen inside a bundle of blankets. The communists didn't notice the baby was missing. They stripped John and Betty of their outer garments, bound their hands behind them, and marched them toward the village center.

The Stams understood they were bound toward their deaths.

Mocking villagers watched the procession. A brave Christian shopkeeper ran toward the Stams, begging the soldiers to spare them. They held a gun to his head and bound him as well. John pleaded for the man's life. The communist leader, furious, abruptly ordered John to kneel, beheaded him, and pushed Betty to the ground, decapitating her with the same bloody sword.

A local Chinese pastor discovered baby Helen thirty hours later. She was wet and hungry, but safe. Money was pinned inside her clothing. It was just enough to provide for her to get to safety. She was eventually brought back to the United States and raised by her grandparents.

Chinese believers gathered John and Betty's bodies, wrapped them in white cloths, and buried them. The gravestone that eventually marked Betty's grave read:

Betty Scott Stam, February 22, 1906
"For me to live is Christ and to die is gain."
Philippians 1:21

December 8, 1934, Miaosheo, Anhui
"Be thou faithful unto death and I will give
thee a crown of life." Revelation 2:10

The Stams' deaths made an enormous impact on Christians across the United States. Betty Howard was only eight or nine when the terrible news reached New Jersey. Within a few years, she'd internalized the story of the brave young woman who'd been the Howards' dinner guest. She painstakingly copied the radical prayer Betty Scott Stam had prayed since she was a student at Moody Bible Institute, a prayer Betty's dad had shared with the Howards. Betty pasted it into her well-worn Bible.

> *"Lord,*
> *I give up all my own plans and purposes,*
> *All my own desires and hopes,*
> *And accept Thy will for my life.*
> *I give myself, my life, my all,*
> *Utterly to Thee, to be Thine forever!*
> *Fill me and seal me with Thy Holy Spirit.*
> *Use me as Thou will,*
> *Send me where Thou will,*
> *And work out Thy whole will in my life,*
> *At any cost, now and forever!"*

It was a prayer that would become Betty's own.

CHAPTER 5

Cutting Diamonds

"My friend, the truth is always implausible,
did you know that? To make the truth more plausible,
it's absolutely necessary to mix a bit of falsehood with it.
People have always done so."
—Fyodor Dostoevsky

*H*ampden Dubose Academy, a Christian boarding school in Florida, invited Betty's Uncle Charley to speak at one of their assemblies in the early 1940s. He brought a copy of HDA's yearbook back to the Howard home, and Betty pored over the photos of palm trees, white sand beaches, aqua lakes, girls in formal dresses, boys in white suits, and small classes of students sitting on a lush lawn with their young, pretty teachers. Betty had been a bit of a loner during her first year at Moorestown High School, though she'd made the local newspaper when her poem, "My Mother" took first prize in a contest. It included slightly overwrought lines like

> When I look at my mother I think
> Of angels.
> Her hair is like spun silk.
> Her eyes surpass
> The beauty of limpid lakes.
> Her hands, though worn with toil
> Are like the lilies.

Poetry aside, at her public school Betty had no Christian kids in her classes, few friends, and zero chapel services, afternoon teas, or warm breezes. She could just see herself at Hampden DuBose Academy, wearing a sweeping long gown, sipping tea from a china cup, banked by vermillion azaleas. She did not beg—Betty was never a beggar—but she let her parents know of her deep desire to attend this lovely boarding school.

Then Uncle Charley passed away, and Betty's father was now the editor of the *Sunday School Times*. His new, higher salary enabled him to pay the three hundred extravagant dollars to cover the yearly room, board, and tuition at HDA. Betty was thrilled, though the experience would be hard. She would be on her own for nine months: there would be no coming home for Thanksgiving, Christmas, or Easter. No phone calls home: those were a luxury only for the rich or those in the most severe emergencies.

So it was that in September 1941, fourteen-year-old Betty Howard boarded the train at Philadelphia's 30th Street Station. It was the Tamiami Champion, a streamlined red and white passenger train with a dining car, observation and tavern coach, and sleeping accommodations.

Meanwhile, the world stood on a brink. Adolf Hitler had become chancellor of Germany in January 1933. His first concentration camp for political prisoners, Dachau, opened in March of that same year. Mussolini swaggered through his Fascist Italy, initiating anti-Jewish laws and aligning himself with Nazi Germany's expansionist aims. Emperor Hirohito, perceived by many of his subjects as divine, occupied Japan's Chrysanthemum Throne. His Imperial Japan had invaded China, Manchuria, Mongolia, Southeast Asia, and oil production zones in the Pacific.

Though Betty may not have followed the latest newspaper headlines and radio reports regarding these Axis powers threatening from both East and West, she was certainly aware of the effect of these geopolitical struggles in her Christian world. Missionaries throughout Asia fled from advancing troops; some were put in prison camps or under house arrest, including several of her closest family friends.

In August, President Roosevelt and British Prime Minister Winston Churchill had met aboard a U.S. warship off the coast of Newfoundland. In the midst of attacks from Germany, Great Britain feared that Imperial Japan would take advantage of the situation to seize British, French, and Dutch territories in Southeast Asia. Britain desperately needed the U.S. to enter the war.

Roosevelt publicly affirmed solidarity between the U.S. and Great Britain against Axis aggression; he and Churchill shared a common vision for the (inevitable) post-war world. But the President was constrained by public opinion at home: the majority of Americans opposed U.S. intervention in the war.

This would change, of course, on December 7, 1941, when Japan would execute its unprovoked attack on the U.S. Navy at Pearl Harbor. Three hundred fifty-three Imperial Japanese aircraft would scream into the blue Hawaiian skies that quiet Sunday morning, dropping bombs, and killing 2,403 members of the Navy, Marines, and Army, as well as civilians.

But in September 1941, that nationally unifying maelstrom was still three months away, and it's unlikely that international tensions were at the forefront of Betty Howard's teenaged mind. She was fourteen, dreaming of life among the azalea blossoms in Florida. She stared through her train's wide windows, watching towns, fields, and cows flit by, excited about her new adventure away from home.

She arrived in due time at the Orlando railroad station, a tall, shy, blonde girl sporting a New Jersey-appropriate beige felt hat, a blue wool dress, and brown suede pumps. She sweated profusely in the Florida humidity. As she emerged from the train, surveying the sea of faces at the station, a slim, dark-eyed woman—appropriately attired in a light summer dress—approached her.

"Hello! You're Betty Howard and I'm Miss Andy. We're so glad you're here!"

Miss Andy took Betty's suitcase, led her to a wood-paneled station wagon, and drove her to her new academic home in Zellwood, about twenty-five miles northwest of Orlando.

Hampden DuBose Academy had been founded in 1934 by Pierre Wilds DuBose, the son of missionary parents in China. As an adult he empathized with kids who were separated from their parents and sent to boarding school at an early age. He and his wife, a formidable woman named Gwen Peyton DuBose, created an environment where Christian kids could grow in their faith, receive a liberal arts education, and learn southern social graces. Dr. DuBose named his school after his father, an activist character named Hampden Coit DuBose.[1]

The DuBoses' school had large, gracious bedrooms, an underground passageway, swimming pool, lake, stables, a bowling alley, laundry, tennis courts, and formal gardens. The public rooms were decorated with invaluable antiques from China. Students' rooms had ruffled curtains and white bedspreads . . . which some students augmented with treasures from their homes on the mission field, such as tiger skins on the floor or African spears on the walls.

The school, like Betty's home in Moorestown, was a crossroads for missionaries on furlough, internationally known Christian speakers, and pastors who stopped into town to visit their kids. Christian leaders like Billy Graham sent their children to HDA. There were vespers (evening prayer services) every night, a private church service for the school on Sunday mornings, and a service open to the public on Sunday afternoons. Students signed pledges to abstain from alcohol, tobacco, cards, dancing, the theatre, and movies. Instead, they were to spend plenty of time swimming and canoeing on Lake Margaret, picnicking, playing tennis, basketball, and other sports, and frolicking in outdoor games under the royal palms.

The one hundred students at HDA in 1941 were divided equally between MKs (missionary kids), PKs (preacher kids), and OKs (ordinary kids). The teachers, like Miss Andy, lived in the dormitory with the girls. They were unsalaried, and not only taught school, but ran errands, planned menus, and pitched in whenever and however they were needed. Similarly, students were assigned jobs like waitressing, dishwashing, housekeeping, and ironing. The most select female student would be given the honor of hand washing Mrs. DuBose's underwear and daunting array of girdles, as well as serving her breakfast each morning on a silver tray with a starched white linen placemat and a delicately embroidered napkin.

Gwen DuBose was tall and amply endowed, a former opera singer whose statuesque form was typically swathed with scarves. She often carried a hand-painted silk and ivory fan, which she would crack open like a Ming empress if she had a pronouncement to make.

However, the school's motto was Latin rather than Chinese. *Esse Quam Videri: to be rather than seem.* This integral authenticity of character that had been modeled at Betty's home in Moorestown now came into full focus for her at HDA.

"Don't go around with a Bible under your arm if you haven't swept under your bed," Mrs. DuBose was fond of saying. Young Betty, already trained as a meticulous housekeeper, further conjoined dust and sin. "What you are now is what you are," Mrs. DuBose would continue. "It's those tiny, little things in your life which, if you don't correct them now, will crack you up when you get out of this school." Dust under one's bed was bad enough, but what it represented—sloth in one's spiritual life—could run mortally rampant if left unchecked.

Mrs. DuBose encouraged Betty to write—poetry for special occasions, articles for the school paper and yearbook, speeches. Students were expected to be well-read, poised, and proper. While other high school's yearbooks might show woodenly posed rows of awkward students for their club photos, Hampden DuBose had the boys and girls artfully arranged in choreographed groups, chatting with one another as if they're on a Hollywood movie set. One would almost expect male students to be gallantly lighting female students' cigarettes in silver holders, were this not a *Christian* institution.

At Hampden DuBose, Betty learned how to arrange flowers in a Venetian glass vase, to pour coffee in delicate demitasses after dinner, to set out gleaming silver salad forks at exactly the right angles on starched, white tablecloths that she had ironed herself. She also learned how to properly pluck and prepare a fresh-killed chicken. HDA was not producing debutantes, but missionaries and Christian leaders who could bring both culture and practical competencies to the most exotic foreign setting.

Mrs. DuBose had her favorites. She honed in on students like Betty Howard, young people who could excel in spiritual commitment, education, work, study, athletics, music, public speaking, and the appreciation of literature. She pressed them ceaselessly in private and public settings, exhorting them to be their very best for God's service.

"We are hand-cutting diamonds," Mrs. DuBose would explain. Relentless discipline, pressure, legalism, and social pain were evidently her tools for doing so. Even as she loved Betty, she corrected and criticized her. She would occasionally call errant students to her bedroom; the student would stand, head bowed, at the end of Mrs. DuBose's big, white bed with its intricate carved eagle headboard. Reclining therein and attired in a pink satin bed jacket, Mrs. DuBose would review the student's sins. The kids called these "White Eagle Sessions." Years later, Betty would remember being so stressed during one of Mrs. DuBose's little reviews that she peed herself. (This did not stop the older Betty from occasionally critiquing the posture, manners, weight, and habits of those she loved.)

Sunday night vesper services were not just worshipful hymn sings; they often included times of confession. Mrs. DuBose would enter the room, unveil herself from her various scarves, and wait for students to confess their shortcomings. If a student had borrowed a roommate's stamp without asking permission, lied, or left a task undone, he or she was expected to acknowledge the sin. If no confessions came forth, these meetings could go on for hours as Mrs. DuBose waited for the guilty to come forward.

Years later, when Betty's younger sister Ginny graduated from HDA, the twenty-four-year-old Betty wrote in her journal, "It would be impossible to express just what my feelings are in this place. HDA is to me the scene of the highest delights, emotional, sensuously. It is also the scene of agonizing conflicts of spirit, devastating fears. . . . It is a world set apart. . . . My heart goes out, almost achingly, to these <u>dear</u> kids. I love my sister as never before. I am proud of her, and almost fear for her, except that I <u>trust His love</u> for her."

After Betty's graduation in 1944, students who came after her remembered the school with a combination of horror and fondness. Some say it took years to heal from the legalism and shame inflicted in the name of Christ. Others remember the love and fellowship among the students, and the great leaders who spoke at chapel services. Some question the leadership's mental health; Betty herself called it a "dictatorship."[2] Over the years HDA flourished, faltered, fell into disrepair, sold off land, and reinvented itself. Gwen DuBose, like all of us, was a mixture of strengths and flaws.

At any rate, just like the atmosphere in her home of origin, the disciplined lifestyle of HDA and its emphasis on decorum and beauty shaped the young Betty. Her first journals from boarding school have been lost, but her diary of the academic years of 1942 and '43 shows an earnest, immature young woman enthusiastically settling into her small, safe pond of academics, work, worship, and an active social life that focused on one particular senior student.

"I am so happy to be here" she wrote as her junior year commenced. "[B]ut I feel so bad. Paul is going with Nona. I like him so much . . . I admire him deeply because he is such a wonderful Christian. I will pray that the Lord will help me to get over him."

After this dark beginning, there were signs of hope. "Herbie . . . says Paul doesn't like Nona at all. I am so glad." "Last night Paul and I helped Mrs. DuBose unpack clothes . . . Paul is too wonderful for me." "He probably thinks I'm stuck-up and silly."

The Paul reports were interrupted by a note about the Duboses' growing silver collection: "Doc and Mrs. DuBose's anniversary today. [Senior High] gave them a silver goblet. They have six now."

Then the pages returned to all things Paul. "[He] was real sweet to me . . . Maybe I have some hope." "Paul is so sweet and _real_. He leads the singing a lot though he can't sing. It shows he's willing to try. It gives me the funniest feeling when he smiles at me."

As the autumn rolled on, Betty's feelings grew. "I had a long talk tonight with Ethel . . . I have felt that I am such a sham and it makes me feel awful, so we talked and cried and prayed about it for a long time. I am certainly unworthy of P."

"I wish he'd ask me [to] the banquet. I'll die if anyone else does."

She did not die. "Paul asked me!"

Uncharacteristically, Betty even threw off the constraints of good grammar to rhapsodize about Paul. "[He] talked about the moon and I liked to died."

"Paul is hot at me, and though I can't say I blame him, I feel mighty awful about it. I really am terrible to him, and he's so good to me." "Tonight Paul and I stayed out in the kitchen cleaning up till 2:00 a.m. We ate a lot of whipped cream."

"Banquet tonite! [sic] . . . absolutely wonderful. Oh, how good is the Lord." And the next day: "Sure hard to get back to studying—I thought of nothing but last night—oh, what a heavenly time I had!"

December 7, 1942: "365 days ago today [the Japanese] started war . . . Paul is so sweet . . . He is getting so serious—the way he looks at me makes me feel so funny, too. I don't know whether we should break up or not . . . He is really swell . . . I know I'm silly, I suppose when I'm older I'll laugh at this."

The journal is not entirely Paul-centric, however. There are notes about friends, staff, studying, debates, musical solos, and other activities. "Holly is darling—I really do love her. Willy Jean is the craziest thing. Ethel is certainly close to the Lord. I love her. Wenger and Carol are skunks. They are more fun—and Sarah, too! I do love Joyce." "Mrs. DuBose has certainly hit home in her vesper talks lately. She is wonderful." "Mrs. DuBose encouraged me so in my music lesson today. She's so sweet."

"I was elected president of the Junior class. It is a wonderful privilege, but a lot of responsibility. I don't feel good enough, but with the Lord I can hold it."

"We played a hot game of basketball after school!" There were also football games, swimming, star and moon-gazing, games like *Kick the Can* and *Run, Sheep, Run,* campfires, hymn-sings, and garden parties, all with remarks like "The Lord helped us wonderfully! What fun we have in Him!"

There was plenty of work as well: polishing the silver, ironing linens, dicing turnips, cutting up pineapples, cleaning carpets and curtains and sheets and dishes. And enthusiasm about the Sabbath: "I just love Sundays. The Lord is so wonderful to me."

There was occasional discord in Paradise. The journal notes that two students got into an argument about cussing, with the result that a staff member cussed them out for fighting. Another conflict merited Betty's cursory mention: "Tonight Holly and Mrs. D. had it out in [the] office. Both of them screaming and crying."

Near the end of the school year, in the midst of casual mentions of blackouts and food shortages, there are clues of the outside world and its war . . . "I may never see Paul again. When I think of [Phil] and Paul going into the army, I almost cry." This is followed rather incongruously by the breezy conclusion, *"C'est la guerre!"*

"What will it be like when Paul is in the Army?" "Paul got a letter from War Dep't. in Washington saying he'd gotten a high enough rating on his I.Q. test to give him Officer's Candidate Specialized

Training!!!! What wonderful news. Think of his opportunities to witness for the Lord!"

Near the end of May, Betty wrote, "Paul gave me a beautiful corsage of red roses! He walked me home and told me this year had been all he wanted. That I was everything to him. Came upstairs and cried on balcony."

The small, worn black diary with the microscopic writing ends with the last day of Betty's junior year of high school. June 1, 1943. "Graduation tonight—Paul was salutatorian, got general excellence award. I got music and debate awards . . . our last night together—he told me he loved me."

Few of us would want our teenage journals published. And for long-term Elisabeth Elliot fans, it's a bit hard to imagine the austere, stalwart, Jim Elliot-loving, *Passion and Purity* author was once a teen girl gushing over a high school romance. It was hard for Elisabeth Elliot to imagine as well. She mis-remembered parts of her own youth, and thought of her younger self as an anti-social wallflower who'd had NO interest in, nor attention from, the opposite sex. When she re-read her own journals much later in her long life, she'd occasionally jot notes in the margins, such as, "had not remembered that I dated this much!"

The most lasting effect of the formative HDA years, however, did not come from a romance, but from the heroic Irish missionary and writer, Amy Carmichael.

Mrs. DuBose often quoted from Carmichael's books in her Sunday vesper talks. Betty was captivated, and Mrs. DuBose lent her the books. They drew Betty with a spiritual magnetism; Amy's bold life gave radical weight to her words.

"She was a down-to-earth mystic whose beautiful writings captivated my imagination," Betty said many years later. "The uncompromising claim of Christ and the cost of discipleship drew me. I was very powerfully drawn by the message of the cross and unconditional surrender and discipleship. . . . There's so much that's wishy-washy . . . but there was something so clean and pure and steel-like in Amy Carmichael's absolutely flintlike determination to be obedient."[3]

Betty felt she owed to Amy Carmichael what C. S. Lewis once said he owed to writer George MacDonald: as great a debt as one can owe another. "She was my first spiritual mother. She showed me the shape of godliness."[4]

Betty had known about Christ's cross, and sung great hymns about its theology, all her life. But now, she saw that being crucified with Christ, as the Scriptures say, was not morbid but in fact the very gateway to life itself. She saw glimpses of an invisible world that she instinctively recognized to be far more *real* than the everyday environment in which she lived her teenaged life.

In Amy Carmichael, Betty had found a worldview as well as a radical life that demonstrated its convictions. Amy Carmichael lived what she believed. Her writings made profound, counterintuitive and yet deeply intuitive sense to Betty, becoming both an evaluative framework for her own perceptions of outside events, and an inner bridle to tame her thoughts and feelings. Both of these were rooted in Amy's countercultural understanding of life on this earth, which Betty took to heart:

> "All that grieves is but for a moment;
> All that pleases is but for a moment;
> Only the eternal is important."

Amy Carmichael was born into a wealthy family in Northern Ireland in 1867. Her parents were sincere Christians who taught Amy about the love of God. As a teenager, Amy decided to follow Christ. Her reading of the Scriptures gave her compassion that first led her to work with "shawlies," poor girls who worked in the mills for fourteen hours a day and were shunned by polite society. She led many to Christ and established a Welcome Hall where they could meet and grow in their understanding of Jesus.

When Amy was twenty, she heard Hudson Taylor, founder of the China Inland Mission, speak about spreading the truth about Jesus around the world. She eventually made her way to the mission field in Japan. There, in her small room, she wrote two words on the paper wall: "Yes, Lord."

She became very ill and had to leave Japan. She recovered over time in England, sailed to Ceylon, and then finally India, where she could better tolerate the climate. (She suffered from neuralgia, which caused debilitating joint pain.) In India, as in Japan, she bucked against conventional missionary trends of her day. She wore Indian clothes, ate what Indians ate, and traveled as Indians traveled. She lived with Indian women who had come to Christ and were threatened by their Hindu families. She suffered what they suffered.

Soon she met Preena, a little girl who had endured one of the great societal evils of the day. Preena's widowed mother had given her to a Hindu temple, where she was "married to the god" and served as a temple prostitute. Preena had tried to run away, but had been caught and branded with a red-hot poker. Somehow she made her way to Amy Carmichael, who took her in . . . and the next child, and the next. The need for rescue and restoration was enormous.

In 1901 Amy established a refuge for children, taking in at first girls, and then boys as well. She called it Dohnavur.

This work of rescue and love did not come easy. Amy wrote,

> I would never urge one to [evangelize among those who don't know Christ] unless he felt the burden for souls and the Master's call, but oh! I wonder so few do. It does cost something. Satan is tenfold more of a reality to me today than he was in England, and very keenly that awful home-longing cuts through and through one sometimes—but there is a strange deep joy in being here with Jesus. Praising helps more than anything. Sometimes the temptation is to give way and go in for a regular spell of homesickness and be of no good to anybody. Then you feel the home prayers, and they help you to begin straight off and sing, "Glory, glory, Hallelujah," and you find your cup is ready to overflow again after all.[5]

Today the Dohnavur Fellowship continues. Led and staffed by indigenous leaders, its website and Facebook page honor Amy Carmichael and the conviction she wrote on her wall during her very first missions posting in Japan, over one hundred years ago:

> *Yes, Lord.*
>
> She went on obeying, although at first she had to face much opposition and danger. . . . As she learnt more of the plight of innocent children, her heart burned with God's own love and indignation, and she wrote words which stirred others to come and join her. . . . From the beginning it was a family, never an institution. Amy was the mother, loving and loved by all. Baby nurseries led on to cottage homes, schools for all ages from toddlers to teenagers, a dairy farm, rice lands, fruit and vegetable gardens, tailoring departments, kitchens, laundries, workshops, and building offices with teams of builders, carpenters and electricians.[6]

Amy Carmichael wrote nearly forty books and lived in India without a furlough for fifty-five years. She died there in 1951, age eighty-three. At her request, her grave has no marker, just a birdbath over it with the simple inscription "*Amma*," "mother" in the Tamil language. (By the year of Carmichael's death, Betty was on her way to the mission field herself, steeled and shaped by her hero's life.)

Over the years, Carmichael received many letters from young people who were considering missions. One young woman asked, "What is missionary life like?"

Carmichael's concise response was not particularly encouraging: "Missionary life is simply a chance to die."

Those words resonated with the young, idealistic Betty Howard when she first read them in boarding school. And certainly she knew from her love of Betty Scott Stam that missionary life could end in death.

But what Betty didn't know as a teenager was that Amy Carmichael's words would be *literally* true in her own life as well.

CHAPTER 6

A Very Small Frog

"I am so tired of getting an education from between the
covers of a textbook alone. What we need is to begin
thinking occasionally instead of memorizing."
—Betty Howard

*B*etty graduated as valedictorian of her class.

"Ah, yes," she would say of this great achievement years later. "There were *ten* in my class."

Next stop, like that for so many Christian MKs, PKs, and OKs of the day, was Wheaton College.

"I was a very small frog in a very big puddle," Betty said of Wheaton. It was not technically a big puddle, with a student body of less than one thousand when she started classes in the fall of 1944. But like HDA, Wheaton College was a puddle producing a disproportionate amount of Christian leaders relative to its size.

Wheaton was founded by Christian abolitionists in 1860 as an institution committed to rigorous intellectual growth and deep, biblically based faith. The school was a stop on the Underground Railroad, and graduated one of Illinois' first African-American college graduates.

Wheaton's motto, *"For Christ and His Kingdom,"* captured the attention and lifelong intentions of students like Billy Graham, Ruth Bell Graham, Carl F. H. Henry, John Piper, and, of course, future missionaries Ed McCully, Nate Saint, Jim Elliot, and one Betty Howard.

As World War II ground on in the fall of 1944, Betty wrote faithfully to male friends in the service: her high school love, Paul, and a fellow HDA student named George Griebenow who'd been inducted into the Army while a freshman at Wheaton. Betty's letters to her family relayed the soldiers' bits of news from the war in Europe— "Paul's in Cherbourg now; that's all he could say."

Betty was more concerned with local matters. "Here is an account of my bill," she wrote to her mother, aghast. "Two hundred twenty-five dollars and thirty-five cents for the semester!"

"I love you lots, and trust you won't be overwhelmed with [it]. I've got to quit worrying about it—honestly, I nearly fainted when I saw it . . . still haven't received my work assignment, but hope to be able to get a good job and decent pay. It is possible to work up to 65 cents an hour. Not too bad!"[1]

Betty needed the money, but she was also heeding a letter sent to incoming freshmen from Wheaton's President Edman: "In war time it is especially patriotic to cooperate in working part-time. There will be many jobs available on the campus wherein you can serve both college and country."[2]

"I had been praying about the expenses and couldn't bear to tell you about it, but after all, the Lord sent me here, I believe, and He can certainly provide," Betty told her mother. "He 'knoweth we have need of these things.' I had to ask His forgiveness for my worrying and doubt."[3]

Aside from her financial concerns, Betty settled right in to life at Wheaton, "I think I'll be majoring in English or philosophy . . . the kids here are very friendly, and we all have a good time . . . things are going very nicely. I . . . just had breakfast—the cafeteria is in the basement of my dorm, and is certainly very clean and attractive. Maple chairs and tables with flowers. No linen, of course, but the tables are waxed and polished. I had coffee, fruit juice, toast with preserves, and an egg."[4]

Things were a bit less orderly in her dorm. Due to the number of young men coming back to college from the war, there was limited housing for women. Betty and her roomie lived in a single room; they had two beds, but only one dresser and one closet. The roommate's father owned a department store, and the roommate had the best the 1940s had to offer: striped cotton sundresses, long, full skirts, plaid jumpers, saddle shoes, loafers, peplum skirts, dozens of flowered cotton dresses, perky little sweaters, pearls, formals, and accessories of all kinds.

"[I]t just took a major effort to hang up a dress or to get anything out of the closet," Betty recalled years later. "With all your strength you'd have to shove the stuff over, and I had about four inches of the closet and she had the rest. It was a bad scene."[5]

Just a few weeks after school started, Betty wrote to her parents about a large meeting in Wheaton's alumni gym—"the Sunday Chapel

Hour, sponsored by Torrey Johnson, the man who started Chicagoland Youth for Christ. . . . I would judge at least 2,000 were there . . . quite a number went up to dedicate their lives and I think some were saved. . . . [Youth for Christ] has secured the Chicago Municipal Stadium for October 21 and they want 1,000 Wheaton kids to volunteer to sing in a choir of 2,500. The stadium holds about 60,000 and oh boy! Is it ever thrilling! What a testimony for the Lord!!! I just can't wait! Please do pray for all the youth meetings—they've had hundreds of souls already and they will have hundreds more if we pray!"[6]

Even as Wheaton offered the type of spiritual opportunities Betty was used to, it also began to open her up to the world of literature beyond the Christian classics she had read at home.

Letters from freshman year show Betty exulting over William Wordsworth's famous "Preface" to his lyrical ballads, written in 1800. Wordsworth's prose—abounding in mind-numbing sentences of stunning length, separated by thousands of commas—resonated with Betty.

> What is a Poet? to whom does he address himself? and what language is to be expected from him?—He is a man speaking to men: a man, it is true, endowed with more lively sensibility, more enthusiasm and tenderness, who has a greater knowledge of human nature, and a more comprehensive soul, than are supposed to be common among mankind; a man pleased with his own passions and volitions, and who rejoices more than other men in the spirit of life that is in him; delighting to contemplate similar volitions and passions as manifested in the goings-on of the Universe, and habitually impelled to create them where he does not find them. to these qualities he has added a disposition to be affected more than other men by absent things as if they were present; an ability of conjuring up in himself passions, which are indeed far from being the same as those produced by real events, yet (especially in those parts of the general sympathy which are pleasing and delightful) do more nearly resemble the passions produced by real events, than anything which, from the motions of their own minds merely, other men are accustomed to feel in themselves:—whence, and from practice, he has acquired a greater readiness and power in expressing what he thinks and feels, and especially those thoughts and feelings which, by his own choice, or from the structure of his own mind, arise in him without immediate external excitement.[7]

Enraptured by Wordsworth's turgid prose, Betty wrote to her mother that it was "positively out of this world" . . . "Imagine being able to express oneself as he does!"[8]

Evidently there was some pushback from home.

"You asked . . . if Wordsworth was not pantheistic," Betty responded to her mother rather patronizingly. "You have the same misconception many people get from reading some of his poetry. A few of his poems tend toward pantheism, but when his motives, ideals, and circumstances are studied, it is discovered that he was definitely not a pantheist. It's too long a story to describe here!"[9]

Katharine Howard must have written further concerns after Betty announced she might major in English. Betty reamed her out. Politely.

"Mother—you seem to have been worrying about my English major. Well, may I straighten you out on the fact that [a book she had read profiling a non-Christian leader] had positively no connection with English. It was . . . for history. . . . The only thing we're required to read for English are *Pilgrim's Progress* and a Shakespearean [p]lay. Anything wrong with them?

"And also—you suggested a Bible major. There is one paramount difficulty there—it prepares you for nothing specific. Why go to college if you're going to come out with no preparation for earning your own living? If I were to study just Bible and relative courses, I should go to Bible school. Kids who are Bible Majors are planning for the mission field and nothing else. I believe that unless the Lord has definitely called a person for the mission field, we should be prepared to meet the world on its own grounds. But mainly—the Lord definitely led me to the choice of English . . . Perhaps He will change my mind again but until then I shall continue in the way He has pointed."[10]

When she wasn't setting her mother straight, Betty was busy with the school newspaper staff, glee club, debating, singing lessons, in addition to her academic and work schedules. Again, there were cautions from home.

"Mother—you need not worry about my having too many irons in the fire. I have prayed very definitely about them."[11]

"Mother, I can't see why you think I ought to eliminate any of these activities—of all things, debate! You've no idea how much fun it is and the wonderful crowd of kids on the squad. I'd hate to give it up. . . . Of course I could eliminate any hope of glee club or singing lessons. But I hate to quit things I'm already in."[12]

Betty and her mother exchanged thousands of letters through the course of their lives. One patient researcher has identified 1,355 letters from Betty to "Dearest Mother," totaling nearly three thousand pages, over thirty-two years.[13]

Like that of many mothers and daughters, their relationship was complex. Betty could be critical and grossly insensitive, as well as loving and appreciative, toward her mom, whom she always called "Mother," while Philip Howard was "Dad" or "Daddy."

Katharine Howard, a helicopter parent before her time, mourned when she felt shut out—even in the smallest ways—from her children's lives. She would comment on how many letters she was or wasn't receiving. When her oldest son, Phil, was in the service, she'd jot him notes like "Phil dear: Do try writing by airmail. No mail has come from you for a long time and the silence is not 'golden!' I am hungry for news of you."

She would count how many letters Phil had sent to his girlfriend, versus how many he had written home. Seeing his mother's need, Phil had counseled Betty about the issue back when Betty was still in boarding school:

"I want to quote to you a piece out of one of Mother's letters to me, and then I'll explain,"[14] he wrote to his sister. He went on to quote some lines Mother had written to him about a piece of news Betty had not chosen to share with her.

"'Betty . . . didn't tell me; I heard it in a roundabout way. It hurt me just a wee bit that she didn't tell me, as I do so long to enter into the joys and sorrows of my children. But somehow I seem to fail where Bets is concerned at least. She is so reticent. However, I love her dearly, as she is.'"

"Perhaps you see already what I am driving at," Phil continued in his letter to Betty. Their mother yearned "that we children tell her everything. I have realized this before, and I do tell her practically everything of my joys and sorrows. I know you love Mother . . . this is one practical way in which you can show your love to her, so do tell her all."

Phil concluded, "I'm not criticizing you . . . I have written this to you as an exhortation, in a spirit of Christian love, for the glory of our Lord Jesus, and the happiness of dear Mother, and the good of your life as a child of God. . . . After all, what better friend on earth has any fellow or girl got than his or her mother?"[15]

Anyone who has ever heard from a sibling that he or she has hurt their mother "just a wee bit" can sense the emotions compressed between the neatly expressed lines of this missive. But the Howard family didn't talk about emotions; they exhorted one another for the glory of God.

Still, Betty felt awful after she'd treated her mother poorly, as a sampling of letters reveals.

"You are wonderful to me, Mother. How you keep going as you do and such a beautiful spirit about all your trials that are <u>many</u>! If nothing else, a daughter like me should be sufficient to drive you crazy. But you've taken a powerful lot, and are just that much sweeter for it. We kids are praying for you (your children, I mean) and I know there are other friends who must be. I am glad you have an even temper and the balance you're made in the family. For the millions [of] other things, too, about you, I'm thankful, but—just for <u>you</u>!"[16]

"I do want to thank you again for all you've done—not only materially but spiritually and every other way. I am really sorry that my continual antagonism and argumentative spirit was such a sorrow to you this summer. I know I say that every year, and every summer I act the same way. But I do thank you for having such a sweet, forgiving spirit. I never could see how you could tolerate me. But the Lord is very real in your life as anyone could see, and I love you, really I do!"[17]

"No—it would not be a <u>relief</u> if you would stop writing, Mother! . . . And I love to hear about you all—even if I seldom mention your letters."[18]

Journal entries show the gap between Betty's intentions and behavior. "My heart aches for the way I treated dear Mother. Oh, I love her so much—this afternoon I wept because I miss her so, and I felt so regretful that I had failed to show her my love. Someday I will go [far away]—perhaps to see her no more. Why do I not appreciate her when I am with her?"

CHAPTER 7

"Let Me Not Sink
to Be a Clod"

*"Humility is perfect quietness of heart. It is to expect nothing,
to wonder at nothing that is done to me, to feel nothing done
against me. It is to be at rest when nobody praises me, and
when I am blamed or despised. It is to have a blessed home
in the Lord, where I can go in and shut the door, and kneel
to my Father in secret, and am at peace as in a deep sea of
calmness, when all around and above is trouble."*
—Andrew Murray

World War II was always in the background of Betty's college life.
Letters were a lifeline for young men serving abroad, and early in 1945
Betty received a gem from a lonely acquaintance—a Private Albert
Somebody she had known at HDA.

"My dear big Betty, You see, I know a little Betty too and am
trying not to get confused. Have you grown any taller? I don't know
why on earth I'm writing to you of all people, but it is said that you
shouldn't forget old friendships . . . or maybe I'm writing because I'm
lonely and just turned nineteen yesterday. Anyway there isn't much
worse that I could be doing."[1]

Albert went on to ask "big Betty" for her picture and maybe a
couple of snapshots of "just your face—a waste of film I know but—
and the other of all six foot of you. I'm asking you because I think you
might send them to me after this nice letter I've written to you and all
the time I've put into it. Love, Al."[2]

Al followed this endearing thought with a three-page P.S. in which
he described troop activities in the Pacific—redacted by the Army

censor—and closed his pleading for a letter from Betty. "Don't be mad at me. I hope that you're old enough to have gotten over those childish things. An old burned out flame, Al."[3]

Betty made sure to write her parents about all the dramatic events of the spring of 1945. Four-term president Franklin Delano Roosevelt passed away in April: "Wasn't the president's death a shock? I heard it 15 minutes after he died and just couldn't believe it. I was thrilled that Truman declared yesterday a day of prayer and asked the newspaper men who knew how, to pray for him. A good start—maybe he won't be so bad after all. [A professor] had just said last Monday that he could think of nothing worse that could possibly happen to the U.S. than if Truman were to have been elected. And now this! We never know how God will use it."[4]

In late April of 1945 she wrote that her friend George Griebenow was "with Patton's Third Army in Germany. Says he can hardly remember what clean clothes are like, they've been marching and taking towns for so long."[5]

Around the same time, Betty's old friend Paul sent her perfume from Paris. George sent her a poem from Germany. It expressed "a great deal—more than we civilians can ever possibly know."

On May 8, 1945, Nazi Germany surrendered to the Allied forces. Though the war in the Pacific dragged on, the horrific conflict in Europe was over. Betty took her transistor radio to her French class, and everyone crowded around to hear President Truman's speech about the surrender. "It was such a thrill to me to hear how he acknowledged God's hand in the Victory. They rang the Tower bell . . . [we] sang the Doxology, a Mighty Fortress is our God and the national anthem in chapel and most of us just sat there and cried. It was so unbelievable but just think of the [war in the Pacific]—we can only pray that the Lord will speed victory there."

In the beginning of her sophomore year, the fall of 1945, Betty met Katherine Cumming, her housemother and new Sunday school teacher. The warm, bubbling, southern Katherine was very different from the reserved, East Coast-bred Betty. When Katherine had chosen to follow Jesus, she had lost favor with her wealthy family, who had disinherited her. She was much older than the students, single, a bit plump, and an enormously comforting and challenging presence—a "spiritual mother"—in Betty Howard's life at Wheaton.

Years later, Betty remembered her mentor's deep southern accent: "[She had] a very ample bosom and she was always clasping her bosom and saying, 'Baa-by, baa-by.'"[6] (Let's just say that if there was anything that Betty Howard was *not* used to as an endearment, it was being called "Baby.") But along with her warm hugs and soft accent, the gracious Miss Cumming had sharp, distinct insights into this complicated girl, and was able to communicate them in a way that the sometimes prickly Betty would accept.

"She is so completely abandoned to the Lord, and so overflowing with the joy of the Lord and a genuine Calvary love for His children," Betty wrote to her parents.[7]

Meanwhile, there were regular evangelistic outreaches at Wheaton. Betty wrote to her parents asking for their prayers: "Please pray that God will work a miracle and revive Wheaton College! We certainly need it and I know He wants to."[8] Betty noted that though some students had been critical of the speaker—"Wheaton would criticize anyone," she wrote in her journal—"the Lord poured out His Spirit in a mighty ways on this campus, and I've no idea how many decisions there were—for consecration and salvation. It is wonderful to see persons whom you did not realize were unsaved go forward. The girl across the hall from me was saved last week. The Lord has been wonderful to me, too!"[9]

She went on to describe the concert the night before in which she heard George Beverly Shea sing. Shea would become a household name in Christendom because of his many decades of solos at Billy Graham crusades.

"Mr. Shea is so real—not one of these self-exalting hail-fellow-well met-bobby soxer evangelistic soloists, but sincere and Spirit-filled. It takes plenty to impress Wheatonites, but kids really enjoyed it."[10]

Aside from spiritual pursuits, if there was ever a college activity that matched Betty's gifts, it was debate. She enthusiastically excelled in her spot on Wheaton's debate team during her sophomore year. Her younger brother, Dave, was on the team as well and they studied scintillating topics like: "Resolved: that labor should be given a definite share in the management of industry" or "Resolved: that the U.N. should be immediately made a superstate."[11]

"Boy," Betty commented to her parents. "Does that ever wear you down! I know of no more strenuous physical and mental exercise than debating. I'll admit (!) I was dead!"[12]

On a debating trip to Bloomington, Illinois, she described her fellow debaters from secular schools. "Most of men have just gotten out of service . . . the girls who are debaters all seem to be real sharp dressers, wear very red lipstick, most of them smoke, wear their hair slicked down in a page-boy or some such. Of course this is the average college girl, except that colored rim glasses and slick hair seem to be especially peculiar to debaters! It always seems so funny to be on a campus littered with cigarette butts, and to sit at dinner with ash trays in front of us!"

In addition to her studies and preparation for debates, Betty constantly read books that sharpened her. "I have been reading the book *Screwtape Letters.* . . . It certainly is clear, and really gives one an idea of Satan's subtle trickery. What a knowledge [C. S. Lewis] has of human nature! . . . The Lord has been wonderful to me lately. My, what patience He has! I don't see how He can forgive me so repeatedly when I am so stubborn, lazy, foolish, and disobedient. I have over my desk a copy of Andrew Murray's *Humility*. How proud and vain we are, I realize as I read it."

"In our prayer group . . . we have had some precious times. I have six of the most popular girls on campus in mine, and I feel so deeply my need of the Lord Jesus, in so great a responsibility. I am so completely opposite in personality and make up, to these girls, and it is a very hard task for me sometimes to correct them as I am supposed to regarding such things as being in the bathrooms after hours, radios on, loud talking, etc. I find myself so sinful, and with such beams in my own eye, that it is very hard to live consistently before them."

Then a speaker from Wycliffe Bible Translators came to campus. He spoke about "pioneer" missionaries; those who seek to reach people who had never even heard the name of Jesus.

"He gave the most unusual and challenging message on pioneering that I have ever heard," Betty wrote. Though working with unreached people groups was tough, the speaker challenged Wheatonites to take this harder road, rather than opting for already established or flourishing mission stations. "May the Lord keep before me His purpose for my life, and may I never be discouraged or sidetracked in any way," wrote Betty. "How I love this from Amy Carmichael—

> Give me the love that leads the way,
> The faith that nothing can dismay,
> The hope no disappointments tire,
> The passion that will burn like fire,
> Let me not sink to be a clod,
> Make me Thy fuel, Flame of God!"[13]

By Betty's junior year in college, several key themes in her life were beginning to coalesce. She had started taking Greek, and found that she excelled in it. She had sensed a continued pull toward the mission field, perhaps in translation work. She had learned more about her deep yearnings for beauty and a deep-soul understanding in any romantic relationship. She doubted she would ever find such a man. She also saw how diffident and distant she could be toward others. And she met, in her Greek class, a hearty fellow student named Jim Elliot.

CHAPTER 8

A Refrigerated Rose

"People cannot become perfect by dint of hearing or reading about perfection. The chief thing is not to listen to yourself, but silently to listen to God. Talk little and do much, without caring to be seen. God will teach you more than all the most experienced persons or the most spiritual books can do. You already know a great deal more than you practise. You do not need the acquirement of fresh knowledge half so much as to put in practice that which you already possess."
—François de la Mothe-Fénelon

*B*ut Jim Elliot was still in her future during the summer of 1946 when Betty reconnected with her HDA classmate, George Griebenow. George was 6'6", with high cheekbones and thick, dark hair. He towered over Betty, which was refreshing for her; she often felt awkward about her height. George had served during World War II with great distinction, and returned home as a decorated hero. He had experienced ordeals few non-veterans could understand, and he would elicit reactions in Betty that *she* couldn't quite understand. Perhaps he represented a no-man's land that she dare not enter. Whatever it was, Betty, for all her intellectual alacrity, remained fairly clueless, leaving George confused, for the rest of that school year.

But now, in the summer of 1946, all was peachy. One warm night in June, George spent the evening at Betty's parents' home, as their families were old friends. It was "heavenly to see him," she wrote in her journal. George must have thought it "heavenly" as well: "[He] wanted to kiss me."

As the weeks went by, George sent her pictures of himself, addressing his letter to "My dearest Betty." She wrote him back, "a very pleasant task." More letters followed. "I should like to see him soon," she wrote in her journal. "He's sweet."

Betty arrived at Wheaton for her junior year in mid-September. She wrote to her mother right away.

"Well, when I got back from town, I found that I'd had a call from "a man" who left no message. Later he appeared—in the person of George—and wanted two or three dates right off the bat. He got one. With that I said goodbye and he loped out."[1]

On September 20, Betty wrote her mother, "You were exasperated by my not giving details of my date! I do not mean to be cryptic; it simply was not a matter of interest to me, hence the neglect. We only went to church, and afterwards I got rid of him by 8:20! I'm afraid he's losing heart by now!"[2]

By September 22, she wrote in her journal, "Saw Geo. this afternoon. He called me tonight for a date. I just can't stand him but I don't know how to ditch him gracefully."

October 16, "The more I see of men, the more I know that as yet I've met no one whom I would care to marry. Phil [her older brother] is an ideal to me, and there are no more of his type, it seems."

A few days later she sang in choir at the Wheaton Bible Church: "Geo came . . . of course he stared holes." A student named Don came into Betty's practice room and sang with her. "He's nice," she wrote. "But what a wolf!"

In the midst of all this romantic intrigue, Betty was taking her first Greek class. It was to change her life.

"I am much interested in the language, though I face the grind of the year with some apprehension! I sat by a girl who has been accepted as a Bible translator to Peru, and attended Wyclif [sic] last summer. She is now a senior and says she felt that she needed Greek rather desperately. But she advises me to attend Wyclif [sic] next summer instead of remaining here for second year Greek, since two years is really all I'd need for a foundation for translation."

Around the same time Betty's beloved housemother, Katherine Cumming, gave her a glimpse of her future, which Betty shared with her mother. "I know you will rejoice with me when I tell you something Miss Cumming said to me today. I only tell you because it is of the Lord's mercy, and I do not feel at all worthy of such a comment."[3]

Betty had led the devotions on Hebrews 12:12 during her Sunday school class. Afterwards, Miss Cumming said, "'Betty—I think you ought to be in some kind of public Christian work. You express very deep things powerfully and concisely. You are a real blessing to me.' Mrs. Evans [another housemother] told Edna that I was one of the most spiritual girls in the school. Mother, you know as well as I do that this could not be true, but I want you to pray with me that this may become true more and more—that I may be only 'to the praise of His glory.' What a devilish thing is spiritual pride, and may the Lord keep me from it."[4]

Around this same time, as she was reading the Bible in her daily devotions, she came to Isaiah 42:6. "I the LORD have called thee in righteousness," Betty read in her worn King James Version Bible. "[I] will hold thine hand, and will keep thee, and give thee for a covenant of the people, for a light of the Gentiles." She felt that God was specifically calling her, Betty Howard, to the work of translating the Bible for people who hadn't yet had access to it.

"It gave me a new thrill to realize that I am commissioned as an ambassador for the King of kings—and new seriousness of purpose here in school, for after all, we do not have tomorrow in which to serve Him—only today! As a young person, it is often hard to keep from living in the future, with the idea in mind that things haven't really started yet—we still have a lifetime ahead. Perhaps—but the Lord gives us a moment at a time, and trusts us to invest it for eternity."

That eternal calling coincided with more ordinary calls.

"On Monday George called me and wanted a date for Oct. 19, and one for the 26th! He sure believes in getting his bid in early! I declined both, saying that it was too early to make plans for then. . . . He told Sarah . . . that he was literally throwing himself at my feet, and getting stepped on. The trouble is he never tells me personally how he feels, (which I hate), so I have no opening to tell him what the score is. I don't want to crush him if he really likes me, but I sure wish I knew how to ditch him gracefully. . . . And I definitely do not want to be "coupled" with him on campus, as the kids automatically do if they see you with a guy twice! There are others whom I should like to date who would never ask me if they thought I was going with Geo."[5]

Decades later, Betty had forgotten all this breathless dating activity. Asked by Wheaton's archivist in the mid-1980s what a "typical date" was like at Wheaton in the 1940s, she responded that, "a typical date in Wheaton was certainly not with me, that's for sure. I was definitely a wallflower. . . . There were certain girls in the dormitory who just always . . . had dates, and I was the one that never went, never had a date for anything."[6]

On December 1, 1946, Betty wrote to her mother, who had called her determined friend "poor George."[7]

"I had a date with George. He gave me a corsage of exquisite talisman [tea] roses, so I wore my blue taffeta formal. Miss Cumming sat right behind us in the concert, and told me yesterday she thought there was something 'unusually fine' about him and she thinks we 'look lovely together.' Most of the girls around here think he is absolutely wonderful and can't see my reasons for not being completely dazzled! . . . He wore a tux, to my amazement, for I never thought he could ever get one big enough."

Betty went on to describe the concert . . . a family that sang "perfectly beautifully together . . . They have very fine faces, portraying strong character and pure lives. All have absolute pitch, a rare quality."[8]

Their names?

The family von Trapp, led by Baroness Maria von Trapp, singing at Wheaton nineteen years before *The Sound of Music* movie would enshrine them forever in American culture.

It was perhaps an ironic evening for young George Griebenow. Captain von Trapp refused to cooperate with the Nazis. George had personal experience with a less principled Austrian, who had sold out his country *to* the Nazis. His name was Ernst Kaltenbrunner.

Kaltenbrunner was 6'4", with a network of scars on his angular face. A rabid anti-Semite, he was head of the SS and had managed Nazi concentration camps throughout Europe. After Hitler's suicide, Kaltenbrunner was named head of all Nazi forces in southern Europe. He had hidden in a remote cabin on an Austrian mountainside—where George Griebenow had been one of the young American soldiers who captured him in May 1945.

Kaltenbrunner was tried before the Nuremberg International Military Tribunal, found guilty of war crimes, and executed in October 1946.

Even as Kaltenbrunner was hanged, George was safe at Wheaton College, attending classes and concerts, but old Nazi memories could not help but flood his mind.

This boy Betty Howard's mother referred to as "poor George" was in fact a multifaceted man who had weathered the horrors of war. He'd been awarded Army commendations for Kaltenbrunner's capture. He received the Bronze Star for dragging a comrade out of enemy fire during a machine gun attack in Germany, and the Purple Heart for wounds he received while crossing the Rhine.

Whatever George carried inside remained a mystery—or an obstacle—in his relationship with Betty Howard. She rarely referred to his wartime service in letters or journal entries, but throughout the winter of '46 and spring of '47, she had a war within herself regarding her relationship with George Griebenow.

December 2, "Saw Geo. Just before chapel. He was sort of funny to me. He came over tonight and wanted that picture of us taken beside his airplane. He refuses to show me the one of me which he carried with him all during the war."

December 20, "On the way home for Christmas break, on the 'Trailblazer' train. Monty drove us to the station. I had to sit by Geo. on train. First I was mad—now we're having fun."

Betty—an old soul, but still a young, immature woman—turned twenty the next day.

In January, Betty's same cycle of indecision continued. She would date George, then wonder why. She wondered if she should "call for a showdown" or "let him work it out." On January 12, she wrote in her journal, "haven't seen Geo. G. to even speak to since a week ago Friday. Nice not to have him around. Oh, golly—wish I would meet the man I'm going to marry—if the Lord wants me to marry at all."

By January 26, George invited her skating. "I had to say yes, though I don't particularly want to. I hate to turn him down again! I'm not so sure I approve of roller-skating."

They engaged in this questionable activity the next day. "George took me to a skating party. I set the tone as to how we would skate, and managed to hold him off. I really do not enjoy being with him at all. Coming home we talked very little, and I know I was rude. Contradicted him. In the vestibule he tried to put his arm around me. Makes me mad."

Most of us wouldn't think of the roller rink as a hotbed of passion, but Betty was very particular about physical contact, even skating with an arm around a partner. She had written to her parents, ". . . I've found that there are few girls around here who realize the importance of chastity in every phase of our lives. No one I know, so far, feels exactly the same thing as I do toward such things as holding hands, necking, etc. I am considered quite unique and, to put it plainly—a 'sad case!' But it doesn't worry me, and I'm thankful for the things the Lord has taught me."[9]

Finally, in April 1947, Betty wrote in her journal that she and George went for a long walk, "and I told him we would have to stop dating. He told me how he had felt there could never be anyone else, and he was very serious about me. Then his eyes filled with tears and his voice broke when he tried to tell me how much I had meant to him. Now I feel terrible—hadn't realized it would hurt him."

The next day she was feeling a bit better, though still fairly oblivious. "Guess I'm getting over George gradually. Still want very much to have a talk with him to express my appreciation for all the hundreds of wonderful things he's done for me." She returned his medals and the other gifts he had given her.

George would move on. Within two years he was engaged, then married and served as a pastor with the Christian Missionary Alliance, eventually becoming head of the Small Business Administration in Minnesota. He was recognized for his lifetime of service to others decades later, when his governor proclaimed March 1, 1987 as George Griebenow Day in Minnesota.

As this romantic drama settled down at Wheaton, Betty's drawling dorm mother took the risk of being honest with her. She gently exposed some walled-off parts in Betty that the relationship with George had revealed.

"I had a long and wonderful talk with Miss Cumming about George, mostly. She certainly analyzes my personality amazingly. She read my motives in telling George off and feels I really shouldn't have done it. She is sure that he loves me deeply. She also thinks I may, because of aloofness, miss the man I should have."

Betty didn't reflect further, in her journal, at least, on the "aloofness" that Miss Cumming saw so well. That sense of reserve or detachment was an organic part of her personality all her life. Because of it, some people dismissed her as stuck-up, pious, or cold. Though her personality had none of those attributes, her abrupt behavior sometimes communicated them to others.

One explanation for this detachment surfaced when Betty was studying Jungian personality theories. "In psychology class the other day we discussed the 13 characteristics of introverts. I find that 11 of these are very true about me. It is rather discouraging to study psychology. I hope it doesn't make a worse introvert out of me. The Lord can change that in me, I know, for it certainly is a bad thing to be an introvert."

Why did Betty see introversion as a bad thing? In a campus setting, particularly in the 1940s, recognized leaders tended to be extroverts. These enthusiastic, people-energized sorts are friendly and talkative—qualities that get attention and attract others more than the introvert's tendency to draw energy from spending time alone. Typical introverts aren't shy but can be perceived so. They like people and are not intimidated by others, but can become exhausted by large parties and gatherings, the settings where the extrovert is in his or her element. They need time to recharge their batteries.

Today, there is more understanding of, and celebration of, the diversity of various personality types. People pore over the results of their Myers Briggs analysis, and post their enneagram test results. Many of us probably classify ourselves as ambiverts anyway, combining, in our minds at least, the best qualities of both personality types.

But back in Betty Howard's college days, she felt it a "bad thing" to be an introvert, and her lack of energy and abrupt silences with others did, in fact, put people off. In later years, when she would confidently appear on speaking platforms all over the world or teach multi-day seminars to thousands, many listeners expected Elisabeth Elliot to be a gregarious people-person. But, as some who would wait in long book-signing lines could attest, one-on-one she would often come across as brusque or inexplicably rude.

Her innate remoteness often hid the fact that she actually loved people, and deeply admired their talents and gifts. She humbly mourned over her gaffes and shortcomings. During college, she constantly invited people who might feel lonely or left out to come home with her for holidays. She loved her friends and looked on strangers with both fascination and curiosity.

On one hand, she had the capacity for a deeply passionate self-giving love without reserve. On the other hand, her emotions ran like a controlled river through firm and deeply channeled banks built by a discipline that grew stronger every year. The girl who wept her way through HDA had already become more reserved at Wheaton College. By the time she'd spent a few years on the mission field and confronted her deepest loss, her tears would be few and far between.

As she grew older she gave little weight to her own emotions, so she sometimes came off as insensitive to the emotions of others. But that did not mean she didn't feel them.

Meanwhile her passions—her deep response to the beauties of nature, for example, or her eventual love for Jim Elliot—were not "just feelings" to her, but a combination of intellectual, spiritual, and sensual responses to her convictions about the truths she sensed around her.

She wrote often of "being sick with loveliness" over the full moon, or a brilliant sunset. Art moved her profoundly. She wrote in her journal, "When I hear a great composition—poetry or music—I am deeply moved by the passion of its author, the pathos—and love seems to me to be too high and glorious a thing to be thought of in connection with any man I've ever known. I wonder if the Lord has someone for me."

At age twenty, Elisabeth Howard had led a disciplined, hard-working, spiritually rigorous life. She loved nature, music, poetry, books, and word play. She'd developed standards on dating and physical affection that were unique in her Christian college. She had lived exclusively among other believers. She kept meticulous schedules with timeslots for everything from devotions to study to work to exercise, 7 a.m. to 11:30 p.m., except for days she got up earlier.

She admired the professor who announced on the first day of class: "There will be no makeup work of any kind, for any reason. Sickness is an economic loss." She appreciated the debate coach who didn't affirm anyone for a job well done: "[w]e were more or less taught that when we did all, we were still unprofitable servants, which is a very healthy attitude to have."[10] She budgeted money carefully, writing about a train trip to visit friends: "I could afford to go . . . but the question is if it would be right to spend so much on mere pleasure. As yet, I'm not sure what the Lord would have me do."

She respected her parents and other authorities, but also perceived their weaknesses, and trusted more in her own analysis of what the will of God was for her. Her character bore the influences of godly— and yet flawed—women she admired. Her organized, sacrificial mother. The martyred family friend and missionary Betty Scott Stam. The formidable yet cultured Mrs. DuBose. The visionary, iconoclastic Amy Carmichael. And the sweet southern housemother steeled by grace, Katherine Cumming.

Though Betty sincerely doubted it would ever happen, she longed for a deep relationship with a soul-mate man, and for marriage. She'd drawn up an eleven-point list of her "ideal man," covering everything from his strong jaw to his love of poetry, music, literature, and nature to his "towering intellect." Her number one characteristic: "Depth of spirituality such as I have never even plumbed. Missionary."

Further, as she reflected on her older brother Phil's wedding, which would take place late in that spring of 1947, Betty wrote: [A friend] "was talking to me again today about love. There are different levels to which individuals love—I should be satisfied with nothing less than a complete and beautiful union of soul—a love of which time could never increase the certainty or decrease the wonder!"

Yearning for wonder, longing for some soaring soul-union, chafing at what was silly and less than fulfilling . . . at twenty, Betty was like a Talisman rose in a florist's refrigerator, chilled, not yet open, and not yet rich with fragrance. Perhaps that would come. Her next day's journal entry read matter-of-factly:

April 23, 1947. "Had a good talk with Jim Elliot—he is a wonderful guy. We both refuse to accept the [conventional] 'Christian life and world view.' May the Lord grant wisdom."

CHAPTER 9

Eunuch for Christ

"Our young men are going into the professional
fields because they don't 'feel called' to the mission
field. We don't need a call; we need a kick in the pants.
We must begin thinking in terms of 'going out,' and stop
our weeping because 'they won't come in.' Who wants to
step into an igloo? The tombs themselves are not colder
than the churches. May God send us forth."
—Jim Elliot

*B*etty knew Jim Elliot, a sophomore and a year behind her in school, because he was her younger brother Dave's roommate. Like Betty, Jim had decided on a Greek major as a way to deepen his own study of the New Testament. He also believed that knowing Greek would help him to eventually translate the New Testament into previously unwritten languages. Jim and Betty shared unpronounceable classes like Thucydides, Herodotus, the Septuagint, and others. Now she regarded him with new interest, noting his gray-blue eyes, his athletic physique, his neat, though worn, sweater, jacket, and gray flannel trousers.

Betty didn't realize it then, but Jim had a reputation on campus as being just a little too spiritual. During his freshman year, he'd turned off many Wheaton students by heartily asking them what they'd learned in their morning devotions, or what their "verse for today" was. Later in his college career, he felt he'd been too extreme; without losing his absolute devotion to Christ, he became far more fun, and popular. Unusually intentional, Jim saw college as a privilege, but one that would be wasted unless he used it to strengthen his soul, mind, and body, all for the glory of God.

Given the various New Testament references to wrestling as a spiritual metaphor, it was no surprise that Jim became a standout on Wheaton's talented wrestling team. Betty's brother, Dave Howard, described it this way:

> In our first match of the freshman year we met the University of Illinois. Jim had the misfortune of meeting the national champion in his weight class. Since Jim had never wrestled before, he was somewhat baffled. The champion put every wrestling hold he could think of on Jim but could not turn him onto his back and pin him. We discovered that Jim was double jointed! No matter what hold the champion tried, it didn't work on Jim, as his limbs would simply bend beyond all belief but would not turn him. From that day on we called him *The Rubber Man.*[1]

The Rubber Man was determined to eliminate all nonessentials from his life. He considered himself—unless God led differently—to be a "eunuch" for Christ, as Matthew 19:12 put it. He could serve the Lord best without the distractions and responsibilities of a wife, family, children, and home. He saw these as a gradual entrapment that could in fact compromise one's full focus on the things of God.

When they were upperclassmen, Dave lived with Jim in the dorm at Wheaton that would later bear Jim's name: Elliot Hall.

"I was dating Phyllis, who later became my wife," Dave wrote many years later. "When I would return to the dorm after a date, I often found him sitting there reading his Bible or praying. He would look at me out of the corner of his eye suspiciously and say, 'Have you been out with Phyllis again?' When I would acknowledge that this was true, he would turn away with a shake of his head implying that once again I was wasting my time.

"One of his firm convictions (at least he *thought* it was firm!) was that celibacy was God's highest calling in life. It was better to be unfettered with a wife and family and therefore to be free to serve the Lord with total abandonment."[2]

Jim's lively—and later, famous—journals bore that out.

"I have been musing lately on the extremely dangerous cumulative effects of earthly things," he wrote after college. He felt that committing to a wife would entail unavoidable trappings, such as "a house; a house in turn requires curtains, rugs, washing machines, et cetera. A house with those things soon becomes a home, and children are the intended outcome. The needs multiply as they are met—a car demands a garage; a garage, land; land, a garden; a garden, tools; and tools need sharpening. Woe, woe, woe to the man who would live a disentangled life in my century, if one insists on a wife. I learn from this that the wisest life is the simplest one, lived in the fulfillment of only the basic requirements of life—shelter, food, covering, and a bed. And even these can become productive of other needs if one does not heed. Be on guard, my soul, of complicating your environment so that you have neither time nor room for growth!"[3]

Part of Jim Elliot's attraction for some, and repulsion for others, had to do with this countercultural bent, sometimes articulated in less-than-thoughtful ways. He loathed the superficiality of a religious life that rested on the American way, rather than the radical call of Jesus.

Jim yearned to preach a pure, New Testament gospel, not one that subtly blended Jesus' teachings with conventional values of comfort and prosperity. After his freshman year in college, he wrote in his journal, "It has been a profitable year, drawing closer to my Savior and discovering gems in His Word. How wonderful to know that Christianity is more than a padded pew or a dim cathedral, but that it is a real, living, daily experience which goes from grace to grace."[4]

Jim came from a Plymouth Brethren tradition that eschewed denominational structure and hierarchy as it sought to adhere to a New Testament model of the early church. His father, Fred, was a "commended" or recognized Brethren teacher and evangelist. The group did not believe in ordained clergy.

Jim's anti-establishment faith had motivated him to register as a conscientious objector—a countercultural idea in the patriotic World War II era. But Jim was an iconoclast who relished rocking the conformist boat. Since high school, he had carried a Bible nearly everywhere he went. His knowledge of the Scriptures' content was deep and wide. He was outspoken about his faith. His views regarding absolute devotion to God were not for the faint of heart.

Lest we think Jim was simply annoying or "otherworldly," it's good to remember his big grin, hearty voice, and ebullient personality. During the latter part of college, he went through a self-described "Renaissance" in which he overflowed with wit, poetry, songs, and jokes; he loved to prank his friends and go to parties. He reveled in nature and loved hiking, fishing, trekking, stargazing, climbing, and swimming. There was something bracing about him, as if he wanted to soak up and fully experience every moment. Jim Elliot did not passively pass the days; he *lived* them.

Dave Howard invited his buddy to spend Christmas break, 1947, at the family home in New Jersey.

Howard family, Christmas, 1947
Phil, his wife Margaret, Philip, Jimmy, Katharine, Betty, Tom;
Dave and Ginny in the back row

————

Betty wrote many years later, "My family was enchanted with Jim. As staid Easterners . . . we found his sudden wide smile and strong handclasp, his complete ingenuousness, refreshing. He fixed everything that needed fixing. . . . He wiped dishes for a little old lady who was then a kitchen helper for my mother. . . . He knew hundreds of hymns by heart, and was quite uninhibited about breaking forth at any moment in his hearty, unmodulated baritone."

Jim went sledding and ice skating with the kids, and shoveled snow for Philip Howard. Late at night, after the rest of the family had gone to bed, he'd stay up and talk with Betty. Topics ranged from New Testament principles regarding the church, poetry, women, and "many other subjects on which his views were, I thought, out of the ordinary. I enjoyed these sessions partly because at that time I disagreed with him on so many things. At any rate, I decided Jim Elliot was a 'character,' and I liked him."[5]

Though Betty didn't know it then, the feeling was mutual.

As 1948 began, Jim Elliot began to spend more and more time studying Greek with Betty Howard. Perhaps this was because she was picking up Greek more readily than he was. Perhaps this was because his interest, kindled during the Christmas visit in New Jersey, was growing.

During that Christmas break, Betty had glumly written in her journal, "Here I am, 21, and no prospect of marriage."

Like few twenty-one-year-olds, however, she thought in drastically biblical terms. She saw her life as a sacrifice to be put on God's altar, consumed for His purposes. "My life is on Thy Altar, Lord—for Thee to consume. Set the fire, Father! Bind me with cords of love to the Altar. Hold me there. Let me remember the Cross."

At the early spring wedding of two close friends, she felt "a calm assurance that I am not to be married. I am grateful to my Lord for winning the victory in that realm."

In March she clarified, "I do not mean to say that I see the whole plan of my life. God may change it all. I only thank Him for the joy of resting in Him, and trusting Him for every step."

A few weeks after Betty wrote that, on April 30, 1948, she and Jim actually had a conventional date . . . though of course it was to attend a large Christian conference in downtown Chicago. They were both thrilled by the reports and challenges of a variety of missionaries from around the world. "It was a blessed, encouraging meeting," Betty wrote. She was moved by two strong, but very different emotions: a deep concern for those who never had a chance to hear the gospel, and deep respect for her fine companion (as her jumbled journal entry makes clear).

"But O, those 100,000 souls who perished in 'blackness of darkness forever' today! What am I doing about it? God give me love! Jim is without exception the finest fellow I have ever met."

Since Jim and Betty were both prolific writers, their developing feelings for one another—and more important to them, their convictions about God— have been well documented in Elisabeth's books *Shadow of the Almighty* and *Passion and Purity*, as well as their daughter Valerie Shepard's skillful compilation of her parents' journals and love letters, *Devotedly*.

Suffice it to say, two very different, yet strikingly similar, souls had come together. Two intense, articulate, unconventional people who saw themselves as perpetually single, serving God on the mission field, found themselves simmering and sleepless, surging with a love they had thought they'd never know. Their individual torrents of prose and poetry brim with the same biblical imagery—altars, crosses, sacrifices for the glory of God. They were strong, stubborn people who shared a radical, intentional submission to Christ. Stunned by love, they were both determined, if God so willed, to sacrifice it for Him.

Certainly other Christian couples they knew were willing to sacrifice anything for Christ, like the other missionaries with whom Jim and Betty would later serve in Ecuador. But few—aside from the seventeenth-century mystics they both loved—*articulated* their sacrificial mind-set with as much detail, passion, intensity, and struggle as did Jim and Betty. We can all be glad they found each other.

"Often we are startled," Betty wrote, "that our ideas so perfectly coincide—things which neither of us has discussed with anyone before."

As Jim and Betty began to actually acknowledge their feelings, they did so privately. By the time others found out, some were less than thrilled to find out about the roiling emotions in the "eunuch for Christ."

Dave Howard—Jim's best friend, roommate, and, of course, Betty's younger brother—was at the top of that list. Many decades later, he sputtered to an interviewer: "He went out with her [Betty] every night for two weeks, and he didn't dare admit it to me. He didn't dare admit that he, the great celibate, was being attracted to a girl."

It was hypocritical, said Dave—who loved his friend but didn't want others to put him on a pedestal after his death. "Jim would make all the rest of us feel like second class citizens for even looking at a girl, [or for] dating . . . but . . . that same period of time when he starts falling in love with Betty he is writing some of the steamiest things in his journal about his imaginations."[6]

On June 9, 1948, Jim and Betty took a walk, meandering south of Wheaton's campus. They passed near the spot where Jim had nearly lost his life eight weeks earlier on the train tracks. It was a sweet, early summer evening, teasing of warmth to come. They knew now that they cared deeply for each other. They knew that anything they loved in this life had to be laid on the altar—yielded to God, since His will was supreme.

Fittingly, they wandered through the gateway of a graveyard, most likely St. Michael's cemetery about a mile and a half walk from campus.

As Betty described it, they sat on a stone slab. "Jim told me that he had committed me to God, much as Abraham had done his son, Isaac. This came almost as a shock—for it was exactly the figure that had been in my mind for several days as I had pondered our relationship. We agree that God was directing. Our lives belonged wholly to Him, and should He choose to accept the 'sacrifice' and consume it, we determined not to lay a hand on it to retrieve it on our own.

"We sat in silence. Suddenly we were aware that the moon, which had risen behind us, was casting the shadow of a great stone cross between us."[7]

Sometimes such scenes are illumined with meaning only *after* subsequent events. Not so in this case. Betty wrote in her journal that night, "Tonight we walked up to the cemetery and by chance (?) sat beneath a great cross. How symbolic it seemed! I made known the decision of yesterday. There was great struggle of heart for both. Long spaces of silence—but communion. 'What is to be done with the ashes?' It has cut very deep—therefore we dare not touch it. O inexorable Love!"

Jim Elliot set the same scene in his own journal: "Came to an understanding at the Cross with Betty last night. Seemed the Lord made me think of it as laying a sacrifice on the altar. She has put her life there, and I almost felt as if I would lay a hand on it, to retrieve it for myself, but it is not mine—wholly God's. He paid for it and is worthy to do with it what He will. Take it and burn it for Thy pleasure, Lord, and may Thy fire fall on me as well."[8]

They were both perceptive enough to note the shadow of the cross. They just did not know what particular form their crosses would take.

CHAPTER 10

Patience in Alberta

"Love is spontaneous but must be maintained by discipline."
—Oswald Chambers

Betty spent the summer of 1948 at the University of Oklahoma. There, via the Summer Institute of Linguistics, under the auspices of Wycliffe Bible Translators, she studied language structure, syntax, phonetics, and other skills she would need to translate the New Testament into as-yet-unwritten tribal languages.

As many recent college graduates can relate, she often felt isolated, missing the warmth, bustle, and community of university life. And she felt a bit random; perhaps she had envisioned a tidy, efficient, straight line from Wheaton College right to the mission field. Like most of us, Betty's life unspooled in chapters that at times seemed unrelated to her highest goals. As she wrote from the vantage point of a few decades later,

"The truth is that none of us knows the will of God for his life. I say *for his life*—for the promise is 'as thou goest step by step I will open up the way before thee.' He gives us enough light for today, enough strength for one day at a time, enough manna, our 'daily' bread."

She went on to describe the mundane, unremarkable multitude of steps in the long journey of the children of Israel as they headed toward the Promised Land. "The stages of their journey, dull and eventless as most of them were, were each a necessary part of the movement toward the fulfillment of the promise."[1]

This was tediously the case as she studied linguistics at the University of Oklahoma campus after graduating from Wheaton. In the summer evenings she would climb to the top of the bleachers in the empty football stadium. There she would read and pray, a tall, solitary figure poring over her Bible, finding herself spending too much time "thinking of J." yet yearning "for that burning passion whose sole object is Christ!"

It was both a comfort and a tease for her that Jim's brother Bert was also studying linguistics that summer. They spent enough time together that people started to assume they were a couple. Betty, not able to let Bert know her true feelings for his brother, relished his physical resemblance to Jim. (Meanwhile, ironically, Jim was off speaking at college campuses in the Midwest with Dave Howard, Betty's brother.)

Betty's correspondence with Jim Elliot explored, at the slow pace of a postage stamp, the intricate inner workings of their minds and spirits, metaphysical musings, their unrequited physical passion, and their meticulous search for the will of God regarding marriage or singleness. It was a courtship that is perhaps almost as excruciating to read about as it was to endure, although those enduring it in real time were being sanctified along the way, and I'm not sure that's true for the rest of us.

Betty and Jim spent a rare few days together in the late summer of 1948 as she made her way to Prairie Bible Institute. Jim told her he loved her, which for both of them was not simply a declaration of emotion, but a declaration meant to pave the way for marriage. But they both also knew that his deeper intention was to go to the mission field as a single man.

Jim was a year younger than Betty, and as summer waned, he returned to Wheaton for his senior year. He went back to school excited about living the college experience to the hilt. He regretted the "priggish little laws whereby I used to govern my conduct . . . I experience new fellowship, new freedom, new enjoyment."[2]

He had reflected on 1 Timothy 6:17: "'God . . . gives us richly all things to enjoy . . .' [and] woke up to the fact that there was a lot of life given freely to us by God that he was not enjoying."

Dave Howard said later: "He saw that his restricted 'holier than thou' attitude was cheating him, as well as his friends, out of a lot of fun. So the pendulum swung to the other extreme, and Jim began to pull out all the stops and enjoy life to the fullest. He wrote in his journal, 'Wherever you are, be all there. Live life to the hilt every situation you believe to be the will of God.'"[3]

So Jim studied the Bible with all his heart, soul, and mind. He dove into academics and would graduate as a Greek major, *summa cum laude*. He threw himself even more wholeheartedly into wrestling, winning many medals. He loved his friends, went to parties, and played pranks. Regarding the last, he sometimes did not know when to stop. (In their correspondence, Betty, who had heard about some of his adventures through the grapevine, had some choice observations about this tendency.)

During his senior year, Jim served as president of the Student Foreign Missions Fellowship. He made a prayer chart divided into fifteen-minute segments; students could sign up to pray for the Wheaton College campus, asking God to stir men and women there to commit themselves to foreign missions.

One tangible result of that prayer effort, Dave Howard reported, was that "in the 150-year history of Wheaton College, more students from the classes of the late 1940's and early 1950's went to the mission field than at any other period."[4]

Jim also recruited in more direct ways. His friend Ed McCully was a football player and track star, tall, handsome, senior class president, and winner of the national collegiate oratory championship his senior year. He planned to go on to law school.

One day when Jim and Dave were in the locker room after a workout, they saw Ed. Jim grabbed him by the neck, and said,

"Hey, McCully! You won the national championship, didn't you? Great stuff, McCully. You have a lot of talent, don't you? You know who gave you that talent, don't you? So what are you going to do with it—spend your life making money for yourself? You have no business doing that. You should be a missionary, and I'm praying that God will make you one!"[5]

The determined Ed did go off to law school for a year . . . but then he believed that God was indeed calling him to become a full-time missionary. He quit law school to study missions, and eventually went to Ecuador . . . where he would serve—and die—with his buddy Jim Elliot.

As Jim bustled through his busy year at Wheaton, Betty arrived at Prairie Bible Institute. At the time, it was a stark set of wooden buildings on a bleak prairie in Three Hills, Alberta. She was feeling displaced and lonesome one afternoon when there came a knock on her door. She opened it to find a beautiful rosy-cheeked woman, her face framed by white hair, evidently a housemother of some sort. She spoke with a charming Scottish burr:

"'You don't know me, but I know you. I've been prraying forr you, Betty dearr. I'm Mrs. Cunningham. If everr you'd like a cup of tea and a Scottish scone, just pop down to my little apartment."[6]

Betty spent many wintry afternoons in Mrs. Cunningham's cozy space. The older lady would pour out tea, and Betty would pour out her soul. Mrs. Cunningham's rosy face showed sympathy, love, and understanding as she listened. She would quietly sip her tea, nodding. Then she'd pray, look up, and strengthen Betty not with sentiment, but with strong words, words straight from the Scripture.

Mrs. Cunningham remained an encourager and model for Betty the rest of her life. This was not just because Mrs. Cunningham had wise things to say. It was because of *who she was.* "Above all, she herself was the message."[7] (Betty would later muse that being a missionary, for example, was not a matter of *declaring* a message. It was a matter of *being* the gospel, incarnationally, as "Mrs. C." had done with Betty.)

During college, Betty's earlier mentor, Miss Cumming, had cautioned her about her "aloofness," and how her remote ways had caused her to unintentionally hurt George Griebenow. Now, in Canada, Betty's mother wrote to her about the same issue. Katharine Howard felt rejected and isolated because Betty shared so little with her, and wondered if this distance was her own fault.

"You have failed me in no way whatever," Betty wrote to her mother. Any distance between them was Betty's fault. She asked for forgiveness . . . and then, bravely went on to disclose things about herself she'd never articulated on paper.

"You must just realize that my nature is reserved, my feelings mostly bottled up. I am a hypocrite of the first order, for a long time in my life priding myself on the fact that no one knew how I felt or what I was thinking. Too often I would not reveal my true feelings in order that people would think me . . . perhaps wiser or more mature than I really was.

"Often I myself was a bit ashamed that things should affect me emotionally, hence would not admit it. I considered the show of feelings or revelation of thoughts pure weakness, and I so desire to be strong!"[8]

Of course she didn't think one should go about divulging everything at once to everyone. But she had carried her own reserve too far. Jim had told her the previous September he would do anything in the world to see her cry. "So you see he knows something of your feeling," Betty consoled her mother. "I have never shed a tear in his presence."[9]

Having thus cracked a window into her heart, Betty went on, and now the floodgates opened. Her feelings about Jim poured out. "I love him, as I never thought I could love anyone," she cried out to her mom. She couldn't think of him without longing for marriage. If she didn't marry Jim, she would marry no one. She thought the latter far more likely. "I have never told Jim that I loved him—in fact, I have never told anyone, not even my diary. It is not easy to go on in such darkness, loving him, and contemplating the future without him."[10]

Then, she asked her mother to pray that she would not be weakened by "<u>sentimentality</u> and vain imaginations."[11]

After her academic term at Prairie Bible Institute, Betty went on to fieldwork. She lived in a rickety trailer on a farm in the tiny village of Patience, Alberta. Roosters roused her at 4:30 in the morning; she rode a bicycle on dusty roads to invite farm folk to Sunday school meetings. The locals were poor, uneducated, and found relief from their hard lives in alcohol, fights, and vulgar gossip. Betty sometimes wept as she rode her bike. One evening the prairie wind was so strong she could scarcely pedal; she "came home to my dark little house, cold and very tired. 'No reward save that of knowing that I do Thy will.'"

Overwhelmed, she took comfort in words from missionary icon Hudson Taylor: "It is not what we set ourselves to do that really tells in blessing, so much as what He is doing through us when we least expect it, if only we are in abiding fellowship with Him."

By the end of her dreary time in the aptly named Patience, one of the rough farmers had warmed to her: "Spent the a.m. packing and cleaning up trailer. It was pathetic to see poor Mr. K. bid me goodbye. He has been kind and polite, yet he tried to apologize for anything 'bad' he had said . . . The kids all cried and cried when we left. So did I!"

CHAPTER 11

"You Made a Universally Horrible Impression . . ."

"It does not matter how great the pressure is. What really
matters is where the pressure lies—whether it comes between
you and God, or whether it presses you nearer His heart."
—Hudson Taylor

*T*hroughout her impatient months in Patience, Betty received prodigious, tender, thoughtful, shocking missives from Jim Elliot. He cited his readings in Freud, Nietzsche, Nehemiah, Hebrews, Ephesians, and everything in between. She disciplined herself to write back sparingly. She, too, was a prolific writer; she could have splurged tomes of prose on Jim. But she bridled herself. She didn't want to move ahead of his pace.

She wrote in her diary, "I suppose, really, that I am writing this journal in some sense, for him. . . . It has not been conscious, but perhaps I am recording some of the things I wish I could say in my letters to him, but cannot. Why can I not say them in letters? Because (I'm not sure if this is true—that is, I'm not sure it is all the reason, or the <u>real</u> reason) we are not engaged. . . . But I love him now—I love him. And it is strong, constant, and pure. . . . I cannot say these things to anyone. So I feel that I must <u>write</u>."

Jim also used his journals to pour out his deepest passions, jotting some of his deep and prescient prayers in notations that became famous after his death.

Many of Jim's writings, threaded through the years, show a magnetic, mystical pull to the thought of dying in Christ's service. Jim would have echoed the famous assertion of Dietrich Bonhoeffer, the brave German pastor who was hanged by the Nazis while Jim was in college: "When Christ calls a man, he bids him come and die."*

Death to self, yes. But, like Bonhoeffer, Jim was willing to be killed, if God so willed:

> "God, I pray, light these idle sticks of my life and may I burn up for Thee. Consume my life, my God, for it is Thine. I seek not a long life but a full one like Yours, Lord Jesus."[1]

> "Was much encouraged to think of a life of godliness in the light of an early death."[2]

> "Prayed a strange prayer today. I covenanted with my Father that He would do either of two things—either glorify Himself to the utmost in me, or slay me. By His grace I shall not have His second best. He heard me, I believe, so that now I have nothing to look forward to but a life of sacrificial sonship . . . or heaven soon. Perhaps tomorrow. What a prospect!"[3]

> "I must not think it strange if God takes in youth those whom I should have kept on earth till they were older. God is peopling eternity, and I must not restrict Him to old men and women."[4]

> "When it comes time to die, make sure that all you have to do is die."[5]

Jim's most famous quote of this sort, one that has inspired and galvanized thousands of young people toward Christ's service, comes from his journal of October 28, 1949.

At the time the twenty-five-year-old had likely been reading selections from Matthew Henry, the well-known Bible commentator and preacher. In 1699, Reverend Henry wrote fondly about his father, Philip, who often said, "He is no fool who parts with that which he cannot keep, when he is sure to be recompensed with that which he cannot lose."[6]

---

*"The cross is laid on every Christian. The first Christ-suffering which every man must experience is the call to abandon the attachments of this world. It is that dying of the old man which is the result of his encounter with Christ. As we embark upon discipleship we surrender ourselves to Christ in union with his death—we give over our lives to death. Thus it begins; the cross is not the terrible end to an otherwise god-fearing and happy life, but it meets us at the beginning of our communion with Christ. When Christ calls a man, he bids him come and die." From Dietrich Bonhoeffer, *The Cost of Discipleship* (1937; repr. New York: Touchstone, 1995).

But Jim Elliot's version was punchier. He jotted in his journal, "He is no fool who gives what he cannot keep to gain that which he cannot lose."[7]

Most of Jim's well-known eloquent and passionate writings emerged from his college and post-college days and his pre-marriage mission work in Ecuador. During this he had the luxury of reflection, the long solitary evenings with Bible and journal by the light of the lamp.

Once Jim and Betty were finally married, living in a leaky tent in the rainforest, the paper trail thinned. Conversation replaced correspondence. And there was less time to ponder the possible will of God in one's journal. When His work is right in front of you, you do it. You administer the injection for the dying Indian. You teach the children at the indigenous school. And when you have your own new baby, there are no mysteries about God's will for its care. You feed, bathe, clothe, and comfort it; you don't agonize about whether you are on the right path or not.

It's beyond our scope to try to fathom everything that was going on inside of Jim Elliot in the late 1940s and early 1950s. Clearly, he was a young man determined to subsume every vestige of self in the flaming service of God. His journal entries and letters, well documented elsewhere, simmered with physical passion. (In recent years at least one determined blogger has claimed that Jim's deep friendships with other men indicate that he was sexually attracted to them, and that his indecision about Betty was the by-product of homoerotic repression. Perhaps if you're a revisionist with a hammer, everything looks like a nail.)

Twenty years after Jim's death, Elisabeth Elliot—granted, not the most objective analyst—wrote, "He was determined to prove God's strength and grace sufficient to overcome the ordinary weakness of a man's flesh. He knew his own great attraction for women. He was determined also to serve the Lord without entanglements. But when the time came when marriage was for him a clear command, and he knew then that it was a gift, given by the same Giver who gives for some the special gift of being single."[8]

It just took Jim Elliot a rather long time to see that God, designer of marriage, smiled on Jim entering into His invention.*

---

*Decades later, when she wrote *Let Me Be a Woman*, Elisabeth Elliot would quote Martin Luther to her long-deceased young husband, tweaking him just a bit: ". . . It is said that it takes a bold man to venture to take a wife," wrote Luther. "What you need above all else then, is to be encouraged, admonished, urged, incited, and made bold. Why should you delay, my dear and reverend sir, and continue to weigh the matter in your mind? . . . Stop thinking about it and

Few of us would have had Betty Howard's patience. Her own trust in God's leading, no matter what, reinforced her endurance. She hung in there for a five-year courtship that was not for the faint of heart.

She could endure because she cast all her anxieties on God. She gave up the most enormous hopes of her life and the smallest details of her schedule to Him. If she was cautious in her relationship with Jim Elliot, or reserved with others, she was not so with God. She threw herself open to Him, wholeheartedly, without restraint.

In this tendency, Betty Howard was the opposite of those of us who've thrown ourselves completely open to people who may or may not be trustworthy, yet have held God, the very Lover of our souls, at a discreet and dispassionate arm's length.

She was determined not to do what was easy, but to wait for God's leading, whatever it was. As she wrote many years later, "Waiting on God requires the willingness to bear uncertainty, to carry within oneself the unanswered question, lifting the heart to God about it whenever it intrudes upon one's thoughts. It is easier to talk oneself into a decision that has no permanence, than to wait patiently."[9]

Certainly her love for Jim Elliot made her hope that they might get together and consummate their relationship some time before they both reached retirement age. But her love for God made her willing to give up that hope, should God so ask.

At the end of the summer of 1949, Betty accepted Jim's parents' invitation to visit the family home in Portland, Oregon, for Labor Day weekend.

Who could know this much prayed over, much anticipated, thrilling, tender visit would be, in human terms, an unmitigated disaster?

It started well. Jim and Betty picnicked, paddled canoes, explored islands, and watched the moon rise over the Columbia River. They swam in the icy ocean, dug under rocks, found sea anemones, built a fire, and watched the sunset. They hiked the Timberline Trail five miles up Mt. Hood to the Alpine Meadow, crossing glaciers and marveling at wildflowers. They worshiped God with Jim's Plymouth Brethren assembly, ate meals with his family, sang, and played the piano.

They both mourned as Jim drove Betty to the bus station, giving her bundles of fruit and sandwiches for the ninety-eight-hour marathon that took her from Oregon through California, Denver, Kansas City, and finally to New Jersey.

---

go to it right merrily. Your body demands it, God wills it, and drives you to it . . . It is best to comply with all our senses as soon as possible and give ourselves to God's Word and work in whatever He wishes us to do." Elisabeth Elliot, *Let Me Be a Woman*, 27.

Soon after Betty's arrival home, a jaw-dropping letter arrived from Jim. Evidently, his family debrief after her visit had been something less than positive. Jim spared her nothing as he related his family's feedback.

"You made a universally horrible impression," he wrote. It "could not have been worse . . . Mother seriously concluded that inviting you here was 'a flop.'"[10]

"She thinks you uncommunicative, possessed of a 'meek and quiet spirit,' but a very poor maker of friends, and hence a poor prospective missionary."

"She tried to warm up a 'conversation.' Your retort that you didn't mind being alone 'froze her inside.'"

"Mom asked, 'Do you sew?' Your response, 'Not if I can help it—Mother has always done it.' Hence you are to [Mrs. Elliot] still an immature 'institution child' who sadly lacks any sense of home responsibility and who possesses little domestic adaptability . . .'"

Meanwhile Jim's dad not only criticized Betty's character, but her appearance. "'I see nothing in her that would appeal to me—no face, no form, a spindly dreamer who has cleverly set her cap for you, and you have bitten.'"

In spite of this, Jim told Betty earnestly, his dad had come to acceptance with his son's doom. "Though he can't understand our attraction for a minute," he was willing to entrust his son's grim fate to the Lord. If God so willed that Jim end up with this "spindly dreamer," then so be it.

Younger sister Jane "never saw you reading your Bible and taking the lead in spiritual converse. Registered effect: disappointment."

Two other family members were more charitable, saying only: "I admire her for not putting on a show for us," and "These quiet people feel more deeply than those of us who say so much."

Jim well knew his beloved's personality. He said he had borne the criticisms "mostly in silence, telling only what I *know* you to be with me." He urged his family to put themselves in Betty's shoes, to think how intimidating it must have been for her to know they were evaluating her every conversation.

But, he concluded, "I don't know why I should have to defend you against such charges as uncommunicativeness," he said. "I will not defend you further. You, knowing their present bias toward you, must do the rest."[11]

One is torn between absolutely giving up on Jim Elliot as a callous, clueless clod, and wanting to know how Betty responded. Many of us would have called off all further contact, streaming tears, or left for the furthest mission station available, leaving no forwarding address and slamming the door behind us.

Betty mulled it all over. "I could hardly believe what I read," she wrote in her journal. ". . . utterly crushed by it. Oh, truly, I am an unimprovable, helpless case. *Help*, Lord!"

Was the "aloofness" Miss Cumming had warned her about in college coming to roost? Her introversion and habitual reserve had played as poorly as possible in the expressive, spontaneous Elliot household.

She wrote to Jim humbly, but with spunk—her debating skills at play.

"I fully expected you would be hearing 'the worst' of me after I left, but I did not expect a detailed account of the criticisms . . . do not fear that you 'betrayed' your folks—I sensed their feeling toward me after I had been there a day or so.

"The criticisms you made of me are just. I am greatly in need of openness in meeting new friends. But, oh, Jim—if you knew the discouragement that swept over me as I realized this so poignantly at your house, for it had seemed that God had won so many battles for me on this very line this summer . . . He had given me such wonderful entrance into hearts and such overpowering love for the people of Patience—why did not His love have free course in Portland?"[12]

Even as she grieved over her own failings, she also let Jim know she couldn't understand why his parents would so freely tell him their critiques. "I think if my folks *hated* a person they would not say such things about him to one who loved him, supposedly. Moreover, I cannot imagine your folks talking that way about anyone.

"The accusations which you quoted to me are things which you said you hoped would help me in the end. Look them over, Jim. Not one is capable of being remedied . . . You said it is up to me to do the rest. There is nothing I can do. I have sealed my image in their minds, even if I do improve, which by the grace of God I have purpose to do. Letters would accomplish nothing now—I am the faker who writes high-sounding letters and is a different person in actuality. I don't expect your mother will be writing me anymore anyway."[13]

Jim's return letter reassured Betty that he had talked with his mother at length, and she had remarked, "Well, we must have her back again, I have misjudged."[14]

He went on to remind Betty that their families were very different. Though they both practiced family devotions in the evenings, for example, the Howards did so in their perfect parlor, after dinner dishes had been properly cleaned and put away. The Elliots just pushed aside their dishes on the plastic tablecloth, brushed the crumbs away, and pulled out their Bibles. While the Howards would silently observe events and contemplate their reactions, the Elliots would "blurt right out at the dinner table their feelings." Jim also let Betty know, with dubious comfort, however, that in spite of any objections, "should I choose to go on and marry you, they would stand by to help."[15]

The drama continued when Betty's brother Dave wrote a strong letter to his best friend and former roommate. He warned Jim that he would unequivocally ruin Betty if he was not careful, and to stop leading her on by writing to her if he had no intention of marrying her.

Betty wrote back to let both of them know she was no shrinking violet, and to please stop treating her like a helpless child. "You speak of *your* liberty, *your* choices (e.g., 'If I should choose to marry you . . .') *your* decisions. Rest assured, Jim, my consent to correspond was based on the liberty the Lord gave *me*. Don't worry about whether I can 'endure.' This is a two-sided proposition. If you can, I can. I am not so fragile a thing as you and Dave would make out."[16]

Over the years, some have questioned Jim Elliot's pursuit of the will of God, wondering if perhaps God's will changed conveniently when the Rubber Man got to certain points in his own development. As one historian wrote, ". . . for Elliot the specifics of God's will seemed to be a moving target, often coming down to his inner convictions at any given time."[17]

It's an understandable critique when we outsiders examine the voluminous trail of letters and journal entries that paper the path of Betty and Jim's five-year courtship. Many of us would have gone running after the first year or so.

But as Betty's biographer, chafing at the tortured days and weeks and months of waiting for an outcome that seemed long-ripe for the plucking, fully within the smile of God, I'm reminded that it's difficult to ascertain just how God leads *any* of us. Within the revealed wisdom of Scripture's riverbanks, the Spirit's particular leading can sometimes be difficult to explain to someone else. The key fact, and the great transferrable truth that comes from these sometimes maddening people, is this: Betty and Jim were determined to obey God's leading as they discerned it, whatever the cost.

At some point in her journey, Betty had determined that Jim Elliot was unique, and she was willing to wait him out. Perhaps she thought back to her idealistic journal entry back at Wheaton, when she had longed for "nothing less than a complete and beautiful union of <u>soul</u>." Now she was finding out that living such unity in real time, in a real relationship, was not gloriously ethereal, but just plain hard. "Jim is incorrigible," she wrote in her journal. "[B]less his heart!"

She continued: "And inimitable. Never have I been treated like this before—especially by a man! What worries me is that I seem to *thrive* on it. I could sit down and answer it tonight. But I must wait a little while. O discipline—thou art a jewel, but cumbersome."

CHAPTER 12

Sitting Still

"Self-seeking is the gate by which a soul departs from peace; and total abandonment to the will of God, that by which it returns."
—Madame Guyon

The year 1951 found Betty living at home in Moorestown. She'd spent the prior months teaching public speaking at Hampden DuBose Academy, where throngs of azaleas still bloomed, Spanish moss swayed lightly in the breeze, and the students still polished silver and confessed their sins as the need arose. Now, in New Jersey, Betty tutored high school girls, led children's Sunday school and afternoon Bible clubs, and worked at a women's department store in Philadelphia.

Betty knew that none of these endeavors was her life calling. Where did God want her to serve? She turned over possibilities in her mind. She thought of people whose steps seemed to be like paving stones, each one illuminated by the Lord like a lighted path, people who experienced "miracles," "surprises," "open doors," and other clear indications of God's will unfolding in a tidy sequence.

The temptation, she said, was to expect God to guide her as He guided other people she knew. But the Bible "abounds in examples of His separate leading of His sheep. For me, He has not chosen to give signs that may be shown to others. He has not led in any spectacular way, or by steps which could be proved to another. Rather, my Father has quietly opened the way, often after much 'sitting still' on the part of His daughter; repeated disappointments; 'hope deferred'; and finally, a revealing of some plan which does not at all fit my expectations."

As Betty waited for God's plan, she felt divested of the things that gave her purpose and meaning. She wrote in her journal, "I truly believe there comes a time in the progress of the soul who truly desires to be conformable to Christ's image, when God strips him not only of earthly props in the form of friends, possessions, talents, or whatever he may have outside of God—but also a time when the all-wise, all-loving Father strips that soul of even His own conscious and evident blessings and gifts."

These include things like joy, a sense of God's nearness, fruits of one's ministry . . . but when one is stripped of all outward evidences of God's blessings, there is a deeper comfort. "The soul who loves God only for Himself, apart from His gifts, knows indescribable peace."

Perhaps Betty had been reading Jonathan Edwards, who nailed the same thought in his famous distinctions between various forms of gratitude. Or perhaps not, and the Holy Spirit brought her to the same conclusion as the great preacher.

Edwards wrote in his *Religious Affections* that most thoughtful human beings feel a sense of gratitude for God's gifts: life, health, a crisp, sky-blue day. He called it *natural* gratitude. That, while a common good, is not enough to stir us to true, deep love for the Giver. If people love God only because of what He gives, Edwards points out that "even a dog will love his master that is kind to him."[1]

As Betty Howard wrote, there is a deeper, more mysterious, more sustaining sense of thankfulness: gratitude to God not for what He gives, but who He is. Edwards denoted this as *supernatural* gratitude, and said that it is the mark of the Holy Spirit in the life of the believer. This radical, gracious gratitude can thrive even in the midst of times of pain, trouble, and distress. It is relational, rather than conditional, drawing the human being who knows God into closer intimacy with Him.

Even in her early and mid-twenties, Betty Howard was practicing this radical form of gratitude.[2] In the years of her epistolary relationship with Jim Elliot, her isolation in Oklahoma, her perseverance in Patience, her foray in Florida, and her wearisome work in New Jersey, she had a foundation that was stronger than her feelings.

Early 1951 found Jim Elliot in a small town called Chester, on the Mississippi River not far from St. Louis. He and his Wheaton buddy, Ed McCully, were sharing a $40-a-month, two-room apartment and launching a radio and teaching ministry, while they traveled and spoke at various churches. Jim had been considering mission work in India, and had been offered a job teaching seventh and eighth grade in Canada. But he had also been corresponding with a British missionary in Ecuador, one Wilfred Tidmarsh. Dr. Tidmarsh was from a Plymouth Brethren background, like Jim and Ed. Tidmarsh's doctorate was in philosophy, not medicine, though he was trained in homeopathy. He was looking for dedicated, competent young men who could continue his work among the Quichua Indians after he eventually retired.

Ed was not long for this single life, however. During his speaking engagements, he'd met a sparkling young woman named Marilou at a church in Michigan. She and Ed became engaged and were married by that summer.

Betty was not to enjoy such alacrity. She was still at her parents' home in New Jersey, spending a lot of time alone.

Her 1951 journal represents a transition of sorts. Its early entries show a near-constant conversation with God, steadily offering her devotion and praise to Him. She reflected at length on the redemption of nature and the daily nature of faith. She saw God's unfolding will like a "'mystery thriller' (though so far better) . . . One does not have any idea what the next may unfold, and it has something of the adventure spirit in it, though, unlike the connotation of 'adventure,' there is no element of <u>uncertainty</u>. The very word 'faith' precludes the possibility of doubt."

She cited various truths gleaned from her constant and often arcane reading, like the biography of Frances Ridley Havergal, a nineteenth-century British hymn writer. "It did what other Christian biographies have done—deepened my hunger for knowing Christ in His fullness, for living wholly 'unto Him who died for us.'"

She absorbed books like *The Life of Madame Guyon*, and Fénelon's *The Maxims of the Saints*, and a seventeenth-century book called *The Life of God in the Soul of Man*, by Henry Scougal. She read Dostoevsky and Thomas Mann. She reflected on the great influence of Amy Carmichael's life and writings when Amy passed away early in the year.

That spring she "followed the Lord in the waters of baptism. O, it was sweet." She prayed often for her older brother, Phil, who was going through a spiritual crisis of sorts. She contemplated going to a mission field in the South Pacific.

Then, about halfway through 1951, Betty had a change in tone.

Her journal is still spiritually serious, of course, and recounts a life committed to Christ above all else. Its author is still powerfully cerebral in her personal reflections. But the tenor is different. The pages show less of a sense of careful Christianity and more of the heartbeat of a flesh-and-blood human being, in love with Jesus . . . and Jim Elliot. "My heart is at peace, more than I have known, concerning Jim. I love him with all my heart, and it seems that God has once more guided us each aright."

Some months earlier, the Elliots had visited with the Howard family, and the scorching reservations they'd had about Betty during her disastrous Portland visit seem to have eased. Jim utterly regretted his heartlessness in revealing their critiques to Betty—"I really wonder at myself, being able to write so."[3]

In early October 1951, Jim and his buddy Pete Fleming traveled to the East Coast. Pete, also from a Plymouth Brethren tradition, was an old friend of Jim's from Oregon; their families knew one another. Pete had studied literature as an undergraduate, gotten his MA, and planned on getting his PhD and teaching at the college level. Then he'd thought seriously about seminary instead. Now, Jim's influence was pulling him toward the mission field. With Jim, he'd talked at length with Dr. Tidmarsh when the veteran missionary had visited the Pacific Northwest, and now they believed that God was calling them to work with Tidmarsh among the Quichua Indians in Ecuador. Like Jim, Pete was also intrigued by the thought of reaching tribes that had never heard of Jesus—like the violent Waodani of the Amazon jungle.

Betty, Jim, Pete, and Phil and Margaret (Betty's older brother and his wife) spent a "glorious" time of hiking and mountain climbing in New Hampshire.

After the hike, Betty wrote, "The enjoyment of nature—all the loveliness our Father has made with His hands—is doubly rich sharing with Jim. Our minds run quite in similar patterns—complementing each other, dovetailing and meeting . . . Just to be with him is peace, peace."

"There is no question in my heart anymore—I love him. I love him as I never thought I could love anyone. The thought of going on without him almost chills me."

But.

"Jim is sure that God wants him on the [mission] field as a single man. May the God of all peace grant to him the great grace that will be needed, the strength to withstand the temptations which abound in such a stronghold of Satan."

After Jim's departure, Betty wrote, "Alone. Jim has gone . . . I feel absolutely empty, hollow, aching with loneliness. I want Jim. I love him strongly, deeply, powerfully. He is my life. . . . Our passions and natural affections are awakened, vivified, channeled by the love of God."

Even as Jim had spoken with Betty of the possibility of engagement but knew that "it is not yet the Lord's time," he was also wondering bemusedly in his journal about "leaping over all the old barriers I've raised against marriage. Is it to be, after all, the conventional life of rugs and appliances and babies? Is [the apostle] Paul's example of single intensity beyond me? Am I at last not one of those who make themselves eunuchs for the kingdom's sake?"[4]

"No settlement in my mind one way or another," wrote the miserable Jim, "though I feel strongly that for my own stability, for Betty's ease, and for most folks' tongues, I should buy a ring.

"Lord, which way? . . . What shall I say to all the liberty I've been given to preach adherence to Pauline method—even to single men working on the field and illustrating it from Pete's intention and my own? Rather, what will men think who have heard me say, 'I go single, in the will of God' when, if I were really engaged, my plans would be otherwise? Well, it is in God's hands. He gave direction to speak that way. And after all, an engaged man is still single, but purposing to be married. And Paul would have me free from care . . . did he ever love a woman?

"I want her more today than any day since leaving her. I need her to purify my desires, to lift me above lust. I need her counsel, her attitude, her strength, her fingers, her forehead, and her breasts. My God in heaven, how am I made! Oh, that I had never tasted woman at all, that thirst for her should not be so intense now, remembering. It is not good that man should be alone—not this man, anyhow."[5]

CHAPTER 13

"I Don't Feel Much like a Missionary"

"The secret is Christ in me,
not me in a different set of circumstances."
—Elisabeth Elliot

*E*ven as Jim struggled with his wretched realization that he was no apostle Paul, his ministry plans were coming together. He and Pete Fleming would sail soon for Ecuador to get started with Spanish study so they could work with their correspondent, Dr. Tidmarsh, among the Quichua Indians.

At the same time, Betty's heart was turning toward Latin American ministry as well. And in the fall of 1951, the Spanish-speaking Plymouth Brethren community in Brooklyn, New York, invited her to come live in the city, learn Spanish, and work in the ministry office there.

As her relationship with Jim Elliot had grown, so had Betty's exposure to his Plymouth Brethren tradition.* The Brethren originated in Great Britain during the early 1800s as small groups that worshiped

---

*Betty Howard was not a particularly denominationally-driven person. Because she'd grown up in the context of her father's work with the *Sunday School Times*, she had connected with missionaries and lay leaders of many flavors within the broad context of evangelicalism.

"Evangelicalism" is a word that doesn't have as much currency or meaning today as it did in the mid-twentieth century and earlier. Broadly speaking, it then connoted Christians who adhered to a high view of Bible exposition, seeing the Scriptures as the authoritative template for theology and faithful living as a follower of Christ. Evangelicals had their roots in the revivals of Charles and John Wesley, George Whitefield, and Jonathan Edwards, and prioritized evangelism,

in homes and sought to replicate the purity of the early church in the first century. They viewed themselves simply as Christians, and rejected the structures and divisions of denominationalism.

Even though Betty's introduction to the Brethren was through Jim, by 1951 she had adopted the tradition as her own. "I was persuaded by the truth of it . . . the idea that it was a literal attempt to imitate the New Testament church," she told an interviewer many years later. "I read E. H. Broadbent's *The Pilgrim Church*" and was "quite convinced by that. . . . I liked the strong biblical emphasis and the Plymouth Brethren that I knew knew their Bibles backwards and forwards, even better than I did. . . . That impressed me."[1]

Later, she wrote in a letter to a friend, "Carol, you can hardly imagine the difference between the assemblies [the Brethren gatherings] and the average denominational or fundamental 'church.' Especially blessed is the breaking of bread meeting Sunday morning. It is a purely worship service, contrary to anything else I know. We go to give, not to 'get a blessing.' It is only for pouring out our hearts in praise to God, very simply, very scripturally. . . . How I would love to know that you were fellowshipping in this way, and I shall pray that God will make His will very clear."[2]

---

with great enthusiasm for both global missions and personal "sharing of the gospel."

Some evangelicals, like those in the fundamentalist tradition, removed themselves from the rest of the world, shunning drinking, smoking, movies, dancing, or other "worldly" activities. Others engaged with culture, seeking to bring the gospel to bear on issues of social justice—as in Wheaton College's founding by God-fearing abolitionists, and the school's welcome of black and female students in the nineteenth century.

In the twentieth century the movement splintered a bit as the many evangelicals became suspicious of the "social activism" of modernists who'd rejected orthodox biblical beliefs. Many evangelicals, certainly not all, turned inward, creating bastions of purity within a decaying culture. And then in the 1970s and '80s, some fastened their hopes on reviving culture through the political process. With a resurgence of that in recent years, the word "evangelical" is today associated by many secularists as a synonym for rabid followers of a particular political party or candidate.

Betty Howard's earliest understanding of the Christian life came not just from her parents and the focus of their tidy, God-fearing home, but from her Uncle Charley Trumbull's 1912 book, *Taking Men Alive*. Its themes focus on the "victorious Christian life" centered on crucifying the flesh and finding new life in the risen Christ. Betty's early love of Amy Carmichael reinforced these same refrains, especially Carmichael's vision that missionary life was all about "a chance to die," which Betty later titled her biography of her hero.

So when Betty Howard would eventually go to Ecuador, she would do so as a Brethren missionary, having received a "commendation" from the assembly. The Brethren mind-set about funding fit with her faith-based view of finances, practiced throughout college and after. So Betty—and of course Jim Elliot and Pete Fleming as well—would sail off to Ecuadorian missions work with no set salary or guarantee of financial support. They would receive money whenever Brethren assemblies in North America felt moved to send it, in whatever amounts God had indicated to the folks back home.

As Betty prayed for God's leading in the fall of 1951, she asked God "that I may be prepared in body, mind, and spirit for the task of a missionary, a 'sent-one.'" Within a few weeks, she wrote, "As He seems to be leading, I'm planning to go to New York on Tuesday, where I will be working with a Spanish [Plymouth Brethren] assembly. They have an apartment ready for me, and Mr. Montaloo is going to teach me Spanish."

That same morning, after a worship service, a young woman Betty did not know well approached her and pressed a $10 bill into her hand. "She is one who hasn't very much, and it meant so much to me," Betty wrote later, touched by such sacrificial funding of her first missionary posting in New York. There she would be working with the Brethren missions magazine, Voices from the Vineyard, and would receive her commendation to go abroad from the Hasbrouck Heights Assembly, in nearby New Jersey.

By November 28, she had moved into a $17-a-month New York walk-up with occasional heat, rare hot water, a brewery next door that blessed the neighborhood with the aroma of beer, and enormous black rats. But her journal entries showed a chipper mind-set: "Imagine me—living in a tenement in Brooklyn! More fun!" She was "alone in a little flat in the Spanish section, The Lord is here, too, and I am happy."

The days that followed were a mix of spicy Latin cuisine, meetings with other missionaries, and the inevitable crash that follows an exultant beginning.

"Lonely. What do missionaries ever do who go to a foreign field alone?" She had friends nearby but felt isolated and dismal. She was freezing all the time, wearing her winter coat to sit on her hard bed and write in her journal. The flat was filthy, dark, and looked out on a dank courtyard with clotheslines stretched between the dingy windows of other apartments.

She peered out her little window; a small bit of gray sky was visible. Flocks of pigeons whirled above, until she felt dizzy watching them—"lovely, graceful creatures in flight, stupid and pedantic on foot."

Perhaps she saw the pigeons as a metaphor. It was one thing to soar the great heights of God's love, another to serve Him on the ground, in the field. "I don't feel much like a missionary," she concluded. "Lord—help."

God did help. Elisabeth got to know a Plymouth Brethren missionary named Katherine Morgan, who would become a lifelong friend, inspiration, and example for her.

The hearty, dark-haired Katherine Morgan was on furlough in New Jersey, while Betty was living in Brooklyn in 1951. Katherine taught a Bible class to South American women there every Wednesday. Betty loved her humor, her spunk, her care for the women, her fluency in Spanish, and her deep knowledge of the Scriptures.

A widow when Betty met her, Katherine had been happily married to one Lester Morgan. During their early ministry in Colombia, Lester had pioneered five churches in southwestern Colombia. The Morgans had four young daughters; life was challenging, busy, and sweet. Then Lester fell mysteriously, gravely ill in mid-1940. It was rumored that those who were hostile to his ministry had poisoned him. The family returned to their home in New Jersey, and in spite of advanced medical care there, Lester died in December 1940.

Katherine Morgan had grieved his loss, prayed . . . and then she packed up her four daughters and returned to Colombia in 1941.

Her home served as a clinic for the sick, poor, and mentally ill people of her community. She performed routine dental procedures. She rode on horseback into the Andes to care for people in need; she paddled canoes on the Amazon River, deep into jungles, to preach the gospel and plant new churches.

In April of 1948, the popular president of Colombia was shot to death on a Bogota street. The fleeing assassin, a volatile young man in his twenties, was torn apart by an outraged mob. Crowds filled the streets, including a young Fidel Castro, then a student attending a Pan-American Conference taking place in the city. The rioting ignited political clashes, and a period in Colombia's history known as *La Violencia*, during which an estimated three hundred thousand people would be killed across the country.

It took a while for the unrest to reach Katherine Morgan's town of Pasto, about five hundred miles southwest of Bogota. A huge crowd assembled, shouting, among other things, "kill the Protestants!" They surrounded the Morgans' house.

One of Katherine's daughters, Lois, was about eight years old at the time. "I remember thinking, this is the last day of my life," she said years later. And "I didn't know if I was going to heaven, I told my mother 'I'm not ready to die.' She asked me if I wanted to pray. As she prayed with me, a sense of peace came over me."[3]

After praying with her daughter, Katherine walked out onto her balcony, looked down at the crowd, and unfurled a huge Colombian flag. "The next word you say, or stone you throw, is against your flag and your country," she shouted. First in small numbers, then in groups, the rioters melted away into the darkness.[4]

Whether in such tumultuous times, or in the everyday work of teaching Bible classes and caring for the sick, Katherine lived by faith. On some days she and her four daughters would have little food left in their home . . . and the Colombians Katherine cared for would bring them eggs and fruit. Their ancient car failed, and she had no money for repairs. Katherine prayed, went to the post office, and there was a check from America, for just the amount she needed.[5]

Over the years of her long life and service in Colombia—she died there in her nineties— Senora Catalina became a legend in the Andes. University scholars studying Colombian culture would stay at her home, as did visiting missionaries and needy neighbors. There was always vigorous discussion at the dinner table, with much laughter. Katherine built relationships with anyone and everyone. As one historian put it, "Although her life was spent in Brethren missions, in later years she emerged as a very public, but controversial figure . . . celebrated as a spiritual mother to Catholic priests and charismatic evangelicals alike."[6]

Katherine Morgan not only specifically encouraged Betty toward ministry in South America, she was also "an icon of what a true missionary was supposed to be," Betty said later. "Tremendous sense of humor, one of the funniest people I've ever known in my life and yet deeply spiritual and very powerful."[7]

She was also hearty. A few years after Betty met her, Katherine was in a bus accident in a mountain pass in Colombia. The driver went to sleep and shot off a cliff 1,500 feet high. The first ledge splintered the bus, threw out all the people, and sent the motor careening down to a raging river below. As the rest of the bus crashed toward the river, it collided with trees and ledges, crushing a number of the far-flung passengers. Katherine regained consciousness to find herself caught on a ledge fifty meters below the road, bruised from head to foot, a rib broken, a lung bruised, blood pouring from a deep cut in her head. Two dead men lay shattered on the ledge next to her. She fainted twice before she could make it back up the hill. It took her twenty-four hours of agony to get back to where she had started from. Being Katherine Morgan, she got patched up and went back to work.[8]

Betty admired—and found a kindred spirit in—Katherine's matter-of-fact commitment to tenacious obedience rather than focusing on how she was feeling. Many years later, Betty quoted a letter from Katherine in one of her books, in a chapter titled, appropriately, "The Discipline of Feelings."

"I agree with you that feelings are untrustworthy," Katherine had written to Betty. "Our feelings were conducive to doubt as to the reasons why our husbands were taken, but we knew inside we had to do as the Lord had commanded. In my estimation there was no particular virtue to what we did. We had received our orders, and we had to stick by them and carry our feelings in our pockets. Many times my feelings would have led me to throw in the sponge here in Pasto. I 'felt' the people were unresponsive . . . and the effort was fruitless. I 'felt' everything but the desire to stay here and work. Nevertheless God's plan has to be carried out. This is a hard lesson to learn, and it takes a lifetime."[9]

What Betty didn't know during that last month of 1951 was that Katherine Morgan's steely example would be exactly what she needed, given what was waiting for her in Ecuador.

Betty left her gray Brooklyn flat for a festive Christmas at home at Birdsong with her family. In late December, Ed Torrey, a doctor in his early thirties who attended the Howards' church, died from injuries sustained in a car crash on his way home from a prayer meeting. "I have been trying to imagine what it is like for Ann, his wife," Betty wrote. "Can the Lord bring peace to such a stricken soul? Surely, oh surely, He can, but it passes imagination.

"Once more, I see that there cannot be love without suffering."

CHAPTER 14

"I Wonder Sometimes If It Is Right to Be So Happy"

"For the special thrilling quality of their friendship was in their complete surrender. Like two open cities in the midst of some vast plain their two minds lay open to each other. And it wasn't as if he rode into hers like a conqueror, armed to the eyebrows and seeing nothing but a gay silken flutter— nor did she enter his like a queen walking on soft petals. No, they were eager, serious travellers, absorbed in understanding what was to be seen and discovering what was hidden— making the most of this extraordinary absolute chance which made it possible for him to be utterly truthful to her and for her to be utterly sincere with him."
—Katherine Mansfield

Jim Elliot and Pete Fleming sailed for Guayaquil, a port city on the southwest coast of Ecuador, in February 1952. After a long and colorful journey, they connected with Dr. Tidmarsh and settled in Quito in the home of an Ecuadorian family. There they soaked in Spanish and learned homeopathic medicine in preparation for jungle work among the Quichuas.

Betty Howard started 1952 feeling "alone again" in her small, gray New York apartment. She felt useless, close to tears, and far from God. "I know that in reading over this entry later on, I shall say, 'What a way to begin a new year.'" But time means nothing to God, she thought, and the fact was, "My desire for 1952, the prayer of my heart—oneness with the Lord."

Within a week a fellow missionary named Dorothy Jones had moved into Betty's tiny flat; Betty was no longer alone with the pigeons. A week or so after that, she met with an enthusiastic British missionary, Doreen Clifford, who was on furlough from the Ecuadorian jungle. Betty listened with fascination as Dorothy told her about her concern for the "yet untouched Waodani tribe of Indians on the Napo River. Humanly, it would be impossible for women to do such a work. Men have tried, and been killed." Doreen told Betty that she believed God had given her a love for the tribe for some purpose, if only to pray. "Or perhaps she might be a stepping stone for someone else to go in. . . . She asked me to pray about whether He might want me to go with her.

"I would hardly dare mention it to others," Betty wrote. "It would seem so fantastic and visionary. . . . If He leads this way, I am ready . . . six years ago, when I asked His will for my life pursuit, I felt that He wanted me in pioneer work, especially with a view to linguistic work. If this is a glimpse of His ultimate life purpose for me, I am glad."

So, though some would later think that Betty's desire to go to the Waodani emerged from her husband's ill-fated encounter with them, it began far earlier . . . in a New York conversation with an ebullient British missionary who dared to dream, like Betty, that women could pioneer where men could not.

Betty set her sights on Ecuador. She would work with Brethren missionaries there. She spent the next few weeks speaking to various Brethren women's groups in New York and New Jersey. She struggled with how to articulate the missionary calling in real terms, rather than just using familiar Christian clichés. What did it *really* mean to be a "witness" for Christ? "There is so much that appears that is not true, and so much that is true that does not appear. I long for utter child-likeness, to be a true child of God, entering fully into sonship. And the quality of truth is radical to such a state."

She felt the pain that she had read about in Amy Carmichael's writings. "Oh, it is one thing to declare, in giving a brave talk, that there is no such thing as sacrifice, in the light of eternity and its rewards, but it is quite another thing to believe, in my heart of hearts, that it is not sacrifice."

She longed for Jim, for the comfort of his arms and strong body. She longed for a child, a little boy that she might give over to God's service, like Old Testament Hannah. "I am past 25," she wrote. She'd read that age twenty to twenty-five was the ideal season for childbearing. "That prime of life is gone for me," she moaned. Lost forever.

No, she told herself sternly. Nothing was lost. The things she missed were stored in heavenly storehouses. Someday she would see God's glory in eternity, rather than the apparent losses she felt so keenly on this earth.

Besides, all musings went toward the dark side in that gray New York flat, with its tiny prison patch of sky and philosophical pondering of pink-footed pigeons. By March, Betty got to bid her Alcatraz a grateful "adieu without tears." After some time in Moorestown with her parents, she sailed on a large cargo-passenger ship called the *Santa Margarita*, bound for Ecuador.

It was the typical missionary departure of the day. Family members would cluster on the dock; the ship's horn would blast. A final round of farewells. The slow, dramatic casting off of restraints, the anchor raised, the gradual progress away from the city, the loved ones' faces growing smaller and smaller in the widening distance. Then the squaring of one's shoulders, and turning one's face toward the open ocean, toward the unknown adventures ahead. After two days of rough sea and rain, Betty exulted in sunny, blue-sky days and serene slate seas through the Panama Canal and on to Buenaventura, Colombia. On April 14, at 2:45 in the morning, Betty arrived at Guayaquil, Ecuador. There she had to wait ten days for the arrival and unloading of her baggage, a common occurrence in 1952. She wandered the streets of the "wretchedly poor town" and watched men unload cargo on the docks.

Betty Howard sailing for Ecuador, 1952

"This was excellent experience," Betty reported philosophically in a letter home. "The Ecuadorian mind seems not to comprehend haste, and each day, upon inquiring about the progress of my gear, I received the same answer, '*Mañana*,'" Tomorrow.

Miraculously, *mañana* eventually came, and Betty and her baggage took a Pan American flight to Quito. She was breathless with the capital city's beauty. "Set 9,500 feet above sea level, it still seems a great valley in comparison with the great rolling hills all about it, and the brutally grand peaks in the distance. . . . The homes are of whitewashed adobe . . . it is not uncommon to see burros, cows, dogs, mountain ponies and llamas roaming the streets, along with Cadillacs and pushcarts, busses and hundreds of Quichua Indians, each with his or her great burden, dogtrotting along on bare feet. The women all wear long, full, hand-woven skirts, [fedora] hats, and shawls."[1]

Reflecting its Spanish influence, Quito retained a certain Old World grace . . . "narrow cobbled streets over which jutted carved balconies of lovely dark wood festooned with geraniums. There were delicate wrought iron gates with heavy handmade hinges and door knockers. The green squares and parks had fountains and statuary and some were bordered by graceful colonnades."[2]

Dr. Tidmarsh had arranged housing for Betty and her fellow missionary and roommate from New York, Dorothy Jones. They settled into the home of a slim, glossy-haired, upper-class Ecuadorian couple, Señor and Señora Arias. They did not speak English; Betty's facility in Spanish would grow enormously over the course of the late spring and summer. Betty's room was above the garage. Two Quichua women with long, black braids cooked and did housework. Betty noted they were "fascinated with the gigantic, pale foreigner." And soon after the "pale foreigner" arrived—oh, happy day—Jim and Pete Fleming moved to lodgings across the street.

It was the first time since college that Jim and Betty could see each other every day. They explored the city, practiced Spanish, picnicked, and read poetry to each other. They took in a bullfight. Jim wrote in his journal, "I don't know why I love bulls. Nothing has quite the fitness to act bravo, it seems to me, as a well-built bull." He compared the spectacle to a western rodeo, though "somewhat bloodier . . . the whole thing seems to fit the Latin mind . . . gold braid and blood . . . exultation at death . . . paper ribbons and 'picks' . . . gracefulness and brutishness . . . a bull and a pair of ballet shoes. These people are extremists."[3]

Jim and Betty, summer 1952

One night, starting at about 2 a.m., Jim, Betty, Pete, and a few other male missionaries hiked up the incline of Pichincha, an active volcano. The moon shone brilliantly. By 11 a.m. they reached the almost sixteen-thousand-foot summit. On the way down, they rested in the warm, soft grass on the slope of the valley. Jim allegedly dozed, his head in Betty's lap, as she "drank in the incredible beauty of the vast vistas" in front of her.

During this idyllic period, Jim and Betty both seemed overwhelmed by the simple pleasures of being together. In a letter to a mutual friend from Wheaton, Jim wrote, "The Lord has brought Betty and me over some happy ground. . . . Oh, Van, I couldn't have asked for more than God in deliberate grace has surprised me with! We didn't ask to be sent to the field together. We didn't ask to be sent to live in such close proximity. . . . It seemed unreasonable to ask such things, six months ago. Dreams are tawdry when compared with the leading of God. Betty and I are agreed that the will of God for some time is to be undeclared to one another, though our feelings are clear.

"I wonder sometimes if it is right to be so happy. Day follows day in an easy succession of wonder and joys—simple, good things like food well prepared, or play with children, or conversation with Pete, or supply of money for rent or board within hours of its being due. Grace upon grace . . ."[4]

From Betty's perspective, she and Jim were coming to know one another "in a new way. We both feel now that there is perfect freedom between us, as far as sharing everything that concerns us. I feel that I not only want to share, I have a great need to share. I love him beyond telling. I desire him more than anything in the world. When I think of his manliness, his strength, his kindness, tenderness, and oh-so-undeserved love . . . I am prostrate with gratitude to God."

Still, she knew that this man could be taken from her at any time. First, Jim was clear that mission work might well require the ultimate cost. He talked with Betty about his desire to go to the Waodani. They were not known for welcoming outsiders with anything but spears and death. She wrote in her journal, "Jim said, 'Do you realize what it may cost?' [Speaking of the possibility of his going into work among the Waodani.] Yes, I realize what it might cost—death."

To her, this was no reason not to be engaged and married. Still, Jim worried that he would take less risks of utter obedience to God if he was encumbered by a wife and family. "To me," Betty wrote in her journal, "this is a pure technical difference." She already loved him with all her heart.

But, since the anguished Jim could not yet commit to her, she held herself back from letting her emotions flood their relationship. Her inner acidity kicked into gear as a defense mechanism. "Every so often, when I want with all my heart, to take his arm or tell him that I love him, in order to restrain myself, I say something sarcastic or cutting, or very off-hand. This is what happened Thursday night. He reproved me for my attitude (it was only an apparent attitude, for such a thing never represses my feelings toward him) and finally in some measure, I brought myself to explain the reasons. He seemed to understand in part, and almost melted me with his gentleness. Oh, it is agony—to act unconcerned and distant when I am all but overwhelmed with tenderness toward him. When shall I be free to tell him???"

Not any time soon. Jim still believed he must go to the jungle both single and unencumbered by a commitment.

So when Betty got news of her sister Ginny's betrothal, it was tough going. She wrote stoically in her journal, "8/6/52. Received word today of Ginny's engagement [to Bud DeVries]. I am stunned— but oh, so happy for her—my 'little' sister, 7 years my junior."

Yes, yes, she was properly happy for her little sister, and also properly glad for her brother Dave, whose new baby was born around the same time. But their gain highlighted her own sense of loss, and though she could control just what she properly wrote in her journal, she wasn't as successful mastering her emotions. She unloaded to her mother. "Sometimes I feel that I cannot stand it any longer, that I literally cannot <u>live</u> without <u>him</u>. . . . I cry at the drop of a hat. . . . When I am in bed, I want him <u>desperately</u>. It is as though every inch of my body just aches for <u>his</u>."[5]

She wept when she and Jim went for a walk that same evening. She told him about her siblings' news, and then sobbed some more.

"It's just that I can't see why they should have it so, and we have it this way," she told him.

"I cried too," wrote the sometimes obtuse Jim, who had spent hours feverishly studying the apostle Paul's writings in the original Greek, trying to discern if he was being disobedient or obedient in his interactions with Betty. He wrote of "wanting to be fair to her, wanting to marry her, wanting, wanting" . . . but he felt "no guiding from God, not even for engagement."[6]

Betty mourned. She was in relationship purgatory, with no public commitment from Jim. All she had was "the censure and lifted eyebrows" of everyone who knew, or knew of, Jim Elliot and Betty Howard. She imagined what people were saying. "'She chased him from one continent to another,' 'she'll get him yet,' etc., etc."[7]

Pete Fleming wrote home about Betty's turmoil, "She is moody and quiet and obviously under a strain. Senora Arias says that she has come across Betty crying alone at night and wants Jim to do something about it. Jim said late last night he and Betty spent more time crying than talking and it was really a heart-rending time. Betty had received word of Ginny's engagement and of Dave's new baby and it just broke her up, I guess. All these joys came to her brother and sister younger than she is and still she has no *firm* promise, no engagement, and no prospected wedding time."[8]

Pete—brilliant scholar, friend to Jim, committed follower of Christ with prodigious Bible knowledge, and sometimes clueless in his own romantic relationship—was perhaps sensitized to Betty's emotions because of insights from Olive Ainslie. Pete and Olive had known one another since childhood back in Seattle, and had come to an understanding of marriage in the spring of 1951. Some months later Jim Elliot had swept into Seattle, infectiously excited about missions in Ecuador and a vision of single brothers working together for Christ. Jim had cautioned Pete to make sure his call was from God, not Jim, but Jim's personality was pretty persuasive. Pete decided to go to the mission field. He broke up with Olive, so he would be unencumbered, like Jim.

This had been not only painful, but confusing for Olive . . . especially when she had gradually discovered, as it dawned on Pete, that Jim Elliot in fact was *not* a free man. Pete now saw that though Jim wasn't formally committed to Betty Howard, his heart was woven with hers. Jim knew *who* he would marry, if it came to that. But as we've seen, he was in a constant jumble as to whether God wanted him to be married in the first place.

When Olive had learned of Betty's arrival in Ecuador and that she'd settled in Quito for language training, right across the street from Pete and Jim, the drama intensified.

This was no subterfuge on Jim and Betty's part. As far as they were concerned—though perhaps they were in a bit of denial—they were pursuing missionary work as *individuals*, and it was just a fortunate blessing that they both ended up in Ecuador. This happy coincidence, their deep love for one another, and Jim's uncertainty if God would ever call him to be married created an understandable muddle for onlookers.

In the midst of the muddle, Pete began to come to his senses about his own relationship with Olive. He re-established contact and began to slowly rebuild the trust he had broken.

The summer of 1952 drew to an end. Jim and Pete were now ready to move to the great jungle southeast of Quito, and commence work in a settlement called Shandia at the headwaters of the Amazon basin. Dr. Tidmarsh had established the station a few years earlier with a school for Quichua boys, but the buildings had fallen into disrepair, and the airstrip overgrown by rapacious jungle vegetation. The Indians there would welcome Jim and Pete, who were determined to build relationships with the Quichuas and work side-by-side with them. Pete wrote in his journal, ". . . in order to reach these for Christ we will have to be like them . . . able to meet their problems with them and help them develop Christ-likeness in *their* environment—not give them an unrealistic goal of Christ-likeness in our controlled environment in their midst."[9]

As Pete and Jim departed, Betty had recovered from her desolation and tears. She bid Jim farewell—yet again—with equanimity. She credited her mother's fervent prayers for her change in attitude. "Yours is a sympathy that fortifies. It is not the simpering, weakening kind. You cannot possibly know how much it does for me just to know that you stand with me in these things. I am perfectly sure that it was your prayer this past week that did this for me."[10]

Betty, without latitude to plan her future *with* Jim, decided to plot an independent course. Her roommate Dorothy was committed to working with Ecuador's Colorado Indians, but lacked linguistics training. Betty could be a huge help in that area. She prayed about it, and gradually felt that God was calling her to the Colorados, far to the west . . . in the exact opposite direction from the eastern jungle where Jim Elliot would be.

CHAPTER 15

The Colorful Colorados

"There are grave difficulties on every hand,
and more are looming ahead.
Therefore, we must go forward."
—William Carey

Today the journey from Quito to the hamlet of San Miguel de los Colorados takes about three hours by car. In 1952, however, the roads were perilous or nonexistent. The trip took several days for Betty and Dorothy. They set out early in the morning, perched on the tailgate of a pickup truck driven by an Ecuadorian believer named E. T. After crisscrossing Quito for several hours, picking up a vehicle part here, or a letter to be delivered there, they at last made their way onto the narrow, winding road west, down toward the jungle.

The road allowed only one-way traffic, which changed directions according to unknown and unpredictable rules throughout the day. This occasionally resulted in tension between truck drivers— *"Caramba! Don't you see that I'm on my way down?"* *"Caramba! Don't you see that I'm on my way up?"*

Then the drivers would get out, yelling and pawing the ground like bulls. Onlookers would weigh in with passionate opinions about who should have the right-of-way. Dogs barked. Chicken feathers floated down on the motorists. And in the end, everyone would get back in their vehicles and somehow eventually get to where they were going, though not in a timely fashion. E. T. drove on, through waterfalls, shallow rivers, and down, down, down, into sugar cane and banana plantations, and the dense, misty jungle.*

---

*Elisabeth Elliot wrote about her work among the Colorado Indians in a slim volume called *These Strange Ashes*, published in 1975. I think it's one of her

The pickup arrived in Santo Domingo, which looked like a "set for a Hollywood western," late on the first evening. Betty and Dorothy slid off the back of the tailgate, rubbed their bruised derrieres, and helped E. T. and his wife, Vera, unload the truck. They would spend the night at E. T.'s small home before traveling to San Miguel the next day.

The house was "unpainted wood that had blackened with the dampness and mildew," observed Betty. "There were four children who appeared to belong to E. T. and Vera, though no introductions were made. . . . One or two other people who apparently lived in the house spoke no English. Where they all slept remained a mystery . . . the house was furnished with the barest essentials of tables and chairs or benches of shoddy construction, and Vera cooked on a *fogon*, a sort of sandbox on legs with a fire built on it. Smoke filled the house . . . everything was dark, and there were unidentified bodies stretched out on the floor of the kitchen-living room. The place smelled. It was a mixture of burned grease, onions, smoke, mildew, unwashed people," and human waste.

"There was an outhouse used by the family, a crazy tall shack emitting a most lethal effluvium, but a steady parade of townspeople were making use of an empty lot next door as a bathroom. They were not seeking privacy, that was obvious, but only space, and judging by the caution with which they stepped, there was little enough of that remaining."[1]

"The depression [the house] brought me made me feel guilty, for I thought at the time that the ugliness and squalor and lack of privacy were sacrifices appropriate for a servant of the Lord. If I did not like the atmosphere it must mean that I was not yet prepared to lay down my life as I had promised."[2]

After a dismal night, Betty and Dorothy got up the next morning, hired two small horses—going rate, 90 cents a day—and rode for about three hours south, toward San Miguel. The trail was deep and wide; at some points the mud almost reached the horses' bellies. The giant trees and ferns and elephant ears of the jungle crowded each other "in unimaginable luxuriance, draped with vines and flowering plants that gave forth unexpectedly sweet scents. The great breadfruit spread its huge, dark, glossy leaves beside the trail and drooped its heavy brown globes into the mud."[3]

In the early afternoon, the two women arrived at San Miguel de los Colorados—a clearing the width of two football fields, with

---

best books; her superb descriptive skills as a writer, and her dry wit, are on full display, and the story lacks the didactic tone of instruction that marked some of her later books.

a scattering of houses. They guided the horses toward a neat frame structure with a fence . . . and a young woman in a flowered cotton dress came flying out, hailing them with a stream of British English . . . "Oh, I say! Welcome to San Miguel-on-the-mud!"

This was Doreen, the energetic British missionary who, while on furlough in New York, had dreamed with Betty about possibly reaching the Waodani one day. Doreen had been working among the Colorado Indians for several years. Doreen's colleague, Barbara, lived in a small house on stilts across the clearing from Doreen. The two Brits invited Betty and Dorothy to sit down for lunch: spinach soup, rice, fried eggs, and of course tea. There was a proper pitcher of cooled boiled milk for the tea, covered with a scalloped doily weighted around the edges with glass beads. Civilization, in the jungle.

"Here we were, drinking tea together over the green and orange tablecloth, discussing the work we would all do," Betty wrote years later. "At last, at last, I thought. Under God we would surely do wonders."[4]

Wilfred Tidmarsh, the missionary who had first encouraged Jim Elliot and Pete Fleming to come to Ecuador, had started the mission work in San Miguel. His main focus was the Quichua Indians in Shandia, to the east, but he had hoped that San Miguel could be a launching point for evangelistic work among the Colorado Indians here in the western rainforest. The Indians lived scattered throughout the jungle; the little clearing was as close to their habitat as missionaries could hope to get.

At this point there was a small group of non-Indian congregants who came together for worship services, complete with dogs, spitting, and crying children. But the mission's focal group, the Colorado Indians, remained peaceful, tolerant of outsiders, and utterly aloof.

But Betty felt a strong sense that God had sent her and her colleagues. All would be well. After all, the Great Commission commanded that the gospel go to all the world. "The Good News . . . is meant for everyone, and the Colorados of Ecuador's jungle had a right to hear it."[5]

She also believed "that God blesses those who obey Him and works things out in "beautiful, demonstrable ways for those who have given themselves to do His work . . . I, as far as I knew, was here in obedience and my purpose was to do God's work. There was every reason to expect that God would grant us success."[6]

Her words sound naïve. After all, she'd read missionary biographies; she knew the stories of men and women who had lost their lives, like John and Betty Stam, or lost their health, or lost their minds, in the service of Christ. She was ready to pay any price to be obedient to His leading.

But, like many, she believed that God would surely take her sacrifices and make them into *successes* for His sake . . . glorious victories that human beings could *see*, that could be reported to supporters back home, bringing glory to God.

But in fact, Betty's time among the Colorado Indians stripped her, in some shocking and violent ways, of her tidy assumptions about God's will. Among the Colorados, she confronted, perhaps for the first time, the monolithic, impenetrable mystery of God's ways.

CHAPTER 16

The First Death of Elisabeth Elliot

"God's favorites, especially God's favorites, are not immune from the bewildering times when God seems silent. Where there is no longer any opportunity for doubt, there is no longer any opportunity for faith either. Faith demands uncertainty, confusion. The Bible includes many proofs of God's concern—some quite spectacular—but no guarantees. A guarantee would, after all, preclude faith."
—Paul Tournier

One black jungle night Betty was deeply asleep when she woke to the sound of someone banging on her front door. "Señorita! Señorita!"

A frantic man paced the porch. His wife was giving birth and about to die. Across the clearing, Barbara, a midwife, had already been alerted. She'd asked the man to wake Betty as well. Barbara had delivered the couple's last child, approximately the eleventh in a long string of births. She had pleaded with the man to take his wife to a hospital; any further pregnancies would be very high risk. He had contemplatively smoked a cigarette, nodded, and not done so. Now the wife, Maruja, was in desperate condition.

When Betty and Barbara arrived at the house, Maruja was writhing on a bloody bed surrounded by pools of blood on the floor. Betty heard a snuffling sound, and turned to see that the baby had been born and was lying on a pile of filthy rags on another bed. Someone— perhaps one of the two men present who might have been the father— had halfheartedly wrapped a rag around it and deposited it there so it could die in peace.

Doreen examined Maruja. She had a prolapsed uterus and was in shock, with hardly any pulse. "I can't stand it, help me, I'm going out of my mind," she gasped. "O God! O holy Virgin! O most holy Virgin, have mercy! I'm dying!"[1]

She quieted, then began to speak again, bidding farewell to her family, then lapsed into guttural noises, her jaw working back and forth and finally settling into a chilling grin. Her husband came back in, howling.

She was dead.

A day or two later, the men brought the baby to Barbara and Betty. It was thin as a skeleton, showed signs of syphilis, and soon died. Its "two fathers" had fed it only water.

Even as Betty mourned over such losses, her particular work here was to render the Colorado language into written form. To do so, she needed an "informant." The term can be jarring; it sounds like an insider who disseminates confidential information so the government can prosecute mobsters or drug lords. But in the missions world it denotes an indigenous person from whom a missionary can obtain otherwise unknowable information about language, dialect, and culture.

Betty hoped to hire a Colorado Indian who would sit with her for hours, reviewing vocabulary words and slowly repeating them over and over so she could get the phonetics right and write them on her neat notecards. It was tedious work . . . but surely one of the Colorados, in need of money, would take on the job.

The first Indian Betty met made an indelible impression.

"He seemed to be wearing a vermillion-red visored helmet . . . on top of this a ring of white cotton. His face, arms, and all I could see of his body were painted brilliant red. There were black horizontal stripes beginning at his forehead and painted all the way to his toes, and in between the stripes, black polka dots. He wore a black-and-white striped skirt . . . [and] several bright yellow and turquoise cotton scarves. . . . He smiled, revealing black-stained teeth and tongue. His lips, too, were stained blue-black. We shook hands, and if his hands seemed small and hard to me, mine must have seemed startlingly huge and uncalloused to him."[2]

Privately, Betty asked Doreen what he needed a helmet for.

"Helmet?" Doreen shrieked. "That's his *hair*!" She explained that Colorado men plastered their hair with a thick mixture of Vaseline and *achiote*, a red dye made from the seed-pod of a jungle tree.

The man was polite, but had no interest in helping Señorita Betty learn his language. Neither did any of the other Indians who came across her path. They were proud, independent, and a bit disdainful about the white women's presence in their world.

Betty chafed at the Indians' detachment. They didn't seem to have felt needs the gospel would address. But she "had no doubt that God was on my side. . . . I would get ahold of the language, make it my own, harness it into an alphabet, and make of the Indians readers and writers."[3]

So Betty prayed. "The work I hoped to do was God's work . . . I was His worker. It was all clear and simple. My prayer was as free from selfish and impure motives as any I had ever prayed. I had God's written promises of help, such as that in Isaiah 50:7, 'The Lord GOD will help me, therefore shall I not be confounded.'"[4]

Her prayer was answered. An Ecuadorian named Don Macario had grown up on a hacienda with Colorado children, and was completely bilingual in Spanish and Colorado. He was a believer. He had no job. He was willing to work for what Betty could pay.

Incredible! God had provided an even better informant than Betty could have imagined.

Don Macario taught Betty that the Indians called their own language *Tsahfihki*, "the language of the people." He taught her vowel pronunciations, inflections, sentence structure, verbs, nouns, prefixes. He was a linguist's dream. Over the weeks that followed, an ecstatic and organized Betty made charts, cards, and orthography lists, using phonetic symbols that represented the *Tsahfihki* sounds. The work was going well.

She duly reported her progress in letters to Jim, which passed slowly—very slowly—across the long miles between them. Working hard in Shandia, Jim was thrilled that his old friend Ed McCully had arrived in Ecuador in December of '52. Like Jim and Betty, Ed and his wife, Marilou, were Plymouth Brethren missionaries, anxious to serve jungle tribes. They were studying Quichua in Shandia, living in a shack near Jim.

One warm morning in January 1953, Betty sat in her bedroom, reading a Bible passage in 1 Peter about believers undergoing "fiery trials." She heard gunshots nearby. This wasn't unusual; men often hunted in the vicinity. Then there was screaming, the sounds of horses' hoofs and people running, and then Doreen's British voice shouting over the din: "They've killed Don Macario!"

Betty ran outside.

"Macario has been shot!" people were yelling. "Murdered!"

A friend came running to the clearing, out of breath. He'd been clearing brush with Macario when a group of men showed up, claiming the land belonged to one of them. Macario had insisted the property was his. One of the men had whipped out a gun and shot him in the head several times.

Betty's colleague Barbara had run to the scene of the shooting. Now, she and a group of men arrived, carrying the body between them on a big poncho. They laid it on the porch of Barbara's house.

Betty and the rest of the crowd gazed in silence for a long time. "There was a great hole in Macario's forehead—he'd been shot point-blank. . . . Rigor mortis had set in, and one arm stuck up stiffly from the side, an accusing forefinger pointing off into space. . . . Flies crawled around the wound, around the slightly opened mouth and eyes."

Someone galloped away on horseback, headed to the next town to alert the authorities. A few hours later two men from the sheriff's office arrived, accompanied by a missionary named Bill. They announced that the perpetrator could not be prosecuted unless an autopsy was conducted and the bullets recovered.

It was fairly clear where the bullets had gone in. Bill the missionary volunteered to do the autopsy, since the nearest coroner was likely in Quito. Doreen said she would assist. She ran to her house, changed into all-white British surgical garb that had presumably been on standby for such an occasion, and grabbed a meat saw. She and Bill perused the body. The crowd pressed in. After some hemming and hawing, Bill commenced sawing the corpse's skull. Not an easy task. Mothers called their children to come and watch, Bill sweated, and eventually, the skull, which had been cracked by the blast of the bullet, fell into several pieces. Bill extracted smashed bullet fragments, the investigators took them, and the crowd dispersed.

Bill and Doreen tried to put poor Macario back together, fashioning a sort of turban for him to wear to his grave. He had no family nearby, so the small Christian community held a wake, singing hymns and drinking coffee through the night as the corpse ripened. They made a coffin, nailed the lid shut, and carried it away for burial.

Betty Howard wrote to her parents that it had been the most nightmarish day of her life. She could not quite grasp the sudden horror of her friend's death, the rank injustice of it, and what his loss meant for the Colorado translation of the Bible.

Macario had been God's answer to prayer, the key to all of the language work, probably the only human on the whole planet who spoke both Colorado and Spanish with equal ease. Did God not care about the salvation and discipleship of this jungle tribe?

The poncho on which Macario's improvised autopsy had been conducted hung on the fence adjacent to Betty's house, so rain would wash off the bloodstains. Every time Betty looked at it, it mocked her. She thought "of the sight of those spilled brains, the only brains in the world that contained the languages" she needed. Had she left so much behind to come to this remote spot of Ecuadorian jungle simply on a fool's errand?

She could not find meaning in the shattered pieces of Macario's head, or in her own shattered mission. She had promised to obey God, and had known that such obedience might well lead to "tribulation." After all, that was biblical. And she had prayed for holiness. But this kind of "answer" was startling and repugnant to her.

"I had desired God Himself and He had not only not given me what I asked for, He had snatched away what I had. I came to nothing, to emptiness."[5]

A few nights later—while still reeling from the bizarre events of Don Macario's death—Betty was sitting at her desk, sadly reviewing her language notes, when she heard the sound of horse's hoofs.

She grabbed her lantern and ran outside. A friend from the town of Santo Domingo handed Betty a telegram. She ripped it open.

It was from Ed McCully. Betty knew from correspondence that Jim had conferred with Ed about marriage in general, and about engagement in particular.

"Jim will come to Quito Friday," Ed had wired. "Come."

It could mean only one thing.

Betty flew into action. Early the following morning, she rode on horseback to Santo Domingo, then caught a ride to Quito on a banana truck. The ten-hour, jolting journey felt like approximately forever. The driver left her at a truck stop in Quito, where she hailed a cab and made her way to the friends' home where Jim was staying.

After years of discussion, anticipation, doubt, and longing, after reams of journals and letters and written prayers, the paper trail about the engagement itself is surprisingly sparse. Betty wrote to her parents:

a. A fireplace,

b. A soft rug on the floor in front of it,

c. The proposal,

d. The kiss. Yes, absolutely my first. Describe it? Yes—'when apples grow on the lilac bush,'

d. The huge surprise of the ring.[6]

But in her journal, Betty wrote about the kiss, "O, God of stars and flowers . . . The relief of being able to tell him my love, of feeling free for the first time, is simply unspeakable. I literally ache with love for him and long now for the day when he will be my husband. Oh, I want to be possessed. I desire him, and his desire is toward me—Oh, perfect love, all human thought transcending."

Jim wrote his own parents about his own joy about the engagement, with just a touch of understatement, "It has certainly not been done in a hurry."[7] He wrote to Betty's parents, as well, thanking them for "bringing Betty into the world, and building into her all that makes her now such a very delightful companion with whom I can share everything I have." He also acknowledged the long incubation period of their relationship, and thanked her parents for the "patience and wisdom you showed through the whole affair."[8]

Jim, being Jim, told Betty he wasn't sure of the timing of their wedding. But he did know one thing: she must learn Quichua before they could marry. If she were to wait until after they were joined, there might well be distractions that would preclude her study, and then she couldn't be a full partner in his work.

She agreed. She was ready to pay any price for this man . . . and how hard could Quichua be?

The next few days were probably among the happiest in Betty's life. Her abbreviated journal entries only hint at the overwhelming joy and release she felt, after five years of loving Jim without being able to express much of anything *to* Jim.

Feb. 1—Church, breaking of bread, radio station HCJB in the evening. The whole choir burst into "I Love You Truly" as we entered the studio![9]

Feb. 2—Broadcast: we announced our engagement to whoever was listening. [At the time, HCJB had an audience of millions of listeners throughout Latin America, the U.S., and far beyond.]

Feb. 3—Lunch in bodega [a flat the missionaries had rented to store their bulky possessions and supplies from the States] with the whole gang. McCullys, Cathers, Barbara and Emma, Jim and I. Dinner at Bill and Marie's.

Feb. 4—Dinner at Betty and Joe's, with McCullys.

Feb. 5—Some shopping and running around town, supper together at Wonder Bar, evening at bodega.

Feb. 6—Afternoon in bodega, dinner with McCullys at Colon Hotel. Hors d'oeuvres, artichoke soup, filet mignon, mashed potatoes, mushrooms, beets, carrots, pie a la mode, coffee! [Betty was always good at recounting what she ate.]

Feb. 7—More shopping, letter writing, lunch with Arias, and in the evening we baby-sat while Gwen went to a meeting.

Feb. 8—Jim preached in church, I sang, meeting at Gwen's; Jim had supper with Youth Camp committee, met me at bodega, we went to a second church service, and then came home.

Feb. 9—Shopping together throughout the day. Dinner with Jim's host family. Mail from home. Our families had gotten our letters. Everyone thrilled with the news.

Feb. 10—Had supper together at bodega by the fire. Toasted ham sandwiches, cream of mushroom soup, peas, tea.

Feb. 11—Went to bodega for just a few minutes after supper. Jim wanted to go home and write letters. We ended up on a hill above the city.

Feb. 12—Whole day at hot springs with Gwen, Jimmy, McCullys, and Emma. Lots of fun. Sunburn. In the evening, bodega again, and a bottle of wine.

Friday 13—To Otavalo (a city known for its Indian textiles, volcanos, and waterfalls) with McCullys. Stayed in Imperial Hotel. Marilou and I had one room, the men another.

Feb. 14—Home from Otavalo after a grand time at market. Jim bought me a gorgeous blanket.

Feb. 15—Dr. Fuller informed me today of an active tubercular lesion in one lung. Jim was with me when he told me. We faced it together. I have never been so crushed by anything in my life. It may mean going back to the States for three months of absolute bedrest. How can I leave Ecuador? How can I ever marry Jim? I cannot be a hindrance to him. Have to have tests made this week.

Feb. 16—Awoke crying. Jim and I had a letter from Dave and Gibby of congratulation on our engagement which brought tears to both of us. Little do they know this latest dark cloud that comes on the horizon.

Feb. 19—The "tuberculosis" proved to be only a shadow which disappeared in the third X-ray. [The diagnosis had either been a mistake, or, as Jim believed, God had healed her of the shadow in her lung.] In the evening of the 18th, our last together, we were at Gwen's. O fiery passion . . . and at 6 a.m. Thursday, he came into my room in the dark to kiss me good-bye. It was a dismal day without him. Oh, God—how long can I endure? I need him, so very much. And my longing for a home with him never slackens. How I need his strength and love, his arms around me, his dear face against my own."

Betty made the long, jolting trip back to San Miguel. "Oh, it is lonely," she wrote after she arrived. "I can't stand it. <u>How</u> can I put heart and soul into Colorado work? <u>How</u> shall I ever learn Quichua here?"

First things first. She set her formidable mind to the task of completing groundwork for the translation of the Colorado language. With Don Macario gone, she feverishly spent time with everyone, anyone, who could possibly give her any shred of help. Samuel, the brother of the chief of the tribe, agreed to meet with her, graciously staying sober long enough on Saturdays to give Betty more of an understanding of the language. He was "a handsome Indian, better painted and greased and perfumed than anyone else I know, and spoke exceptionally good Spanish."[10]

Samuel, Betty's Colorado language informant, 1953

With Samuel's help, Betty was able to complete a phonemic alphabet of *Tsahfihki*. Characteristically concerned about others inflating what she had done, she wrote to friends, "now please do not go around saying that I have 'completed' the alphabet of the Colorado Indian language! I am not at all satisfied with some of my conclusions, as they had to be based on hypotheses rather than pure science in one or two instances."[11]

This hard-won material could be used by Doreen and Barbara and any other missionaries as a base to understand and communicate with the Colorados. Linguists could build on it to eventually translate the New Testament. Wishing it could have been more, or better, Betty carefully packed all her linguistic papers, cards, charts, and notes into a suitcase, so it would be easy for others to have it all in one place. Barbara and Doreen consulted the materials often, and began to make a bit of progress in the Colorado language.

In early summer, Betty moved from San Miguel to Dos Rios, a Christian and Missionary Alliance mission station in the eastern jungle near the town of Tena. The missionaries there had graciously invited her to come and study the Quichua language.

She immersed herself among Quichua speakers. While not as colorful in appearance or personality as the Colorados, the local Indians were ready to help her however they could. She studied, practiced, listened, read, ate, drank, and dreamed in Quichua. After *Tsahfihki*, it was remarkably easy. Soon she was beginning to both understand and converse in the new language.

Then she received a letter from Doreen. She eagerly tore it open, and sat stunned, unable to breathe.*

Doreen reported that Barbara's luggage had been stolen off the back of a truck. This included Betty's suitcase full of her handwritten notebooks, file boxes, charts, and laborious linguistic notes on the Colorado language. All of them.

There were no copies of anything. In one stroke, everything Betty had done in nine months in San Miguel was gone. Her unique, irreplaceable work decoding the Colorado language for an eventual New Testament translation. . . . *No!* This could not happen. There must be some way to get it back. She kept rereading Doreen's letter, as if its contents might change upon review.

What was God doing? It made no sense. Didn't He want the Colorados to have the Bible in their own language? Why would He so casually allow the loss of nine months of painstaking work for His kingdom?

As with her questions after Don Macario's death, there were no answers.

Many years later, Betty referred to the first nine months of her official missions experience in Ecuador—late 1952 through mid-1953—as a "school year."

---

*When Betty later wrote about these traumatic events, it appears that she conflated them for the sake of clarity and narrative flow. In *These Strange Ashes*, she wrote that the materials were in a suitcase that had disappeared from the top of a bus, and that she was told this via letter in the summer of 1953. In her journals and correspondence, however, it appears that the letter from Doreen arrived on April 7, 1954, and reported that the suitcase with all Betty's language materials had been stolen from the back of a truck. Either way, the loss of those many months of painstaking language work shaped Betty's understanding of God's sovereignty for the rest of her life.

During that course of study she certainly acquired a lot of new information. She learned two languages. She learned many practical skills that were essential for missions work.

But this school year was not just about facts and skills. In it, God began to teach her truths she would probe deeper and deeper over the ensuing decades, multi-faceted aspects of His will that could not be charted, categorized, or listed in an index. God's sovereign will was a mystery that could not be mastered, an experience that could not be classified, a wonder that had no end. It wove together strands of life, death, grace, pain, joy, humility, and awe.

In short, the San Miguel "school year" had brought the first of four distinct, almost soul-crushing deaths over the course of Elisabeth Elliot's long life. Macario's death, and the subsequent theft of the language notes, gouged a fatal hole in the usual smooth surface of her correct Christian answers and created a conundrum for the dutiful, devout, curious, and high-achieving new missionary. The question "why?" not only remained unanswered in practical terms, it also could not be neatly resolved by the skillful re-arrangement of facts to produce the proper "spiritual" answer. This death, this loss, defied the usual religious formula: *Well, this bad thing happened so God could do x, y, and z, beyond what we could have asked or imagined.*

Of course Betty knew the glorious, huge themes of life trumping death in the end, as in Jesus' triumph over the grave. Her view of the end of history, of the new heaven and the new earth, of Jesus' ultimate victory, was unaltered. But in her life experience, these particular earthly events just seemed like an inefficient waste for the kingdom of God, with no explanation that could make anyone, particularly Betty, feel better, let alone "victorious."

It was Betty's "lesson one" in the graduate school of faith . . . "my first experience of having to bow down before that which I could not possibly explain. Usually we need not bow. We can simply ignore the unexplainable because we have other things to occupy our minds. We sweep it under the rug. We evade the questions. Faith's most severe tests come not when we see nothing, but when we see a stunning array of evidence that seems to prove our faith vain. If God were God, if He were omnipotent, if He had cared, would this have happened? Is this that I face now the ratification of my calling, the reward of obedience? One turns in disbelief again from the circumstances and looks into the abyss. But in the abyss there is only blackness, no glimmer of light, no answering echo.[12]

"It was a long time before I came to the realization that it is in our acceptance of what is given that God gives Himself. Even the Son of

God had to learn obedience by the things that He suffered. . . . And His reward was desolation, crucifixion."[13]

Amy Carmichael wrote of a believer asking God why one's hopes would come to ashes. "But these strange ashes, Lord, this nothingness/ This baffling sense of loss?" to which the Lord asks, in return, "was the anguish of my stripping less/Upon the torturing cross?"[14]

Betty mulled over it all. "Each separate experience of individual stripping we may learn to accept as a fragment of the suffering Christ bore when He took it all," she wrote. ". . . This grief, this sorrow, this total loss that empties my hands and breaks my heart, I may, if I will, accept, and by accepting it, I find in my hands something to offer. And so I give it back to Him, who in mysterious exchange gives Himself to me."[15]

Betty saw a similar lesson in an apocryphal story told about Jesus and His disciples. Walking along a rocky road, Jesus asked each of His friends to carry a stone for Him. John chose a big one; Peter selected a small one. They all climbed a steep mountain path. As they rested at the top, famished, Jesus commanded that the stones become bread. When Peter was still hungry after his small portion, John shared some of his.

A while later, the group set out on the path again, and Jesus asked each man to carry a stone for Him. This time Peter chose the largest. After a long walk, Jesus took them to a river, and instructed them to cast their stones into the water.

They looked at him, bewildered and sweaty.

"For whom," asked Jesus, "did you carry the stone?"

For the rest of her life, Betty remembered the sad losses of 1953; they would presage other, more terrible deaths for her. But she began to learn the mystery and secret of her ancient faith . . . it was not about outcomes, inspiring results, personal fulfillment, or even coherent answers. It was about obedience to the One whose stone she carried.*

---

*God works His will in mysterious ways. More than forty years later, Betty visited with her dear old friend Doreen and her Ecuadorian husband, Abdon. Doreen and Abdon were still faithfully working with the Colorados. Some had become dedicated believers and were part of a small church. The New Testament had been translated into the Colorado language by Bruce Moore and his wife, Joyce, translators with the Summer Institute of Linguistics. Bruce and Joyce had helped to disciple Colorado leaders within the church, including a former hostile witch doctor who decided to follow Jesus, with no small ripple effect in the rest of the community. After a lifetime of faithful service to Christ, the Moores passed away in 2013 and 2014 and can now be found residing in heaven along with Elisabeth Elliot . . . and the former witch doctor.

CHAPTER 17

Finally!

"Love is not all: it is not meat nor drink
Nor slumber nor a roof against the rain;
Nor yet a floating spar to men that sink
And rise and sink and rise and sink again;
Love cannot fill the thickened lung with breath,
Nor clean the blood, nor set the fractured bone;
Yet many a man is making friends with death
Even as I write, for lack of love alone.
It well may be that in a difficult hour,
Pinned down by pain and moaning for release,
Or nagged by want past resolution's power,
I might be driven to sell your love for peace,
Or trade the memory of this night for food
It well may be. I do not think I would."
—Edna St. Vincent Millay

While Betty was in San Miguel, painstakingly developing translation tools for *Tsahfihki*, Jim had been working hard at the eastern jungle mission station at Shandia. He had harvested and hand-planed five hundred pieces of lumber, representing hundreds and hundreds of hours of labor. With high hopes, he had repaired three old buildings and constructed two new ones on the property. All for the Lord's work.

Then, in early August 1953—about the same time that Betty discovered that her nine months of translation work had been stolen—rain poured down day after day on Shandia. The river below the mission station rose higher and higher. Villagers three hours away could hear the sound of the rushing waters. Rocks the size of houses tumbled in the roaring tide. Whole trees rushed downstream. Twenty-two Indians died in the encampment just below Shandia. The river kept rising.

Jim, Pete, and their Quichua friends worked frantically through the night as the river threatened building after building in the compound. The McCullys' house lay closest to the swelling flood and the men pulled everything of value out of it; beds, furniture, aluminum roofing, and the kitchen materials. A teenaged Indian boy dragged out the refrigerator. As the waters rose, there was a great *crrrrack*, and the front porch slipped and crashed into the churning river below . . . followed by the rest of the house.

Over the next thirty-six hours the group worked frantically to empty building after building before each one plummeted into the wild waters. Four Indians went in the night to dig up their father, whom they'd buried a few months before. They took him to a higher location and buried him again; thinking surely the river would not rise to that height. Faster than they could have dreamed, the river rose, swirling and tearing their father's body from the new grave, and down into the rushing flood.

At one point, Jim was trapped in one of the houses the workers were trying to salvage; the cliff below the structure slipped away, in slow motion, into the water.

"He's gone!" the Indians screamed. But Jim, with great presence of mind, had used a machete to cut through the roof of the house so he could crawl out before the whole thing fell into the abyss.

After several days of flooding, Jim and Pete fell into exhausted sleep at 3 a.m. in an Indian's home far, far from the river. They woke suddenly before dawn; the river was rising again.

In the end, all the buildings were gone. Betty, madly studying Quichua in Dos Rios, heard the news over the missionary radio frequency. She and a group of Indians walked for hours, spending the night in the jungle, and arrived at Shandia the next morning. Jim and Pete were filthy, exhausted, sleeping in a tent, with a rescued washing machine in the mud beside them, right in the middle of the swampy airstrip.

After sleep, food, prayer, and consultation, the local missionaries believed that perhaps God was indicating, by the unusually high flood, that they should set up another smaller station in a new area. They would also rebuild Shandia's school, church, and other buildings. Jim, Ed, and Pete were sent out to "spy out the land" on a twenty-one-day canoe expedition to survey Indians on the shores of the Bobonaza River, getting a sense of needs, openness, and possible locations for outreach. (By this point Pete had proposed, by letter, to his girlfriend,

Olive, about five weeks after Jim and Betty's engagement. Pete and Olive would be married in June 1954.)

Ed McCully, Pete Fleming, and Jim Elliot, fall 1953

At the junction of the Pastaza and Puyo Rivers—a place called Puyupungu—an Indian with fifteen children begged the men to come live among them and establish a school. This kind of openness, let alone an invitation from a tribal leader, was unprecedented. Jim, Pete, and Ed agreed that they should accept the request. But Ed and his wife, Marilou, were going to rebuild Shandia, and they needed Pete's help there. So what missionary couple could possibly establish the new mission at Puyupungu?

Ed and Pete looked at Jim, and raised their eyebrows.

"So," said Jim as he told Betty about the expedition and his buddies' conclusions. "How soon can you marry me?"

The long-awaited event took place at 9:30 in the morning on October 8, 1953, in Quito. It was Jim's twenty-sixth birthday. Neither he nor Betty had any interest in a "conventional" wedding with white satin, sequins, long dramatic entrances, and hail to the bride. Still, the relentlessly frugal Betty had written to her mother a few months earlier that she had just happened to bring ten yards of white Swiss organdy when she first came to Ecuador in order to make *curtains*— why not use this to make a long, very simple wedding dress with a full skirt, long sleeves, and a narrow waistline? She could add "the simplest possible headdress—no veil." That way she'd eliminate "all fanfare and foolishness, save a great deal of expense, and still wear a white dress."[1]

But when the great day came, Betty was attired in a street-length suit. Jim wrote in his journal, "We were married without fuss at the Registro Civil" in a "dingy, high-ceilinged room in an antique colonial building" by "a suitably solemn official who read, in rapid monotone, several pages of Spanish, punctuated here and there by our 'si.'"[2]

Dr. and Mrs. Tidmarsh served as official witnesses; Ed and Marilou McCully were the only guests. "We signed our names in an immense ledger, and were man and wife," concluded Jim. The ceremony, the culmination of years of anguished longing, had taken less than ten minutes.[3]

From there the new couple took their friends to the Colon Hotel for coffee and cake. Jim had somehow pulled enough money together for six days of extravagance at El Panama, then Latin America's most luxurious hotel. The Elliots then flew from Panama to Costa Rica, appearing nonchalantly where Betty's brother Dave and his wife, Phyllis, were serving as missionaries—surprising them to the point of collapse. Eventually they flew to Quito to buy supplies for their pioneer outreach in a brand-new area in the eastern jungle of Ecuador: *Puyupungu*, roughly translated as the "mouth of the cloud."

Jim and Elisabeth Elliot's official married life began in a love nest as unconventional as their love story. To get to Puyupungu, they took a wild trip down the Pastaza River, piloted by Indians who skillfully steered the big canoes through terrific rapids every 400 feet. The Indians would get out in the waist-deep water, hauling and pushing the canoes over, around, and through the rocks.

"We'd go roaring through a tiny pass in the boulders, be dashed down into a pool below, and go zipping within inches of a solid rock wall in front of us," Betty reported. "In the middle of a very dangerous rapid, our *puntero*, the man that poles the front position, broke his pole and with magnificent skill, managed to guide the canoe with his foot as it careened wildly through the rocks."[4]

All the newlyweds' possessions—one thousand pounds including a stove, a steel drum, bed, trunk, washtubs, a hand wringer, gas iron and ironing board, table, chairs, one-hundred-pound tent, stove pipe, sacks of flour, sugar, salt, rice, beans—though sealed in rubber bags and covered in plastic, ended up soaked. But nothing was lost. The Elliots arrived around sunset near the mouth of the river. Atanasio, the chief who had invited the missionaries, and several canoes full of friends appeared like a flotilla. They pulled up, grinning and shouting to Jim, "So! You are a word-fulfiller!" and led the way toward their settlement.

The canoes scraped onto the sandy beach. Betty looked to the cliffs above to see Atanasio's family—"two wives, and a veritable battalion of children, peering shyly through the trees."[5]

The children ran down the steep trail, grabbed boxes, bundles, pots and bags from the canoes, and scampered back up the hill to stack these at the Elliots' new home: a cockroach-ridden, rotting wooden structure used by the Catholic priest when he visited the Puyupungu Indians once a year. It wasn't Betty's childhood dream of living in a hut in deepest Africa, but it was primitive enough to fit the bill.

The Indians supplied Jim and Betty with wood, water, fresh eggs, papaya, smoked fish, and plantains. Jim and Betty held a "church" meeting almost immediately. Ten adults and a gaggle of children came, ready to listen. Within a day or so Lucas, an Indian man whom the Elliots had brought with them from Shandia, began a new Christian school, with seven pupils enrolled.

After a few wet days in the moldy cockroach shack, the Elliots graduated to a small tent with barely enough room for their slanted single bed, which unkindly assured that at least one of them would get wet when it rained. They sometimes fought about just who that should be. Outside the tent, Betty had a tiny kitchen: a roof made of small slabs of aluminum to shield her little cooking stove, rusted and dented from travel, on which the new bride baked biscuits for the first morning's breakfast. There was an outhouse, populated by all sorts of crawling creatures, a discrete amount of yards away.

From their cliff-top dwelling Jim and Betty could see El Sangay—then the world's most active volcano. "It spits out smoke nearly all the time, and quite often at night vomits up huge red hot boulders which roll down its sides," wrote Betty. To its right was Ecuador's "most magnificent snow cap, El Altar," and to the right of that "another active volcano, Tungurahua, the mountain which caused the terrible earthquake in '49."[6] Miles of rolling jungle, mountains, sunsets, river: the landscape was as wild and dramatic as the adventurous Betty could have wanted.

Jim at the shack, 1954

Missionary pilot Nate Saint would drop supplies and mail now and then, even as Jim and the Indians worked to clear a small airstrip. Betty sent pictures home. Her inexorably attentive mother (often wondering why she didn't receive more correspondence, or if Betty was tiring of her letters) responded to every detail. In that subtext one can feel the tension that sometimes marked their relationship. "Sorry you don't like the hairdo, Mother. Neither do I. I am in despair about this hair problem in the jungle. Permanents get frizzy, straight hair looks like a broom."[7]

Mother kept going, so Betty responded, "Why don't I wear my hair [in a certain] style? It's not long enough, and besides, my face is too round. Furthermore, no hat will fit a head fixed in that style (Not that hats are in vogue in Puyupungu!)."[8] "Your next comment—I look so thin. I have not lost a single pound since you saw me. . . . I weigh . . . the same I've weighed for the last twelve years. It's the hairdo."[9]

Hair crises were not the only jungle challenge. Jim killed a tarantula near their sloping bed; its body the size of a mouse, its thick, furry legs as big as the span of a man's hand. One night Betty woke up feeling something cold and clammy on her bare back, reached around, and came up with a long, gooey earthworm. The tent leaked all night long, but only when it rained . . . which was roughly every night.

Indians brought gifts of armadillo legs, wild duck, and flanks of capybara (a rodent of unusual size). Betty roasted, pressure-cooked, and boiled just about anything, grateful for the Indians' generosity.

She also drank what they drank. Chicha. The Indians would gather manioc root, divide it up, and everyone would sit around a wooden bowl on the ground, chewing manioc and then spitting it into the common bowl. The longer it sat, the stronger the fermentation.

Betty and the other missionaries would gamely drink it before it became highly alcoholic. "Just as they hand you the half-gourd from which it is drunk, the Indian woman puts her hand in it and gives the wad of manioc pulp a squishy squeeze, and then puts it to your lips. It is a milky fluid, with lumps and string in it, a very sour taste, to say nothing of the aesthetic idea that I for one, cannot forget! . . . [but] it is the custom, and would be a serious offense if refused."[10]

One day in December, Jim and a friend were carrying a long palm pole through the forest, and Jim stumbled and fell into a slippery mud-pit at the edge of the trail. As he landed, a sharp stick pierced him under the left arm. The gash exposed muscle and tendons, and bled profusely. If the thick, spear-like stick had punctured his chest, it would have killed him.

But in December 1953, that was not yet to be.

"We are very grateful for the guardian angels," concluded Betty.[11]

As Christmas approached, Jim told the school children the Bible story of Christ's coming. "Some of the Indians from upriver will come, and it will be the first time they hear why the whites celebrate Christmas."[12] The next day, Jim and Betty left Puyupungu to join their fellow missionaries in Shell for their own celebration. They left their possessions in Atanasio's care. "We trust the Indians 100%, and haven't a worry in the world about them, but there are occasional whites who pass through."[13]

The sucking mud was deep, the rivers frothing, the cliffs steep and slippery. After a grueling ten-hour trek, Jim and Betty arrived at a small clearing, and there was Marj Saint, pilot Nate Saint's wife, the aptly-named, ultimate trail angel. She was waiting for her exhausted friends with a pick-up truck, ice-cold Cokes, and generous, moist slabs of freshly baked chocolate cake.

The town of Shell, on the banks of the Pastaza River at the edge of the Amazon rainforest, had been established in 1937 as a base for the Shell Oil Company. The Ecuadorian government was eager to see virgin jungle opened up for possible development as well as transportation infrastructure. It granted Shell permission to establish a base in remote territory that was both environmentally and sociologically hostile. The company constructed roads, blasted through granite, and cleared swamps. Shell built small homes, storage shacks, and a five-thousand-foot airstrip.

But by 1949, jungle Indians like the Waodani had killed too many of Shell's workers. With a growing focus on oil elsewhere, like the Middle East, Shell Oil abandoned its efforts in that part of Ecuador.

The newly formed Mission Aviation Fellowship took advantage of Shell's road access to Quito and its airstrip, and made the outpost its base of operations for jungle ministry. Other ministries like Gospel Missionary Union profited from Shell's withdrawal, buying Shell buildings and land to use for ministry. The former oil town became a center for mid-century missionary activities.

Nate Saint had served in the military during World War II, receiving flight training through the Army Air Corps. After his discharge in 1946, he studied at Wheaton College for a semester, but was anxious to get to the mission field. He joined Mission Aviation Fellowship in 1948 and he and his wife, Marj, settled in at Shell. The home they built there would become Mission Control for many jungle missionaries of various denominations.

When Nate and Marj arrived in Shell in 1948, some twelve missionaries served in six jungle stations. (By the end of 1954 there would be twenty-five missionaries in nine stations.)[14] As Nate flew supplies to those scattered missionaries reaching out to scattered people groups, Marj Saint was a supremely organized one-woman nexus back at base. (Nate called her his "partner with a brain like a filing cabinet.")[15]

Attired in the usual mid-century womanly garb of a freshly-ironed dress, curled, tidy hair, and a big smile, Marj sat at Nate's bank of radio equipment and manned the air waves all day long. Nate would call in with progress reports and weather conditions; she'd pass his information down the line to the various missionary outposts. She'd also relay short spurts of the news of the day and prayer requests; the tribal woman dying in childbirth, the man on the trail who'd been bitten by a viper, the need to evacuate a desperately sick little boy.

As the Elliots rested, laughed, and enjoyed Christmas with the Saint family, Betty wrote home. "I am happier than I've ever been in my life, and grateful to God. I can ask nothing more than what the Lord has given me, in showing me His will, leading me, and giving me Jim."[16]

But back at home in the jungle, by early 1954, Betty *was* asking God for one more thing. The Elliots had stopped using birth control, and Betty longed to bear a child. She yearned for a son, noting her hopes and disappointments regarding pregnancy in her journal.

Jim's days were full of counseling the young men he mentored, and managing and working on construction projects like a fence to keep the cows from wandering onto the new air strip. He settled disputes between the Quichua Indians, who, though normally stolid and easy-going, could erupt into brutal violence if they felt someone had violated their rights. Betty sometimes mourned that Puyupungu was not exactly yet a New Testament church, where members were tenderhearted and forgiving one another. That could only come with grace, and time.

Betty wrote with admiration about Jim's patience, wisdom, and kindness. Knowing her love of flowers, he planted a half-dozen varieties of orchids for her, tending them with great interest. He was buoyant, cheerful, and mature, though "just boyish enough to be lots of fun." It seemed he was in his element, and Betty wrote of herself: "No one could ask more of life than to be loved as I am loved."

Soon Atanasio invited Jim to become the "chief" in Puyupungu. Jim could have the new canoe he had just made, and the other Indians would gladly keep the Elliots supplied with food. He was so grateful they had come. "Before," said Atanasio, "I lived like a donkey. I didn't know anything.* . . . Now, hearing your teaching, it is like waking up. Before, the priest used to come for just three days a year. He'd make a few masses, say a few prayers, charge me forty sucres, and—zas! Away he'd go, back to Puyo. . . . How can anyone learn anything in three days a year? We want you to stay for always."[17]

By Easter, Jim wrote to his family that Atanasio had told him that even though he was old—about forty-seven—his eyes were beginning to open to faith. A heavy drinker, he had lived "like a burro and a savage" till now. "We pray earnestly for his conversion," wrote Jim. "Pray that the family will wholeheartedly accept the kingship of Christ and that the work will spread to the other Indians who live one and two days away, too far for us to reach up until now."[18]

"I really love this place," wrote Betty. "The Lord gave us such happiness here. . . . The Indians are so kind and thoughtful. . . . [T]hey presented me with ½ doz. eggs, and when Atanasio got back from a hunting trip, he sent over about 10 or 12 lbs. of smoked tapir! Oh that they might come to know Him! Lord, once more I bring them to Thee."

In April, Jim's dad arrived from Oregon—having spent a week in Quito getting his construction equipment and tools through customs—to help with various building projects both at the Puyupungu outpost and rebuilding the Shandia home base. He was "flabbergasted" by the jungle. "Dad just drinks it all in," Betty wrote, "shaking his head

---

*It's interesting that Atanasio, who knew nothing of the Bible at the time, basically quoted Psalm 73:22 in his description of himself without God. "I was senseless and ignorant; I was a brute beast before You" (Ps. 73:22 niv).

constantly, saying 'My, oh my, oh my. What a country. What a country. Well, for any sakes! Did you ever? I never. You don't mean it? Is that so? My, oh my, o my.'"[19]

One of the Indians, Ushpalito, killed an armadillo and brought it to Betty. "Dad E. was here," wrote Betty, "and I'm not sure he was thrilled by the leg we served him, foot, claws, and all, but he ate it valiantly! The meat is something like chicken,"—of course—"but after I'd had to clean and shell the beast, the meat had lost something of its appeal for me."[20]

At the end of June 1954, Jim and Betty had a small "commencement" program for the school children and their parents in Puyupungu. They, or other missionaries, would follow up later. For now, though, the Elliots needed to be in Shandia so Jim and Ed McCully could work with Jim's dad full-time on construction projects, before Dad Elliot had to return to the U.S.

Jim and Betty lived in a tiny bamboo house that Pete Fleming had built. Pete had left Ecuador to marry his gracious fiancée, Olive. They would return from the U.S. for language studies in Quito in September.

The additional blessing that Betty had prayed for came to be. In late July, Betty wrote in her journal, "I am quite certain I am pregnant. Jim and I are so happy about it . . . we've asked God for a son, and He has given me verses which assure me that He has given what we asked."

Jim spent his days in heavy, exhausting construction. He cleared jungle, hauled sand and rocks, poured concrete, and supervised workmen. Bringing a pitcher of cold lemonade in mid-afternoon, Betty would find him standing by the little cement mixer, stripped to the waist, bronzed and glistening with sweat as he heaved buckets of sand and directed the Indians who were working with him.

He would return to the McCully house near sundown, and bathe in the cool river before supper. He and Betty spent their evenings writing letters, discussing translation issues, preparing Bible teachings, or talking with the McCullys. It was a simple time, and Betty and Marilou smiled when they watched their husbands work together. "Their minds met, it seemed, at nearly every point," wrote Betty, "and they found that the old fellowship of Wheaton . . . had lost none of its joy; in fact, the sharing of work together on the mission field had immeasurably strengthened the bond."[21]

Of course, progress in any mission field is often tenuous. Betty mourned how Satan could use old ways, and old temptations, to pull the local people away from Jesus. One night Jim and Betty were invited to a party, and though they arrived fairly early in the proceedings, the

Indians were worse off than usual. "All the women, as well as men, were just stewed, and staggering around trying to keep their balance with babies tied around their shoulders . . . men laying moaning and crying, women staggered around with blouses soaked with liquor and hair streaming."

Though Jim sometimes had had decent conversations with men who'd been drinking, since alcohol loosened their reserve, this particular night had gone far beyond that point. He broke up a few fights, protected several women who were being dragged away by their hair, and helped out as best he could.

Several Indians decided to carry a fight to outside the Elliots' house. "Jim was able to mediate the difficulties there, too," Betty reported in a letter home. "You never heard such a racket. Dogs barking, children screaming, women shrieking and tugging on the arms and legs of the fighters, men cursing and roaring at each other. . . . It made me feel as though Satan himself were in their midst."[22]

Meanwhile, Betty kept a count of missionary "casualties" who had started work in the field with high hopes, but had returned to the U.S. Some left to get married, or had health issues, and there were many cases of "nerves," or psychological challenges. At one point Betty had counted thirty-four missionaries who'd had to leave the field. If she and Jim ever did so, she wrote, "I can't imagine what we'd ever do in the States," wrote Betty. "This is where God sent us, and this is where we belong."

On his birthday and first wedding anniversary, October 8, 1954, Jim wrote a note to Betty's parents, concluding "Tonight completes the happiest year of my life . . . [Betty] has been all and more than I ever wanted in a wife and I praise God for our having been brought together."[23]

Betty's pregnancy had been confirmed during the summer, but she had waited until fall to share the news with those back home. Predictably, this injured her mother's feelings.

"I love you very much, Mother, and apologize a thousand times for not having told you sooner about my being pregnant," Betty wrote. "We just had a letter from Mom E[lliot] telling us how thrilled she is about it. . . . She said she didn't tell her own mother till she was five months along, and when she finally did, her mother wouldn't believe her! . . . Well, I'm sure you wouldn't have done that, so I certainly should have told you."[24]

Betty wrote sadly in her journal. "Mother is a wonderful, wonderful woman, and I can never be grateful enough for her! Oh that I might <u>show</u> my love for her. Somehow it is beyond me." She found herself feeling wistful about her parents getting older, and wrote to her mother, "It must have been an untold grief for you and Daddy to have a daughter as distant and wrapped up in herself and her own little world as I was."[25]

Having made her profuse apologies, Betty noted that she was, as usual, "disgustingly healthy." She and Jim had decided they wanted to keep things simple. "We have agreed that the baby is not going to run the house. Blocks, toys, junk, play pens, swings, bottles, carriages, potties, rattles, dominating every room. . . . In fact, we are not going to give the child any bought toys! Don't we sound just like expectant parents who haven't had any children yet?"

By the end of October, Jim and Betty moved into a new house in Shandia. (Newlyweds Pete and Olive would continue the work in Puyupungu.) Jim, a gifted draftsman, had drawn detailed architectural renderings, and he and his construction team had brought it to reality. It could serve as a gathering place as well as a solid and expandable home for what he hoped would be his growing family. It had four bedrooms, a bath, a large kitchen, dining room, living room, and several porches: a far cry from the cockroach shack or the leaky tent in Puyupungu. He had harvested fine, dark woods from the jungle and lovingly hand-built a smooth-honed desk, bookshelves, cupboards, and a coffee table created from a single, swirled slice of an enormous tree.

Elliots' home in Shandia, 1954

On one jungle foray, a slim, deadly snake hung on a tree limb just above the trail. The Indians—usually extraordinarily alert to such danger—did not see it. Jim, wearing a long-sleeved shirt with the sleeves rolled up on his forearms, followed close behind. As he passed below it, the snake surged like lightning and struck his arm—right on the thick, rolled part of the sleeve. The fangs did not penetrate. The men moved on.

"We thank the Lord for His promises that no evil thing can touch us without His permission," Betty concluded.

She focused on Jim's thoughtful organizational details in their new house, marveling over the linen closet, the custom shelves that were just the right widths for her various types of canned goods, the clever vegetable storage, with screen-bottomed drawers, as well as the luxuries like screened windows and ample storage space. She loved the 1950s decorating touches like her dark rose chenille bedspread, the white goats' hair rug, and the drapes—a large, tropical leaf pattern in "dubonnet, rose, and chartreuse."[26]

Before she got too carried away with the details, however, Betty reeled herself back in:

> . . . as I look at this beautiful house, with all its comforts and conveniences, I sort of get scared. But I have to remember the Lord gave it to us, unsought, and unasked, and I have asked Him to use it for Himself as He sees fit. But the temptation to be covetous about it—wanting it for my 'own' and fearing lest something happen to it, is dangerous. It is not easy to hold <u>things</u> lightly. Once we have them, we want to keep them.[27]

A person's life, however, consists not in the abundance of things, she concluded. She would be reminded of those words, when she returned to Shandia to live in that house again.

For now, though, she was exceedingly grateful. God gave it "to us, and it is His" she wrote in her journal near the end of 1954. "I want it to be used for His name's sake, and to be a place of peace for the Lord's people, as well as be a lighthouse to those who live around us. I wonder if we shall spend the rest of our lives here? I dream of it being filled with children and guests—Lord, let it be."

CHAPTER 18

In the Company of Saints

*"When all his other gifts could not prevail, he at last made a
gift of himself, to testify his affection and engage theirs."*
—Henry Scougal

*I*n February 1955 the Elliots and their Quichua workers held a conference in Shandia. Ed and Marilou McCully, as well as Pete and Olive
Fleming, came to help Jim and Betty. There were several days of sessions, attended by seventy to one hundred Indians. There were observers, too—Indians who came to scoff, or because they were curious.

Onlookers watched as a group of believers met in the schoolroom
to celebrate the breaking of bread (communion). A small table stood
in the center of the simple room with its thatched roof and backless
benches. The Indians gathered quietly and sat barefooted and rever-
ent around a loaf of bread and a cup of wine. One by one, the young
men would take part. They ended their meeting singing about Jesus'
eventual return: *"kirikgunaga, kushiyanguichi—Cristo shamunmi!"*
"Be happy, believers—Christ is coming!"

The missionaries all continued to work on translation of the
Scriptures into lowland Quichua, since a Bible did not yet exist in that
tongue. Jim was anxious for the Indians in Shandia to learn to study
the Scriptures <u>themselves</u>. He sought to equip them in a method of
Bible study that they could follow when no missionary was there. He
had found several young believers who showed spiritual discernment
and teaching gifts, and he equipped them to take charge of worship
meetings; everything from leading the singing to preaching a sermon.

At the time, it was a novelty for Indians to see one of their own
up front. "To them the gospel was for *gringos*, and for learned people
only. An Indian preach? Absurd!"[1]

Jim showed them in the Bible that Jesus did not choose seminary graduates as His disciples. His early followers were common laborers, from the same strata of society as their listeners. There was no dichotomy between clergy and laymen. Jim determined that in Shandia there would be none. "If the Indians came to meetings only to hear a foreigner, they might as well not come. They must see that the written Word is the oracle of God—regardless of who is preaching it—or the missionary labors in vain."[2]

And the Indian church, of course, could not be compared to the cultural standards of 1950s America. It was much less buttoned-down.

One day Betty looked around during the worship service. The boy who led the singing was decked out in a red and green horizontally striped T-shirt, with a pink and green satin jacket over it. Three girls sat with legs encased in an orange petticoat turned upside-down, for fly protection. One of the older men wore a felt hat, red wool scarf, coat and trousers and bare feet. Another sported a blue and white rayon pajama top, neatly tucked into his pants. Another wore just socks, no shoes, with his trousers rolled into the socks. Not a hat, tie, jacket, or dress in sight.

Ah, thought Betty, as she noted her own conditioned reaction. People look at the outward appearance. God looks at the <u>heart</u>.

After the Quichua conference, Jim and Betty went to Shell. Jim was to help with construction of a hospital built on land Nate Saint had purchased with the aim of serving the various jungle peoples. Betty, great with child, rested at the Saints' home. She wrote in her journal, "I'm sure I have been making life difficult for dear Jim. I have not been the help to him in any way—spiritually, morally, or anything—that I should, and have complained too much of my personal condition. He is such a good husband to me, and very sympathetic and thoughtful. I am ashamed of myself. . . . [I] feel a real sense of unworthiness and responsibility. Marriage has cost him too much, I fear. I am to blame."

Today the Nate Saint house in Shell, Ecuador, is a tourist destination. Christians from all over the world come to see the place where the celebrated missionary pilot originated his flights into the jungle. Several rooms are preserved much as they were in 1955 and '56, when the house was a crossroads for missionaries heading in and out of various jungle mission stations.

Today's "museum," however, can't quite capture the dynamism of the Nate Saint home when it was full of Saints. Betty marveled at Marj's flexibility: "Marj is . . . unperturbed, always ready for two or twenty for a meal, and it doesn't seem to matter if she knows five minutes ahead of time or not." And the enterprising Marj didn't want those guests to eat lite. "Missionaries are usually hungry," she'd say. "So I just plan for what normal people eat, and then double it."[3]

In the mid-'50s, Nate wrote, "Our family has occupied only one bedroom. [Daughter] Kathy is now sleeping on a cot in a closet under the new stairway that cuts through a corner of our room. We recently had nineteen guests overnight . . . foreign missionaries, national workers, a schoolteacher and family, and some Indians! I sincerely believe that you could count the days that we've been alone as a family recently on the fingers of two hands."[4]

When Marj gave birth in December 1954 to her third child, Philip, she did so in the downstairs darkroom that Nate used to develop his film. Why? Well, the rest of the house was full of guests, and Marj didn't want to inconvenience anyone else.[5]

A few months later, when Betty was due to deliver, she got an actual bedroom. This was fortunate, as there were a number of observers. "Jim was by me every minute, which meant more than he will ever know," Betty reported later. Dr. Fuller, and his wife Liz, a nurse, managed the proceedings; Marj Saint and a visitor Betty didn't know (who had asked Betty if she could attend), filled out the birthday party.

The stoic Betty had thought she could make it through delivery without meds. But labor went on interminably, and the pain was "unimaginable." Thank God for a spinal anesthetic. Baby Elliot arrived at 5:40 a.m. on February 27, 1955. Jim, who had told his parents he thought he might be disappointed if the baby was not a boy, swept his tiny daughter into his arms, full of absolute joy and wonder. "Her name is Valerie," he proclaimed.

The Elliots stayed for another week with the Saints. They stayed up late, sipping cups of hot cocoa in the small kitchen and talking, even as they rocked their new babies in the night. Nate's bright yellow Piper airplane nestled in the big garage near the house. The airstrip— gateway to the eastern jungle—lay just across the narrow road. Nate knew more about the seemingly endless sea of rainforest beyond that runway than just about anybody, having gauged its breadth, depth, and mysteries for years. Jim and Betty, Nate and Marj dreamed of more and more unreached people under that green canopy having the opportunity to hear the name of Jesus . . . including, of course, the most elusive tribe of all, the shadowy Waodani.

CHAPTER 19

What Might Have Been

"Teach me never to let the joy of what has been,
pale the joy of what is."
—Elisabeth Elliot

After Valerie's birth, the months went quickly, though the days seemed slow. Valerie was a sunny baby, and her dad delighted in each phase in her development. As the weeks passed, Jim claimed she looked like [then-president] Dwight Eisenhower with her wide grin and almost-bald head.

For her part, Betty wrote, "How grateful I am to the Lord for giving me such a dear husband and baby. How much life means now—living for them, giving of myself to them, feeling myself needed by them. Of all hopelessly selfish people I should have been the worst had I remained single."

Still, like any new season in life, there were new challenges. Jim's days were absolutely full as he continued to work with the Shandia school and church, developing the Indian leadership in both places. Meanwhile he was setting up a water system for the Elliot home, tearing down the old woodshed, and often traveling to lead teaching conferences among Indians in other locations.

Betty felt a bit of post-partum loss in their partings, but, typically, blamed herself. "Lately I have felt that Jim has not wanted to share things with me. It must be that I have not shown him the love that asks nothing in return. O Lord, give me a <u>purer</u> love for him . . ."

In late March, the Elliots got word of a Waodani attack not far from the missionary station at Arajuno.

In April, Jim rejoiced that God was bringing fruit in the ministry. "I've never seen so many Indians openly receptive to the Word," he wrote to his parents. "In Dos Rios at the conference last week there were over twenty, in Pano about the same, and here in Shandia about a dozen. Now to the job of readying them for life in Christ."[1]

During this time Betty and Jim had live-in household help in the form of a married couple, Eugenia and Guayaquil. She was perhaps seventeen, and he was about twelve. Trying not to wonder too much about their marital arrangement, Betty was thankful for the help. The boy was still in school, but he could cut wood, clear weeds, and run errands. Meanwhile Eugenia could help around the house with cooking and cleaning, all for about five dollars a month.

Eugenia, Betty, and Val

Eugenia was about as different from Betty Elliot as two personalities could be. Their cultural habits differed as well. One day an Indian brought Eugenia some pale, fat grubs, about two inches long and fatter than a thumb. While Betty had eaten them fried, it was tough to watch her housekeeper enthusiastically suck the insides out of them, raw, and crunch the hard, pincher-jawed head between her teeth. And Eugenia had nearly vomited when Betty gave her some vegetable soup; she had absolutely recoiled at the taste of fudge. Well, Betty thought, it was just another vivid reminder that one could not assume that everyone thought and felt just like North Americans.

In May, one day after Betty had conducted her usual women's prayer meeting, attended by about twenty Quichuas, one of the young girls came to her, weeping. Catalina, about fifteen, told Betty that her parents were furious that she'd been coming to the Christian meetings. As a punishment they were going to force her to marry a little old man—very ugly—who had a disease that had turned his skin blue. She needed a safe place to stay.

Feeling that no one should be forced to marry an old blue man, Betty sympathized with Catalina. She felt that if the girl's parents were determined to punish her because of her interest in faith, then Betty should give her asylum, at least until her family appeared to reclaim her. Then she and Jim could share the gospel with them.

A week later, the parents had not yet showed up. Betty had tried to persuade Catalina to marry one of the local believers in Shandia, a nice young widower of about twenty-two who wasn't blue and was looking for a wife. But Catalina and the others weren't having it. "It is '*sasi*,' [taboo] for a virgin to marry a widower," they told Betty.[2]

Betty never did see the old blue man, nor was she able to resolve the young girl's dilemma. But she took Catalina with her when she, Jim, Valerie, and Eugenia went downriver to treat a snakebite case an hour or so away.

Eugenia was carrying Valerie, right behind Betty on the narrow trail. Suddenly she screamed in a pitch that Betty had never heard before. Betty went cold. A small, deadly snake was hanging on Eugenia's bare foot, its fangs sunk into her flesh.

Jim came running back, dislodged the snake, pulled out his pocket knife, grabbed Eugenia's muddy foot, slashed the bite, and sucked out the poison. They dragged her to the river, soaking the foot and squeezing the leg to keep the blood flowing. Catalina eyed the ground and held Valerie high in her arms. Eugenia was hysterical. "Leave me alone!" she screamed. "Let me die right here!"

Jim still had to continue on his mission to take care of the urgent snakebite victim further down the trail, so Betty made a tourniquet and somehow got Eugenia home. Catalina carried Val.

As they stumbled into the house, Eugenia's husband—the twelve-year-old—took one look and broke into sobs. "You're going to die!" he cried.

This was not helpful.

Betty wrestled with Eugenia, who struggled and clawed at Betty, drawing blood with her nails. Somehow, Betty gave her a shot of antivenin, and administered a codeine tablet to quiet her down.

A day or two later, Eugenia could still not walk, but she would live. A miracle. Betty thought about how she was no more than three paces in front of Eugenia on the leafy trail, with Jim in front of Betty. They must have walked right over the snake.

"Jim feels that we are justified in taking very literally the Lord's words that we shall tread on serpents and scorpions without harm. God has surely taken care of us, and there is nothing to do but trust Him to continue."[3]

Jim was once away with some Indians near a river pool. A little boy was in the water, splashing happily. Suddenly the child cried out, "What is catching my foot?" Everyone turned to look, even as he disappeared under the muddy water. The adults plunged into the river. Two hours later the Indians found his body. There was no mark on it; apparently a boa had twined around his foot, pulled him under, found him too big to swallow, and let him go.

In the jungle, there were no illusions about the brevity of life.[4]

Betty had just settled in to enjoy the family mail one afternoon when an Indian woman arrived to tell her that her sister-in-law was "dying." Knowing this could mean anything from an ingrown toenail to cerebral malaria, Betty ran with the woman into the jungle under vines, over logs, around bamboo, and through streams as fast as they could go. They arrived in a dripping sweat to find the house full of howling children, weeping relatives, and frantic old women gathered around a young girl in the throes delivering a breech baby. The head was still stuck. One granny was shaking the baby for all she was worth; meanwhile they had tied a tight cord around the mother's waist to "keep the baby from coming out of her mouth."

Betty cleared the room and made the woman lie down. She put on a rubber glove and inserted her hand into the birth canal. She found the baby's mouth, and drew the chin down to the chest, while applying external pressure with her left hand, as she had been instructed in a midwifery class. She worked as hard as she could for an hour, but as darkness was falling, she had to get home to Valerie and Eugenia. She told the men to carry the woman to her home.

Betty ran home. The men arrived with the dying woman. Betty gave the mother a shot of ergotrate (a medication that causes uterine contractions). The dead fetus did not budge. Perhaps there were twins, thought Betty. Another shot finally brought on some feeble contractions, and Betty was eventually able to extract the head . . . that showed that the single baby was hydrocephalic, with a head as big as that of a ten-year-old child. Incredibly, the mother survived.[5]

As Valerie grew, Jim was anxious for another baby as soon as possible. Betty had initially thought, after childbirth, that she would never go through that again. But now she was excited about another; it would be great for Valerie to have a playmate in the jungle. "I trust the Lord has other children for us," Betty wrote to her parents. "We're getting old, you know. I shall soon be 29. Horrors!"[6]

Pete Fleming and his wife, Olive, were still living in the Elliots' former newlywed shack in Puyupungu, working with the growing body of believers there. Olive had had a challenging time since her arrival in Ecuador. Besides the normal adjustments of married life, she had to learn Spanish, then Quichua. She'd had to adapt to poisonous snakes, enormous bugs, and lack of privacy. She had to develop improvisational ingenuity for living life in the jungle. On top of everything else she had an early miscarriage on her first Christmas in the mission field, and then a second during the summer of 1955.

But she and Pete were excited about spiritual developments in Puyupungu. "The Lord has broken things wide open here," Pete wrote to his mission agency. He had preached during church to "a full house, including every adult in the village except the chief's sick wife." He'd spoken carefully about repentance and faith, not wanting any to affirm belief in Jesus without truly counting the cost of following Him.

Twelve people stayed after the service to talk further. Pete encouraged any who weren't actually ready to walk the narrow road to leave. No one did. They prayed out loud. "One asked forgiveness for an angry heart, one for corrupt living, one for drunkenness, one for evil thoughts. All seemed most sincere; the group included the oldest woman in the community, our washer girl, the worst drinker in the village, the chief's two daughters and two sons, and several 12-year-olds." Pete felt an unusual sense of the Holy Spirit; there were several others who stood, literally and figuratively in the doorway of the meeting, close to coming to Jesus.[7]

CHAPTER 20

Cast of Characters

*"People who do not know the Lord ask why in
the world we waste our lives as missionaries. They forget
that they too are expending their lives . . . and when
the bubble has burst, they will have nothing of eternal
significance to show for the years they have wasted."*
—Nate Saint

Even though the various missionary families were based in various
remote jungle outposts, they weren't solitary players. They were connected to their fellow missionaries, friends, family, and sending agencies back in the States. A constant flow of letters assured them that
they were being held up in prayer. Their theology reminded them that
they were a part of the worldwide body of Christ, of all believers on
"this terrestrial ball," as the old hymn put it. Not only that, they were
cheered on by a vast "cloud of witnesses," the saints who had lived and
died and gone on to glory in an unbroken chain of evangelists since
Jesus gave the Great Commission two thousand years earlier.

In spite of this transcendent mind-set, daily reality can be lonely
and isolated (as any modern missionary can tell you), and the pioneering men and women of 1955 didn't have email, cell phones, or the
worldwide web.

But they did have connectivity that *their* predecessors did not,
thanks to the availability of small airplanes. Jungle pilots like Nate
Saint were transforming modern missions, bringing medicine, mail,
supplies, and food to previously inaccessible places, encouraging and
supplying missionaries who had previously been isolated.

As historian Kathryn Long puts it, "Daily flights to jungle stations replaced days and even weeks of ground travel. Goods nearly

impossible to haul or herd over jungle trails—corrugated tin roofing, gas powered refrigerators, stoves, calves, goats, and turkeys—could be transported by air. [Nate] Saint could deliver medicines when missionaries or tribal peoples became ill; in emergencies he could also carry the sick or wounded. Future decades would bring debates over whether aviation represented yet another means of the control missionaries exerted over tribal peoples, but in the 1950s the little planes represented the blessings of technology."[1]

The use of airplanes also presented a new kind of missionary hero: the skilled pilot who loved Jesus and brought supplies for the dissemination of the gospel to otherwise inaccessible places, landing his little plane "on a jungle airstrip that from the air looked not much larger than a Band-Aid."[2]

There were others on the jungle stage in late 1955 as well.

Like Jim, Pete, and Ed, Dr. Wilfred Tidmarsh was from a Plymouth Brethren background. As he approached retirement age, the very British Dr. Tidmarsh had been looking for younger men to take over his work with the Quichua Indians at his missions base in Shandia.

Dr. Tidmarsh had served in Ecuador for about twenty years as a single man. He was slender, with brown hair and a high forehead. He wore short khaki pants, and long, thick British socks with high-topped Keds, or long pants with the cuffs stuck into his Keds, so he wouldn't get chiggers. He wore a scabbard on his hip to hold his machete, and, of course, a pith helmet. He would have looked more at home on safari in Africa than he did the rainforest of Ecuador.

Eventually an American widow had been swept off her feet by Dr. Tidmarsh's charms, and he became a husband and a stepfather to her young boys. Betty Elliot would see him strike off down the trail in the morning to visit Quichua Indians, and not return until the afternoon—just in time for tea.

"Gwen, darling," he would call out to his wife in his high, squeaky voice, "have you got the kettle boiling?"

She was American and not yet up to speed on British traditions.

"Oh, no, Wilfred, do you want tea?"

"Never mind, darling," he'd respond, tipping the pith helmet. "I'll make it myself."

He was eccentric, charming, maddening. One day Jim Elliot stopped by the home and one of the stepsons, a little guy of about four, opened the door for him. As Jim stepped in, the boy burst out in anguish, "Oh, Jimmy, I've got MICROBES in my blood!" Evidently his stepfather had informed him of this unfortunate development. At night Dr. Tidmarsh would direct the two younger boys to put all their stuffed animals in their toy basket, because "if you leave those little wild animals outside, they'll go walloping off!"[3] Once Betty, the mimic, heard and jotted down Dr. T's words as he tried to get his small son to eat dinner. "Weet up, Jimmy boy. If Jimmy boy doesn't weet up, Daddy's going to weet it up! Nice eggie, nice chickie meat, now then Jimmy boy, drink up milkie."[4]

Betty would later note that linguistics work was not Dr. Tidmarsh's strong suit.

"I sat with him on a number of occasions when they were supposedly doing a translation of the Bible and he couldn't really pronounce the words very well . . . not really a linguist himself, but he did the best he could.

"It used to drive me up the wall the way he would just butcher the language . . . but on the other hand you know he had a great ministry, spiritual ministry with a lot of people. And he certainly could speak English!"

"He was a brilliant man," Betty concluded. "He had learned quite a lot about various kinds of [jungle] medicines." Jim and the other guys "loved him, [but] they didn't even consider including him in their [eventual] plan to reach the Waodani . . . he was so eccentric, they just knew he'd ruin everything."[5]

As Jim Elliot wrote in his journal, "That esteemed brother has one grave fault: he talks—too fast, too precipitously, and too much."[6]

Rachel Saint was another strong character on the jungle stage. She was nine years older than her inventive brother, Nate, and was the only girl in their family with seven boys. According to her brothers, she was bossy. She had serious blue eyes, an occasional dimple, a broad forehead, and long, dark hair usually arranged in a bun. She had entertained young Nate with missionary stories of David Livingstone, the Scottish doctor who penetrated the wilds of Africa, Adoniram Judson, the first Protestant missionary to take the gospel to Burma (now Myanmar), and John Paton, who lived and worked among members of a cannibal tribe in the South Pacific.

Rachel studied at the Philadelphia School of the Bible,[7] and then worked for twelve years at the Keswick Colony of Mercy* in New Jersey. There she had run the dining hall with a firm hand, tolling the dinner bell precisely on time. Keswick was—and is—a Christian retreat center and a flourishing ministry to men struggling with substance abuse. At Keswick Rachel had met the young Betty Howard,

---

*Keswick was founded in 1897 by William Raws. Set free from his alcohol addiction, Raws determined to spend the rest of his life helping others escape the bondage that had once chained him. Though he had a grand total of $1.87 in his pocket, he dreamed big. By God's grace, more than 120 years later, Keswick was still going strong.

who spent many summers at the retreat center and whose father often spoke to its Christian conferences.

When she was a young woman, Rachel became traveling companion and helper to a well-to-do older lady. During a summer trip to Europe, the woman, without a family of her own, told Rachel that she had decided to leave her sizeable estate to Rachel. The only condition was that Rachel would take care of her for the rest of her life.

By this point Rachel had sensed a distinct urging from God to become a missionary. She could not spend her life catering to the needs—perceived and otherwise—of a rich, elderly woman. "I can't do that," she told her benefactress. "I've committed my life to the Lord Jesus."

The wealthy woman, unaccustomed to not getting her way, was furious. Rachel retreated from her elegant salon to the bow of the boat, staring out at the ocean. Uncharacteristically, she wondered if her decision was right. *Have I made a terrible mistake? If I inherited that wealth, I could give the money to my family; I could help with all their educations* . . . but then there came another, weightier thought. Actually, it was a picture, perhaps a vision. Rachel saw people with darker skin than her own. They stood against the backdrop of a deep, green jungle. It was just a flash . . . and then she had a sense from God: "If you are faithful, I will allow you to bring My Word to a people who have never heard it."[8]

Rachel Saint never looked back. In 1948—the year Betty Elliot graduated from Wheaton—thirty-four-year-old Rachel attended Wycliffe's linguistic training program; she received jungle instruction in southern Mexico the following year, and then worked among a tribal people in Peru.

In 1951, Rachel was visiting her brother, Nate, in Ecuador. As they buzzed above the jungle in Nate's little plane, she noted that Nate did not take a straight path to their destination, but instead made an elaborate detour around a certain swath of jungle. She asked her brother why, and Nate told her that that particular part of the Oriente was peopled by "Waodani," a tribe so savage that if their plane had mechanical trouble and they had to land in that territory, the inhabitants would kill them.

Few of us would react to that in a positive way. But Rachel Saint felt an immediate sense of kinship and recognition. Here were her people! These were the "brown-skinned" ones whom God had brought to her mind years earlier! Though she continued working in other assignments from Wycliffe, Rachel's heart was now set on the Waodani. This was "the tribe the Lord had for me," she wrote in a letter to supporters in February 1955.[9]

Rachel's dream began to come true when she met a young Waodani woman named Dayuma.

Dayuma had been born around 1930 or so in the Waodani territory of Ecuador's eastern jungle. She was a little girl when many of her family members died by spearing. In March of 1944 she fled the tribe, taking her chances with an outside world that was almost as threatening as the terrors she faced among her own people.

Naked except for the usual Waodani string at her waist, she was taken in by Quichua Indians, and given clothes. She ended up working as an unskilled laborer on a large hacienda where she and the other *peons* were basically owned by the *patron* landowner, Señor Carlos Sevilla. She assimilated into Quichua culture and learned the language. She absorbed bits and pieces of Catholic teachings and fused them with her childhood questions about God. She worked hard on the hacienda, and while there, had a baby (evidently by Sevilla or one of his sons).

A decade or so after her escape from her Waodani roots, Dayuma attracted the attention of Rachel Saint and other missionaries who were anxious to learn everything they could about the mysterious Waodani tribe. Rachel began building a friendship with her. Dayuma obligingly began to teach her the language.

This process was not as simple as it sounds.

Neither Rachel nor any of the other missionaries knew that *Wao tededo* was unrelated to any other tongue on earth. It bore no relation to Spanish, Quichua, or any other languages or tribal dialects. Over the years since she'd left her tribe, Dayuma had unintentionally mixed her childhood language with the Quichua she learned on the hacienda. Consequently, the words and phrases that she taught the missionaries were not particularly helpful in the best of circumstances, let alone the worst.

When asked why the Waodani killed so voraciously, Dayuma had few insights as to their motivations. Her only answer was that they were killers.

"Never, never trust them," she would say, thinking of her own bloody childhood. "They may appear friendly and then they will turn around and kill."

Dayuma was as much of an expert as anyone. In the mid-1950s, little was known of the Waodani, except that they killed all strangers who ventured into their territory.

Their violence was equal opportunity; they killed their own people as well. Anthropologists would later identify them as one of the most homicidal tribes ever studied.

They lived in a region of roughly 8,100 square miles—around the size of Massachusetts—of Ecuador's eastern jungle. It is one of the richest biotic zones on the planet—origin of half the rivers that form the Amazon. The Waodani lands were bordered by the foothills of the Andes, the Napo River to the north, and the Villano and Curaray rivers to the south.

Perhaps they were descendants of the original Incas who had been double-crossed and subjugated by the Spanish conquistadors in the 1500s. In the late nineteenth and early twentieth centuries, rubber traders penetrated deep into the land, kidnapping, torturing, and killing Waodani for sport. The tribe killed as many invaders as they could, though never in open warfare. Their signature attack was an explosive ambush that took down unsuspecting victims without warning. Outsiders feared them as ghosts, shamans, or devils.

Those seeking oil came after the rubber traders. As we've seen, the Shell Oil Company established a formidable presence in the central sector of the Oriente from about 1938 through 1949. But, "[i]n 1949, after investing over $40 million and losing fourteen of its oil workers to spearing raids by Indians, Shell abandoned its Ecuador holdings without pumping a gallon of commercial oil."[10]

If a victory for the indigenous people, it was a temporary one. How long could their way of life remain untouched by the outside world? Those who wanted to develop their land for economic gain would return, and there were rumors that the Ecuadorian government and the oil companies might well solve the "Waodani problem" by using the military.

The Waodani lived a partially nomadic life as hunters and gardeners. They hunted monkeys with long blowguns and notched darts. The men would dab the tip of the dart with poison, load it into the hollow wooden tube, aim and blow with astonishing precision. *Fffffft!* The monkey, high in the trees, would try to claw out the dart, breaking its shaft, and leaving the toxic tip lodged within. Paralysis would soon hit his central nervous system; it was a long fall to the jungle floor. The hunter would recover his prey, and before rigor mortis had set in, he'd wrap the monkey arms over his shoulder and wear his catch home, like a furry purse.

They also hunted and ate various types of pigs, and the many fish that flourished in their unspoiled rivers. They lived in long, oblong huts with mud-packed floors, and slept in woven hammocks, keeping fires going through the long cold nights. If the fire died down, they'd lean out of the hammock, poke the embers and add more sticks, and it would flare up again.

They ate every type of banana the jungle offered. They farmed manioc, the fibrous, starchy tuber somewhat like yucca, full of carbohydrates. Like other tribes they made *chicha*, the lumpy yogurt-like staple that supplied energy for hunters' long days on the trail. The longer the *chicha* fermented, the higher its alcohol content, but the Waodani, unlike other nearby people groups, did not tend toward drunkenness.

They were short, but very muscular. Their broad feet, toes splayed to the sides almost like fingers, gave them powerful trekking and tree-climbing skills. They pierced their children's earlobes, inserting balsa wood plugs of graduated sizes over the years to form large, round holes by the time the kids were teenagers. They wore their thick, dark hair with short bangs (cut with a clam shell), and trimmed behind the ears to show their ear lobes. The men plucked their beards. Women were married shortly after reaching puberty.

They wore only a *kumi*, or G-string made of twine. Wearing this, they considered themselves attired, though outsiders would call them naked. They called outsiders "foreigners," or *cowodi*. They teased each other without mercy, and loved to laugh. They told stories over and over and over, particularly at night. Most of their stories recounted spearing attacks on *cowodi* or on other Waodani family groups. The warriors remembered every move, every spear-thrust, the way people today might tell others the memorable plays of a championship football game. After a killing, they mocked and further speared the dead; their ultimate insult was to toss a body in the river, where it would remain unburied. They loved their children, but sometimes inexplicably followed the custom of burying them alive with a family member who had died—or was in the process of dying.

Unlike many tribal groups, and the caricatures that flourished in North American culture, they had no chief. Though some would later characterize them as matriarchal, they were an egalitarian society. They were extremely practical. They lived in the present. They did not spend time mulling over origins, though they did believe in strong spiritual forces at work in the world.

They lived in family groups. They dealt with conflict decisively. If one man insulted or wronged another, the only recourse was for the offended to ignore the insult, or to spear the other to death. They did not hold back from spearing women and children. By 1956, the tribe was in danger of exterminating itself. Six or seven of every ten deaths were due to spearing; add in their mortality rate in childbirth and deaths due to snakebites, anaconda, and other threats, and the Waodani were dying off.

The missionaries of the 1950s did not know much about the Waodani, beyond the obvious danger of contact with them. All they knew was that God had stirred within them an unlikely love for this tribe that was in danger of extinction. Critics would later accuse the missionaries of being in collusion with American oil companies or the government, or idiots determined to impose Western culture on a pristine indigenous people. But the five men did not go to them for profit, fame, or ignorant cultural imperialism, but simply because they knew that Jesus offered the people eternal life in heaven *and* a new, nonviolent way of living here on God's green earth. Good news. For free.

CHAPTER 21

Countdown to Contact

"All God's giants have been weak men who did great things
for God because they reckoned on God being with them."
—Hudson Taylor

The missionaries' dream of reaching the tribe began to become reality on September 19, 1955. Nate Saint had a little extra flying time on his delivery run to the various missionary outposts. He invited Ed McCully to join him to "go looking for the neighbors" in the expanse of green jungle near Ed's home at Arajuno.

They both peered down from the plane, scanning the vast area below. Nothing but an ocean of green . . . green . . . and then, look, a tiny brown variation in the jungle floor . . . a clearing . . . a patch of cultivated land . . . a few thatched houses. Waodani!

A week or so later, Pete Fleming flew with Nate, and they spotted another group of dwellings. On the evening of October 1, Nate, Ed, Jim, and fellow pilot Johnny Keenan pored over a huge map of the Oriente. They talked late into the night. They prayed. They believed it was God's timing for them to try to reach the Waodani.

The missionaries all had day jobs, so to speak. They knew that their mission agencies would likely discourage their plans to go to the Waodani . . . not because of conflict of interest—after all, everybody wanted the gospel to go to all the world—but because of their concern for the men's safety. So at this point, the plans, and the mission itself, would be secret.

The men were familiar with the outreach made in 1943 when five missionaries in Bolivia traveled deep into the jungle to make contact with the unreached Ayoré people. They were never heard from again, their bodies never found. Nate, Jim, and the others discussed the men's strategy, and what they could learn from their fate.

The main handicap for the missionaries was their lack of any knowledge of the Waodani language. Rachel Saint, Nate's sister, was the person who knew the most about it because of her relationship with Dayuma. But the men felt that it would be most prudent not to include Rachel in their plans.

Nate wrote a letter to Rachel, and held it for some future point when it seemed right to send it.

> "Dear Sis . . . as you know, the reaching of the Waodani has been on our hearts for a long time. It has been heartening to know that the Lord has laid a specific burden on your heart also and that you are currently engaged in work on their language. For this reason it has been hard to decide not to share with you the efforts that we are about to initiate toward the contacting of these people. . . .
>
> "As we see it, you might feel obligated to divulge this information to save me the risks involved. In view of that fact, and since we know that you are already praying for the contacting of these people, we trust God to carry us forward in this effort and you in your efforts to the end that Christ might be known among them. Affectionately, Nate."[1]

When Nate told Betty Elliot of his decision not to include Rachel, Betty was surprised. She asked Nate if he was sure; shouldn't they include his sister in the plans?

"Ah," Nate responded, "You don't know my sister!"

Since Jim Elliot had already met Dayuma, Rachel's language informant, he walked four hours from Shandia to the hacienda of Don Carlos Sevilla to meet with her again. He asked about a variety of simple Waodani phrases without divulging to Dayuma exactly why he needed them. He carefully noted her responses on 3 x 5 note cards, phonetically sounding out words like *"biti miti punimupa,"* which Dayuma told him basically meant "I like you; I want to be your friend."

The men developed a series of weekly "bucket drops," in which they attached gifts in a bucket or basket attached, with a release mechanism, to a long cord from Nate's airplane. He'd keep one hand on the joystick and let the basket, attached to a long line, out of the plane. Then he'd fly in tight circles over the settlement. Thanks to gravity and drag, the basket would eventually hover, almost motionless, three feet above the ground.

The first gift was a bright aluminum kettle, decorated with color-ful ribbons to draw attention to it. As Nate flew home, he thought, ". . . there was our messenger of good will, love and faith two thousand feet below. In a sense we had delivered the first gospel message by sign language to a people who are a quarter of a mile away vertically . . . fifty miles away horizontally . . . and continents and wide seas away psychologically."[2]

Over the course of the next thirteen weeks, Nate and the guys dropped dozens of gifts to the tribe. The Waodani responded with confusion at first. But by the second week, they ran to the site of the drop; by the sixth visit, they started sending return gifts like a pet parrot, food, a feathered headdress, and pottery back to the missionaries, via the bucket. They cleared trees so the plane had better visual access; they constructed a crude model airplane on a platform so their visitors could identify their location. The missionaries, though still cautious, took the tribe's responses as God's encouragement that the Waodani could be open to outsiders.

On October 29, Jim Elliot used a loudspeaker and leaned out of Nate's plane to shout some of the friendly Waodani phrases he had learned from Dayuma. Jim wrote optimistically in his journal that as far as he and Nate could tell from about 1,500 feet up, the people seemed to understand what he was saying.

Betty Elliot wrote in her own journal that Jim and the guys "have been able to sight the Waodani clearly, their houses and canoes. All feel it is time for us to make some definite move in their direction. I have been wondering if I should go—perhaps the presence of a woman and baby would help the initial impression. Lord—I am Thine."

Even as Betty and Jim continued their usual ministry among the Quichuas that fall, Nate Saint approached fellow missionary Roger Youderian about joining the men's top-secret mission to the Waodani. Roger was a World War II veteran, a decorated paratrooper who had fought in the Battle of the Bulge in Germany. He and his wife, Barbara, had come to Ecuador with their infant daughter in 1953 as part of a Gospel Missionary Union team. They had been working with the Shuar people—best known at the time for their skills at shrinking human heads. Now serving a related tribe, the Achuar people, the Youderians lived near fellow missionaries Frank and Marie Drown in Macuma, about 100 miles southeast of Shell. Roger burned with urgency in missionary work; he opened three outstations for tribal work in Ecuador during his three years there.[3]

Nate knew that Roger was resourceful, jungle-savvy, and disciplined. Roger had once run eighteen miles—over jungle ridges and through treacherous trails without stopping to eat, his skin torn by thorns and his clothes in tatters—to save a wounded Indian. Nate concluded, "He was convinced that the cause was worth dying for and therefore put no price or value on his own life. He was trained and disciplined. He knew the importance of unswerving conformity to the will of his Captain. Obedience is not a momentary option . . . it is a die-cast decision made beforehand."[4]

What no one except Roger's wife knew, however, was that he was struggling with depression. He felt he wasn't seeing any results from his hard work among the tribal people. He felt like a failure. His faith was intact. He loved God. He loved his family. But there was something he could not identify, some failure for which he took responsibility, that made him believe it was time to hang up his missionary hat and return home to the States. But, still, Roger was still determined to seek God's will, and "[at] every point I will obey and do."[5]

And now, as far as Roger could discern, God was directing him to join the mission to the Waodani. So he did.

Roger Youderian, January 1956

Meanwhile, Jim's old friend Pete Fleming wrote in his journal, "The Waodani situation is developing fast. A definite attempt at contact is planned for early January. The attitude seems increasingly friendly as the weekly flights are made . . . There is to be a pow wow about it at Arajuno during Christmas. Ed, Jim, and Roger are definitely going . . . I might make up the other one."[6]

As they shared a common desire for the Waodani to know the love of Jesus, the men's feelings about timing varied according to the personalities.

As Elisabeth wrote later, "Pete, who constantly conferred with the other three, did not feel that the next full moon was the right time for the first attempt at contact. It was too soon to assume that a long-standing hatred of white men had been overcome. . . . Ed's reaction that the next move should not necessarily be an effort at contact, but rather the establishment of a usable airstrip" within about five miles of the Waodani settlement.

Meanwhile Jim Elliot, according to his wife, was "'chewing the bit.' If a friendly contact were made, Jim and I were prepared to leave the work in Shandia for a time, and go in and live among the Waodani." Meanwhile Nate felt that the group should continue to make regular contacts, without a sudden move just yet.[7]

But tensions outside of the missionary community pressed Nate to move more quickly. As we've seen, the Waodani spearing of oil company workers had hindered jungle petroleum exploration. Now the missionaries were hearing that oil executives had discussed the situation with the Ecuadorian government; there were fears that the military would find a way to get rid of the Waodani problem once and for all. The missionaries were anxious to reach the tribal people soon, or there might not be any left who could be saved.[8]

"Since recent Waodani attacks," Nate wrote, "there has been some talk of an expedition that would go in armed to the teeth. Chances are, they wouldn't even find the Indians, but if they did there would surely be bloodshed and increased danger for those of us who are willing to labor patiently for a friendly contact for the Lord's sake."[9]

On November 26, Jim Elliot made his second Waodani flight with Nate. "Noted an increased amount of . . . land clearing since my last visit. The second house has a model airplane carved on the house ridge and there we dropped a machete . . . and I saw a thing that thrilled me. It seemed an old man stood beside the house and waved with both his arms as if to signal us to come down. Waodani waving at me to come! . . . God send me soon to the Waodani."[10]

Still, they knew that actual contact would be dangerous. Without revealing details, Nate wrote to a military friend for advice regarding what might happen should a plane have engine trouble in Waodani territory. Should the men carry guns? After much discussion, the course of wisdom seemed to be that yes, it would be prudent to carry firearms. The Waodani had shown a healthy respect for guns carried by Quichuas and others, and would hesitate to attack armed men. The missionaries determined that they wouldn't defend themselves; the presence of the guns, or firing them into the air, would hopefully deter the Waodani.

By December, Nate, Jim, Ed, and Roger were all in. Pete Fleming was still not sure how God was leading him. He talked deeply with his young wife, Olive, prayed, and sought God's will. In the end, he chose to join his buddies on the adventure. "I am glad to go," he wrote in his journal, "and when my heart begins to be troubled at all, the Lord has quieted me."[11]

Meanwhile, Betty shared Jim's excitement. "I, of course, would love to do the Waodani language work. . . . Jim went on the Waodani flight on Saturday. Came back beside himself with excitement. To see them waving their arms, beckoning to them, running around like crazy, jumping with joy at the gifts dropped to them—he feels the time to go to them is now. How I wish I could go—but Ed simply ridiculed the idea, so there is no possibility, I guess."

She sighed, hating missing out on the action and being relegated to writing letters to supporters back home. "And here I am at the desk in the afternoon sun . . . the rude noise of a parrot in the trees, and time to write some letters to some ordinary car-driving, church-going, pizza-eating, elevator-riding, false-toothed and probably good hearted Christians in the USA."

She couldn't even help with her innate linguistic gifts. "Last week Nate and Ed were quite anxious for Jim to . . . get language material from Dayuma. So I made plans to go (as it would be easier for me) and today Nate arrives to tell me he has no peace about my going, nor has Ed. Now I don't know what to do. It is the second attempt I have been ready to make for the language, and Ed decides I shouldn't."

On December 16, a naked Waodani tribesman appeared outside the McCully home in Arajuno, right at the border with Waodani territory. He faded into the jungle, leaving only distinctive footprints behind.

Betty wrote in her journal that this development was "very thrilling to me for some reason. I wonder if God will let Jim and me be the first couple to go among them? We are ready to go at a moment's notice . . . as far as our own desires are concerned. . . . O Lord—purify my heart and motives. Thou knowest the dross, and the alloy which lies in the hidden recesses. Purge and fit me for Thy service."

The plans continued to develop. "Jim went on the Waodani flight Sat.—received a parrot, 2 squirrels, some cooked food, bracelets, and baskets on the end of the line. [In the New Year] he will be going on the first attempt to meet them on the ground."

Betty, who would have plunged into the jungle in a heartbeat, was having an uncommonly hard time managing their housekeeper and friend, the sometimes volatile young Eugenia. Eugenia often refused to do tasks that Betty assigned her; her attitude ran the gamut between disrespect and sweetness. Betty was utterly stumped as to how to work with her to achieve both peace and order in the home. Jim observed that the girl had her "over a barrel."

"I was not proud of you today," he told Betty, having observed her struggles with Eugenia. She wrote in her journal, poignantly, "Has he ever said, 'I was proud of you today?'"

"I am at the end of my rope," wrote Betty. "Eugenia has been very difficult again today . . . I've tried silence, I've tried raising my voice, docking her pay, sending her home for a few days, sending her outside while I do the work myself, etc. etc. Jim sees only the times when I am bawling her out for something (which are frequent, granted) and feels I deal very childishly with her. I don't know what to do. I almost feel that she comes between us. I feel so far away from Jim sometimes—I long to be close, sympathetic with his problems (and he must have far more than I, with the responsibility of everything at the station) but he does not complain or share them with me if he has any."

Christmas 1955: Jim, Nate, Ed, Pete, and Roger had fifteen days left on earth.

The Elliots, Flemings, and McCullys celebrated Christmas together at Ed and Marilou's home at Arajuno. The usual comedy team of Ed and Jim had everyone crying with laughter. Meanwhile the Saints were cozy at Shell; the ever-competent Marj had put up a spangled tree and ornaments, and filled the house with the aroma of fresh-baked cookies. Visitors were in and out at all hours.

Nate took some time behind closed doors, as his sister Rachel—oblivious to the Waodani plans—was staying with them. He wrote a long letter to be sent out after the men's expedition into Waodani territory. It described his discomfort at the disparity between his own celebration of Christmas, and the situation of those who had never heard the gospel. He was thinking of "two hundred silent generations who have gone to their pagan graves without a knowledge of the Lord Jesus Christ . . . these who . . . survive by killing and die by counter killing . . . these have no Christmas!

". . . as we weigh the future and seek the will of God, does it seem right that we should hazard our lives for just a few?"[12]

Nate answered his own question, that the men's foray to the dangerous few was in realization of the Bible's "prophetic word that there shall be some from every tribe in His presence in the last day and in our hearts we feel that it is pleasing to Him that we should interest ourselves in making an opening into the Waodani prison for Christ.

"As we have a high old time this Christmas, may we who know Christ hear the cry of the damned as they hurtle headlong into the Christless night without ever a chance. May we be moved with compassion as our Lord was.[13]

There's no question that these were five dedicated young men, representing the best human beings can offer to God—a passionate abandon to extend His kingdom and multiply His glory by sharing His gospel with those who have never heard it.*

But lest we think that the missionaries lived on a plane none of us can attain, it is perhaps helpful to consider Jim Elliot's final journal entry, written dejectedly on the last day of the year, 1955. His heart and intentions firmly set on Christ, he was nonetheless battling a temptation common to all of us, the lure of the flesh.

"A month of temptation. Satan and the flesh have been on me hard on the dreadful old level of breasts and bodies. How God holds my soul in His life and permits one with such wretchedness to continue in His service, I cannot tell. Oh, it has been hard. Betty thinks I have been angry with her, when I have simply had to steel myself to sex life so as not to explode . . . my unworthiness of her love beats me down. I have been really low inside me struggling and casting myself hourly on Christ for help."[14]

Though they have sometimes been presented as such, Jim Elliot and his fellow missionaries were not spiritual superheroes. Yes, Jim

---

*As Kathryn Long points out with characteristic thoroughness, the five missionaries who reached out to the Waodani "did so as friends, with little concern for institutional affiliations. In part this reflected the Plymouth Brethren tradition of three of the five, who were themselves independent representatives of their home assemblies. Also, to avoid competition the various missionary groups working in the jungles of Ecuador had divided the territory and tribal peoples among themselves. The Christian and Missionary Alliance (C&MA), as well as the Gospel Missionary Union (GMU) worked in the southeastern jungles, along the Pastaza and Bobonaza rivers, among the Shuar (Jívaro) and Achuar peoples. Brethren missionaries took the central and northern area where various groups of lowland Quichua peoples lived. Wao territory also lay in their domain, one reason why Jim Elliot, Ed McCully, and Pete Fleming felt a proprietary interest in the tribe. The missionary station Ed and Marilou McCully established at Arajuno, the aerial jumping-off point for [Waodani outreach], had been deliberately located on the Waodani side of the Arajuno River, the western boundary of traditional Waodani lands. When, at Nate Saint's suggestion, the other missionaries invited Roger Youderian to join them, they were "borrowing" him from the southern jungles, an action that brought the Gospel Missionary Union, his sponsoring organization, into the picture.

possessed energetic faith and unusual spiritual insights. But at the end of his life, when Satan desperately wanted to derail him, it was through one of life's most common temptations. And as we've seen, in spite of their enormous faith, the others struggled as well: Roger, with depression, Pete with indecision, Nate and Ed with all kinds of normal human uncertainties. These firm followers of Christ were not impervious to the cares, afflictions, lures, and demands of this world. Even as they launched on the path that would bring them to martyrdom, they were thoroughly human—which makes their martyrdom all the more heroic.

Jim Elliot's last days were not those of some sterile plastic saint, but a flesh-and-blood man experiencing a cloud of distractions. But the last words in his journal, from that last day of 1955, shed light on his confidence in the ultimate outcome ahead.

". . . though the flesh conspire," he wrote, ". . . Let spirit conquer."

The Spirit would.

CHAPTER 22

The Second Death

*"We believe that in a short time we shall have the privilege of
meeting these fellows with the story of the Grace of God."*
—Nate Saint

On January 3, 1956, Nate ferried his missionary buddies to a clearing
on the winding Curaray River. He'd nicknamed the site Palm Beach; it
was near the Waodani settlement where they'd spent the last thirteen
weeks dropping gifts. The river had left a long sandbar there; only the
most skillful of pilots, like a Nate Saint, could have possibly landed
on it or taken off from it.

On January 4, Betty wrote in her journal, "Jim is gone to the
Waodani now. Nate flew him, Pete, Roger . . . and Ed to a beach
about 3 hours away from the houses where they've been making
the drops. . . . They set up a tree house where they will wait for the
[Waodani] to come and visit them. They are armed, of course, and
since Waodani kill only with lances I suppose it is fairly safe for them.
I have no idea when they will return.

"I have thought a lot about being a widow," she continued. "I
wonder if I would have the courage to carry on here. I feel now that I
would want to. But God doesn't give guidance for dreams."

That same day, Jim Elliot wrote what would be his last note to his
wife. Nate Saint flew it out of the jungle that evening. Jim jotted in
pencil, from the tree house at Palm Beach. ". . . we really feel cozy and
secure thirty-five feet off the ground in our . . . little bunks. . . . We
saw puma tracks on the beach and heard them last night. It is beautiful jungle, open and full of palms. . . . Our hopes are up, but no signs
of the 'neighbors' yet. Perhaps today is the day the Waodani will be

reached. . . . We're going down now. Pistols, gifts . . . and prayer in our hearts. All for now. Your lover, Jim."[1]

By now Rachel Saint had come to Shandia. She was staying in the Elliots' home. Since Nate had decided his sister must not know about the outreach, it was awkward for Betty. When Nate would radio in with updates, Betty would listen in on those transmissions wearing earphones, so Rachel could not hear the reports.

On the morning of Friday, January 6, 1956, Nate, Jim, and friends expected another long, hot day of waiting for the Waodani. It could take weeks. Then, unbelievably, two women stepped out of the jungle on the opposite side of the river from the camp. One was young, the other older, with a torn ear. They were naked except for strings tied around their wrists and waists. They wore round balsa plugs in their pierced ears. Waodani!

Jim Elliot waded into the river to help them across. Nate, Ed, Roger, and Pete welcomed them with much nodding and smiling. Then a Waodani man emerged from the foliage as well.

The tribespeople had no idea what the North Americans were saying, but streamed forth with torrents of verbiage they assumed the missionaries would understand. They ate, drank, and seemed utterly comfortable, to the extent that the man made it clear to Nate, by body language, that he wanted to ride in the airplane. Nate obliged, and as the yellow Piper skimmed over the Waodani village, the Indian got so excited he would have climbed out on the strut, mid-air, had Nate not held him back. (There was little for Nate to grab onto, as the man wore no clothes.) Later, in an elaborate pantomime, the missionaries tried to communicate their desire for the Waodani to clear a landing strip in their settlement, to make further contact easier. Home movies the missionaries took of that attempt show that dramatic portrayals were not exactly their strong suit.

Nate Saint and Roger, applying insect repellent to
their Waodani visitor, January 6, 1956

Later in the afternoon, the man and the younger woman walked back into the jungle. The older woman stayed on the beach, earnestly sharing her unintelligible, deepest thoughts and feelings with Roger. She slept next to the fire that night; when the missionaries awoke in their tree house early the next morning, she had gone.

The missionaries were beside themselves. Friendly contact! With Waodani! Their dream was coming true. They radioed the happy news to their wives; Nate flew pictures and video of this first-ever Waodani connection back to Shell.

The next day, Saturday, the men paced, prayed, and shouted friendly greetings into the silent jungle. They waited all day. No sign of the Waodani. When would their new friends return?

Back at Shandia, Betty had laughed at Nate's descriptions of the Friday's meeting with the Waodani, thrilled that the first contact had gone so well. Clearly, great things were ahead.

It's likely that the missionaries' second visit with the Waodani on Sunday, January 8 would have been as friendly as that first visit on Friday, but for one situation that had nothing to do with the North Americans.

The Waodani man who had visited with the missionaries on Friday was named Nenkiwi. The younger woman was Gimadi, the older woman Mintaka.

In a tribe of killers, Nenkiwi stood out. He had had two wives, and had speared one when she displeased him. Now he wanted to marry the provocative young Gimadi. Her brother, a fierce warrior named Nampa, opposed the match.

As this tension was developing on Friday morning, January 6, Gimadi, a willful sort, had left the Waodani settlement. So did Nenkiwi. The older woman, Mintaka, saw what was happening and went along as a self-selected chaperone. The three of them eventually came upon the five missionaries, and, as we've seen, peacefully spent the day with them.

When Gimadi got up and left the men's campsite, Nenkiwi followed her into the dense tangle of trees and vines. Mintaka stayed with the missionaries until very early the next morning, then made her way back to the Waodani settlement. So did Nenkiwi and Gimadi, but only after spending the night alone together in the jungle—a violation of Waodani mores.

On Saturday, Nenkiwi was more determined than ever to have his way and marry Gimadi. Nampa, furious, did not want Nenkiwi to have his sister. He and Nenkiwi both escalated into a killing rage, which in Waodani culture could only have one outcome: death by spearing. As others gathered around, the tension mounting, Nenkiwi skillfully turned the wrath against him toward the missionaries. He described the visit with Nate, Jim, and the others, but with his own spin on it.

"The foreigners were going to kill us!" he claimed.

The older woman, Mintaka, scoffed at this. She told the other Waodani about the peaceful visit with the five light-skinned men. "We ate their food with them!" she explained. "Nenkiwi's talking wild!"

Gikita, a seasoned warrior and the oldest in the group, well knew Nenkiwi's tendency to lie for his own advantage . . . but he also knew the tribe could not afford to kill one of its own warriors right then. The low-river months of December, January, and February were "the killing season," when other Waodani clans would attack. They needed Nenkiwi for the coming raids. As Nenkiwi's accusations against the five foreigners continued, the tribe's anger and bloodlust started to burn, and soon they were sharpening their spears.

"Yes!" they shouted. "We will spear! We will go and kill the *cowodi*!"

The course was set.[2] The Waodani spent the rest of Saturday making spears, sharpening them with the machetes the missionaries had dropped as gifts. They would attack the next day.

Of course, the missionaries didn't know about this web of lies, intrigue, and rage.

On Sunday morning, January 8, when Nate Saint flew over the jungle, he saw a group of naked tribespeople heading in the direction of Palm Beach. At 12:30 p.m., he radioed Marj that he'd seen the approaching Waodani, and that they would certainly arrive at the missionaries' camp later in the afternoon. "Pray for us!" he concluded. "This is the day! Will contact you next at 4:30."

After Nate landed his yellow plane on the sandbar, and shouted to Jim, Ed, Pete, and Roger about the expected visitors, the five missionaries paced the beach, praying and reviewing their phrasebooks. Waiting. A pot of beans simmered over their open fire. They all had on shirts and khaki pants, except for Roger, who wore blue jeans. They were brimming with anticipation, hoping that the Waodani might invite them to their homes.

The accounts of what happened next have varied over the many years since January 1956. Each Waodani who participated in the killings saw the event only from his own perspective. Each was fueled by adrenalin that both concentrated and soon exhausted his energy, focus, and anger. But the various accounts, and the forensic evidence, agree on the overall course of the attack. And all agree on its quick outcome.

The action unfolded on the banks of the Curaray River. The five men were now under their makeshift shelter from the sun, batting at insects, and waiting for the Waodani to emerge from the jungle.

Palm Beach, January 1956

Meanwhile, the Waodani warriors—Gikita, Nampa, Kimo, Nimonga, Dyuwi, and Mincaye—had stealthily separated into two groups. They were accompanied by several women. The first group hid upriver, a distance away from the missionaries' base camp. A couple of the Waodani women, decoys, came out from the tall sugar cane next to the water, calling out to the foreigners down the beach.

As would be expected, Jim Elliot was first to head in their direction, away from the camp, joined by his old friend Pete. Meanwhile Roger, Nate, and Ed waited back near the shelter.

So the missionaries were separated when the ambush began.

As Jim Elliot smiled and gestured happily, his attention focused on the women, Nampa burst from the thick foliage, running toward Jim with his spear poised. Jim grabbed at his side, where he was wearing a holster with a snap-down cover. He somehow got the pistol out and raised his arm to fire a warning shot into the air. But Nampa had thrown his spear, with deadly accuracy, toward the middle of Jim's chest. One of the women, Nampa's mother, ran at Jim from behind and pulled his arm down. As she did so, Jim's gun went off. The bullet grazed Nampa's head, and he fell, not far from where Jim thudded to the sand, Nampa's spear in his chest.

Simultaneously, the downriver warriors shot out of the jungle near the missionaries' base camp. The warrior Gikita speared Nate, hitting him center chest; the others rushed Ed and Roger. At some point in the chaos, big Ed McCully tried to protect one of his missionary friends by grabbing his attackers' arms from behind; other Indians came behind Ed, spearing him in the back. At the same time one of the missionaries, most likely the battle-seasoned Roger, ran toward the airplane and desperately leaned in to grab the hand-held radio. The Waodani pursued him and speared him in an upward thrust through the right hip. He fell in the sand. Covered in blood, they speared him again and again.

Upriver, after Jim went down, Pete had escaped to a log resting in the shallow river.

"Why didn't he flee?" the warriors asked years later. "He just stood there, calling out to us." It's unknown if Pete's phrases were fully intelligible to the Waodani; it *is* known that they could see he meant them no harm. But in their flow of rage, it did not matter. They ran toward him and threw their spears, piercing his heart.

As was customary in their killings, the attackers circulated among the fallen men, insulting them and plunging more spears in their bodies, so all would share common responsibility for the deaths. The missionaries, bleeding from horrific wounds, did not live long.

The killers: hard breathing, hyped by adrenalin. The missionaries: breathing their last. Blood in the sand. The pull of the warm water. The jungle canopy spinning green, blue, then brilliant, brilliant gold.

The Waodani moved on to Nate's yellow airplane, hacking its tough yet pliable surface with machetes, spearing it, and ripping off as much of its skin as they could.

When they killed like this, the warriors did so from a roiling, diabolical pool of rage that propelled their spears, fueled their insults and drove their overkill. That rage was soon spent . . . replaced by fear.

They picked up the barely conscious Nampa,* carried him onto the trail, and fled for their homes. After setting those homes on fire, as was their custom after killing, they disappeared into the jungle.

Years later, Mincaye (one of the warriors who later came to know Christ) confirmed the consensus among the Waodani at the time of the killings. First, though the missionaries had guns, and several fired those weapons into the air, they clearly did not use them in self-defense. Second, "the short one"—Pete—could have escaped into the jungle; the warriors would not have pursued him since their killing rage was short-lived. But he did not, and so they speared him.

---

*Nampa lived for some months after the Palm Beach massacre. There are basically two schools of thought about his death. Some say that he was merely grazed by the missionary's warning shot and died later while hunting, crushed by a boa. Others posit that he died from complications from the bullet wound in his head.

Several decades later, some who participated in the attack spoke of a strange, additional presence beyond the human beings who were killing and dying on the beach that day. Kimo and Dyuwi, among others, described strange lights above the trees . . . "foreigners" dressed in white cloth . . . and the sound of chanting, which is how the Waodani described singing.

Were they angels? God only knows.

In the agony of their dying moments, in the pain of those last shallow breaths, what flashed through the five Americans' minds? God only knows that as well. All that the brave widows and families, and the rest of us down through the decades, can know for sure is that when they passed through that thin veil separating this life from eternal life, those five missionaries' *next* enormous, exultant breath was in the actual presence of God. They had gained what they could not lose.

CHAPTER 23

Christ the Beginning;
Christ the End

"Distance in a straight line has no mystery.
The mystery is in the sphere."
—Thomas Mann

Betty Elliot, in Shandia, had no indication of her husband's death until the next day. Since Rachel Saint, unaware of the men's mission, had been staying with her, Betty hadn't been on the radio transmissions on Sunday. She had no particular reason to think anything was amiss.

On Monday morning, January 9, 1956, Betty got on the radio with Marj Saint at 8 a.m. Marj told her that Nate and Jim and the others hadn't checked in as usual on Sunday afternoon, and that Johnny Keenan, the MAF pilot who worked with Nate, had taken off to circle over the Palm Beach campsite. Could Betty get back in touch at 10? Betty wasn't particularly worried. She knew that the men were excited about contact with the tribe; they'd probably just gotten absorbed in whatever they were doing.

At 10 a.m., Marj's strained voice came over the radio. "Johnny has located the plane, and all the fabric is stripped off. There was no sign of the fellows."

Rachel, standing with Betty and hearing that message, now understood what was going on, and that she'd been left out of the plan. She burst out and asked Marj if the plane had been burned. "No," said Marj. "We don't know . . . but I don't care anymore about the old airplane! Just about the fellows!" With that her voice broke, and she didn't say, "over" at the end of her transmission.[1]

It was only then that Betty realized things were bad. Very bad.

"Lord, show me the way," she prayed silently. "Give peace, O Thou God of my Salvation."

When Johnnie Keenan radioed his sighting of the ruined plane back to Shell, news of the men's disappearance in Waodani territory exploded throughout the missionary community in Ecuador and far beyond. Quito's powerful Christian radio station, HCJB, the "Voice of the Andes," transmitted the news around the world. The head of the U.S. Caribbean Command, General William Harrison, knew several of the missing missionaries. He marshaled the support of the U.S. military, which brought in two C-47 cargo planes, one carrying a helicopter. The Ecuadorian military offered help. The Associated Press got wind of the story. Christians around the world prayed for the missing men.

The ruined plane

The five wives asked their friend and colleague, missionary Frank Drown of the Gospel Missionary Union, to head the volunteer members of the search party. Missionaries who had jungle expertise offered to join him. They were Morrie Fuller of the Christian & Missionary Alliance, Dr. Art Johnson of HCJB (now known as Reach Beyond), Dee Short of Christian Missions in Many Lands, Jack Shalenko of the Slavic Gospel Association/HCJB, and Don Johnson and Bub Borman of Wycliffe Bible Translators/Summer Institute of Linguistics. Colonel Malcolm Nurnberg of the U.S. Air/Sea Rescue Squadron of the Caribbean Command led the military unit.

Part of the search party

In the end the party consisted of twelve soldiers, six missionaries (including a doctor), and ten Quichua Indians. The Quichuas, friends of Ed McCully's, would handle the long, heavy dugout canoes needed to transport the group into Waodani territory.

Frank Drown presided over the loading of the canoes. He put soldiers, Quichuas, and missionaries in each, so if any canoe was attacked, it would be a mixture of people groups who'd be killed. He spaced the canoes about 300 feet apart. "I wanted it to look like the whole army was coming," Frank said later, "so the Waodani wouldn't try to attack us . . . we looked like the Spanish Armada going down the river."[2]

The exhausted group slept on a sandbar the first night, the soldiers keeping watch.

At dawn the next day they continued along the river. Airplanes flew cover above, reporting on what might be ahead. At one point the crew radioed that a group of Indians was around the bend . . . but when they came in sight, the Quichuas recognized them as fellow believers from Ed's ministry. They told the group that they had found Ed McCully. He was dead. They brought one of his huge shoes—Ed had distinctively large feet—and his watch.

The news passed from boat to boat. Most likely all the men were dead. But still . . . perhaps, somehow, one or more might still be alive.

Frank Drown and his team arrived at Palm Beach. The plane was full of holes, the campsite wrecked, the tree house ravaged.

The helicopter above swept low over the river, and stopped to hover as those inside saw a leg emerging from the water. Several Quichuas waded in, and with ropes, pulled out the unrecognizable corpse. They laid it on the sand. A bit further downstream, there was another. The men carefully drew it out and laid it next to the first.

After the doctor measured the bodies, the group determined that the two were Jim Elliot and Pete Fleming. Jim's body was completely eaten away from the hips up, identifiable by a scrap of material left on the neck of his T-shirt, which had a name tape. His waterproof watch, intact, was still on his wrist.

The helicopter went further. There was another body emerging from the water, stuck on brush and branches, less decomposed than the others. Frank and Morrie, another missionary, went to investigate. "Before we got close we could see a spear sticking out of the head. . . . As we approached I knew it was Nate. The spear had been driven in backwards. He had a big machete wound on his face.

"Then I noticed something else unique to Nate. His wrist watch was pushed up above his elbow. He sometimes did that to remind himself to do something. Perhaps he had not wanted to miss the 4:30 Sunday afternoon contact with his wife. . . .

"I reached over from our canoe to tie a rope on Nate's body, but I couldn't do it. I had no strength. My hands were shaking, and my eyes were full of tears. I just couldn't do it. Morrie saw I was having trouble, so he said he would do it for me. He tied the rope around Nate's body, pulled him back to the beach, and laid him beside Jim Elliot."

About half an hour later, a canoe that had gone further downstream came back, pulling a fourth body.

"I knew it was Roger," Frank said. "His tennis shoes, blue jeans, and white tee shirt identified him. When they laid him beside Nate, I stood there and looked at him. We had walked many trails and ministered in a lot of places together. He had been so strong and capable. But now he was gone from this earth, and I cried and cried. He wouldn't walk the trails with me again.

"I saw the spears in his hips. A great soldier had fallen. Through my tears I had my last look at him. This was his last service done for

God. His body was broken, but his spirit lives on in heaven and in my heart."[3]

The sky grew dark. A huge rainstorm blew in. The soldiers, constantly scanning the jungle for hostile movement, were jumpy. The distraught missionaries and the rest of the group hastily dug a common grave, said a brief prayer, and shoveled the jungle soil over the remains of their fallen brothers.

The story unfolded through sensational newspaper headlines in the U.S. and around the world: "Five U. S. Missionaries Feared Seized by Savages" (*The Los Angeles Times*).

Other news outlets heralded the story: "Amazon Savages Seize Five U.S. Missionaries"; "Wichitans Anxiously Await News of Missionaries' Fate"; "Five U.S. Missionaries in Ecuador Feared Dead"; "Planes Comb Amazon Jungle for Five Missionaries Seized by Savage Indians; One Dead"; "Copter Crew Finds Bodies of 4 Missionaries"; "Missionaries Buried in Jungle: Slain by Indians; All Bodies Found."

The five women—Betty, Marj, Marilou, Olive, and Barbara—prayed constantly. They slept little. They somehow prepared meals, cleaned up, changed diapers, and took care of the children as well as well-wishers and curiosity seekers who had converged on Marj's home in Shell. American soldiers showed up, too, members of the air rescue team that had so heartened the wives when their huge planes painted with the red, white, and blue came roaring down the Shell runway, ready to support the search efforts.

The wives got radio reports about the search as it moved beyond the hope of rescue to recovery, then to the men's hasty burial on the beach where they had died. Later Betty asked Morrie about what Jim's body had looked like. Morrie told her that Jim had been wedged under a log in the river; there wasn't much left of his flesh, which had been "eaten away" in the water. "I wanted to know [all the details], as did all the wives."[4] Betty wrote to her mother and Jim's mom. Somehow the details seemed to help, rather than compound, her hurt.

"The Lord has stood by all of us in a way unimaginable," she wrote. "All of us women are so happy that the men died in such a way—in the 'fullness of their might.' Jim and Ed could have wanted nothing more than to die together—and in such a project. They were ready—every one of them.

"So far I have shed no tears since the final word came. This to me is a miracle. I have been a crybaby since we were married, but the Lord has literally fulfilled His word—[the waters] shall not overflow thee.'

"It was the kindness of God that they were able to find all the bodies easily.

"Some of the future's loneliness began to press on me yesterday afternoon. . . . What will I do? God called me to translation work and to Ecuador. I cannot go home. . . . <u>God keep me from self-pity</u>. . . .

"I must refuse to dwell on all that we did together, on the brevity of our married life, etc. I must refuse each weakening thought. It is true joy to think of Jim, without fault before the throne of God, victor, martyr, overcomer. Oh, the privilege that is mine to have been given such a husband—God 'lent' him to me for 2 years and 3 months.

"They took us out to see the site of the incident today in the Navy C-47. We were all so happy to be able to see where they buried our husbands. The plane was clearly visible on the beach.

"Just one more long day . . . [Marj] and I have kept each other awake every night because we cannot bring ourselves to go to bed.

"I feel perfectly certain that I shall never marry again. No doubt all new widows make that statement, but I feel sure in my heart.

"Who would have guessed that this slim booklet would encompass our whole married life?"

As she came to the last page of her well-worn journal, she closed it with lines from the English poet, Frederic W. H. Myers, lines that she'd actually written on the back inside cover when she started it.

> "'Yea, thro' life, death, thro'
> sorrow and thro' sinning
> He shall suffice me, for He hath suffered:
> Christ is the end, for Christ
> Was the beginning.
> Christ the beginning, for the End is Christ.'"

CHAPTER 24

Through the Gates

"Better those two perfect years of belonging to such a man
than fifty with a run-of-the-mill man!"[1]
—Elisabeth Elliot

Within three weeks of Jim's death, Betty started a brand-new journal, live-streaming in ink both the volatile flow of her emotions and the resolute determination of her intentions.

"Life begins a new chapter—this time without Jim or any hope of seeing him in this life. 20 days ago he was killed by the Waodani Indians on the Rio Curaray.

"Oh, how I pray for conforming to the acceptable will of God. I do not want to miss one lesson. Yet I find that events do not change souls. It is our response to them which finally affects us."

"I find that tho' I am in a new place of yieldedness and utter prostration before Him who has thus planned my life, little things remain between me and Him—big things in His sight, lack of patience with Indians, laziness in myself, failure to discipline myself to prepare properly for school meetings, etc. O God—Thou knowest what they are saying: 'You're wonderful!' 'You're such a rebuke, testimony, challenge, etc.' If only they knew! Thou alone knowest, Lord Jesus. Come Thou, purge, purify, make me like unto Thy glorious self!

"I long now to go to the Waodani. The two things—the only things—to which I can look forward now are the coming of Christ and my going to the Waodani. O, if Christ would only come—but how can He until the Waodani are told of Him. . . . Or if only I could die—what a blessed release. But I do not ask to be released. I ask to be made Christ-like, in the inmost part of my being. . . . Before, I feared to place all before Thee—now, the most precious has been stripped from me. Does this mean I have not so much to put at stake now? I guess it does. But O Lord, Thou knowest. Accept me, in Thy name. And, oh, if it be possible, send me soon to the Waodani!"

The early morning hours were always the hardest. In the old days, she would slowly wake and lie at peace on Jim's strong shoulder. Those days were now forever gone. To wake and feel his place empty beside her was a lance to the heart.

Every time she read the words "Mr. and Mrs." or heard reference to "husband and wife," . . . another stab. "They are allowed to be together . . . and I? Then the Lord shows me that my lot is not to be compared with others," she would tell herself. God had a place in His kingdom and service that no others could fill. Her situation was not by mistake.

"I should rejoice that others are given life-partners for life," she thought; she should gladly accept God's lot for her. But oh . . . the mornings in the dark hours, with great waves of loneliness, oh, to reach out to touch Jim, to dream that he was really there, that his death was not real, that his strong arms were open to her . . . and then nothing but the empty pillow, the cold and solitary bed!

The busy days did not assuage that longing. She felt impatient with the Quichua girls in the school, frustrated that she had to now lead the instruction class for the children's meetings, which Jim had always done. There were seventy-seven letters from family, friends, supporters, and strangers; these must be answered. There was supper to cook. There were concerns about little Valerie, who had stopped eating much during the day, but wanted bottles all night long. "Show me how to be mother and father to her," Betty prayed.

"I feel so helpless without Jim," she continued. "A thousand little things come up constantly—gasoline for the lamps—where did he store it? Someone broke into the [storage]—what did they steal? I don't know what was in it. Hector came up to discuss his salary—such a complicated business, I don't understand it all. . . . I have no one now to take care of the lawn and garden . . . Other women have a man to do these things . . . and they will have heaven too! Lord—forgive me. I write it because I thought it. I cannot hide it from Thee.

"Then I realize that I <u>must</u> instruct the believers. The last thing Jim said when we spoke of the possibility of his not returning was, 'Teach the believers, darling—we've got to teach the believers.' O Lord help me—for I am truly helpless."

Betty was invited to be the speaker at a Quichua Christian conference. She was hesitant; at the time, women did not typically do these things. "I just feel so helpless, at a loss as to whether it would be right in principle. [But] there is no [male missionary] in Ecuador who speaks Quichua."

A Quichua man prayed during a church service of remembrance for the dead missionaries, "Lord, we would not be here doing this if the *señores* had not come all that long way to tell us of you. For this we thank You, we think of Your Son, stuck with a lance, broken and beaten for us."

Elisabeth Elliot, eleven days after the death of her husband

Betty decided to go ahead and speak at the conference. She felt a new urgency; surely Jesus was coming soon. If only He would!

"Mom Elliot wrote yesterday expressing her fears for me—apparently thinking I am repressing my true feelings and will eventually crack. Is it not possible to be kept in perfect peace when one's husband has died? Can God not fulfill His Word?

"Then comes a letter from Marj [Saint] this afternoon—telling me she got weepy talking to me on the radio and couldn't finish. Says each day is harder for her. So the enemy came in like a flood and threatened me with the possibility of cracking up in the future; it was all just nerves and excitement which had kept me from tears, it would soon be different. Perhaps it will, but Jesus Christ is the same yesterday and today and <u>forever</u>. He will meet me there, too.

"I long to be Home. I long to put off this mortal body, to be occupied wholly with things unseen. What a weight things seen are to me now—meals, clothes, my body, housecleaning, etc. . . . I feel frustrated and useless. Cleaning, feeding all these people, caring for Valerie, making bread, etc., etc. Lord—is this what I am here for? Oh, when shall I be free from the body of this death? Help me to be loving Thee in these hours of occupation with things seen."

In mid-March, at a meeting of Quichua believers, one of Jim's mentees preached with passionate conviction, telling the congregants, "If you do not like what I say, I am sorry, for I will keep on tormenting you till I die."

Another preached the next day; nine believers stood spontaneously and gave testimonies of their faith, and four more decided that they were ready to follow Jesus. Eventually sixteen more new believers joined the church as well. "Nothing like that has ever happened," Betty marveled. "It is purely the work of the Spirit—and He has used the Indians themselves for His witnesses!!"

Betty's mother and the formidable Gwen DuBose arrived to visit. The days ticked by as Betty gave penicillin injections, bought 100 pounds of corn, worked with Jim's friend Venancio on his Sunday sermon, and visited with her guests. "Much time spent listening to Mrs. DuBose," Betty noted cryptically. Then: "Could not restrain tears this afternoon as I looked at happy pictures of Jim and me and Val, taken . . . last summer. Ashamed of myself in front of Mrs. DuBose."

Had Betty inferred that tears were a sign of weakness, and that stoicism was a virtue, at Hampden DuBose Academy?

Probably so. In those early weeks after the men's deaths, Betty had scolded Olive Fleming for weeping over her husband's loss, evidently totally tone deaf to her fellow widow's pain. At her core, Betty struggled. From her youth, she'd felt that showing emotion was a sign of weakness; now her emotions were all over the place. It took too much energy to explore, repress, contain, or just plain feel them. Add to that what Jim had called her "natural reserve" and lack of desire to get close to people unless she felt they were an outright gift from God, and she could be aloof to others.

She could also be kind. By April, Betty had gone through all of Jim's stuff. All her letters to him, pictures from high school and college days, photos she'd never seen. Then there were his clothes. She buried her face in his shirts, breathing in the last hints of his presence. Then she packed them up and gave them to missionaries in need. A Mr. Young of the Bible Society had just lost his good coat and suit when his suitcase was stolen. "Jim's coat and suit fit him perfectly," Betty wrote, "also a brand new pair of black shoes. He was touchingly grateful, and said he counted it a very great privilege to wear Jim's things."[2]

By mid-April, Betty sounded a bit like C. S. Lewis. "Today I am thinking how my short time with Jim was not the End of all things. There are times when it seems so—as if it is all over, and I've nothing left now to do but put in time till [Jesus] comes. Not so. Marriage was not in itself the End of Desire—it generated further ones. It was but a segment of the Journey which is Life, and called for obedience. Now, what have I to do? Obey. And my eyes will be opened to the next thing."

There wasn't much doubt what Betty longed for, in terms of that "next thing." "My heart almost cries out for those dear Waodani—how I long to go! Prayed that God either send me there, or take me Home.

"Waodani: how? When? Who? O my heart aches for them. What can I ever do?"

The next day, an altogether different thought popped onto the pages of her journal. "'Single' again, wonder if I will revert to the spinster rut, small mind, self-consciousness, affected mannerisms, off-hand way? Oh—I have known—let me never forget it. Let me go thro' life with the wonder.

"Six months today. Six months of separation from Jim, who was my life. And so it must go on . . . 'Time is a kind friend, and he will make us old.'"

As always, Betty read voraciously. Tolstoy. Marcus Aurelius. And a small book called *The Challenge of Amazon's Indians* by a missionary named Ethel Tylee. Ethel told the story of how she and her husband, Arthur, had followed God's leading to spread the gospel to a remote Brazilian tribe, the Nhambiquara. In 1930, after initially friendly overtures, the tribe blamed the Tylees for the death of their chief, who had succumbed to a jungle fever. They killed Arthur, toddler Marian, and her nurse Mildred with arrows, as well as three of the Tylees' Brazilian coworkers. They bashed Ethel on the back of the head and left her for dead. Miraculously, she survived to tell the story.

To most of us, this would not have been a great encouragement toward work with volatile tribes. Betty's response: "I am possessed as never before with a consuming desire for the Waodani. Can hardly think of anything else when I am not concentrating on translation or something. O Lord—wilt Thou let me go?"

A week later, she mused, I have "utter satisfaction with the present will of God. Now I am shut up to Him. My life with Jim is closed, thus cutting off the past and offering nothing more for the future. No more babies, none of the hoped-for trips we talked of, no improvements on the house, nothing to look forward to but heaven. And this gives me perfect peace. I have no fears, no hopes, no ambition, no regrets, no frustrations now, really—apart from the hope which is in God, and if one must call it 'ambition'—the desire for the Waodani. Well, Lord, Thou knowest.

"Evening. I am left with a vast loneliness for [Jim], for his love— the only answer it seems, for me is that He take me soon. How can I live without Jim, Lord? Thou didst make us one—how go on alone? O Lord, if it be possible, take me to be with Thee. Nevertheless, not my will . . ."

"Sobbed uncontrollably reading Jim's letters."

Then she jotted the moments that made her smile, reporting that one of the Quichua women, reflecting on the lack of clothes among the Waodani, had remarked to her, "Señora, wouldn't the Waodani have very rough bottoms?"

"Why?" asked Betty.

"Why, from sitting on their bare bottoms all their lives."

One evening in September, she wrote, "After supper I went outside to wait for the evening star. A wind came up from the river, and set in motion the giant leaves of the plantains over the hill, and the great plumes of the chonta and bamboo on the stretch between house and river. I stood in thanksgiving to God for this tangible beauty which is, for the beauty which has been in my life because of Jim, and for all of that tremendous substance hoped for which will be. The sky reflected palely the sun, long gone over the horizon, and as the shadows on the clouds finally conquered the lighted tips, suddenly the great red light of the Star burst through, low over the luminous silver of the wide river. For all of this—and heaven too— thanks to Thee, my Father. *Teach me never to let the joy of what has been pale the joy of what is.*"

The other young widows faced their own struggles and challenges. Marilou McCully, eight months pregnant when her husband was killed, returned to the U.S. to have her baby in early 1956. She would return to Ecuador with her three small sons in December of the same year to run a home for missionary children. Marj Saint and her three children went on to Quito, where Marj exerted her endlessly gracious gifts of hospitality and ran a bustling missionary guest-house. Barbara Youderian and her children went to a small jungle station to work with the Jivaro Indians. Olive Fleming helped her fellow widows in their endeavors, and then sensed that God's call for her was to return to the United States in March of 1957.

Marilou McCully, Barb Youderian, Olive Fleming,
Betty Elliot, Marj Saint, and children

None of the widows had the luxury of making such decisions in privacy. They found themselves the objects of much attention, elevated to "celebrity" status in the Christian subculture. On the positive side, condolences poured in from all over the world, letters full of prayer support, empathy, and encouragement. So many in the U.S. wanted to give money to support the slain men's children and widows that a "Missionary Martyrs' Fund" was set up through the auspices of Wheaton College.

But there was unwelcome attention as well: hundreds of letters full of spiritual advice, remonstrations, and directives of the "God told me that you should do x" variety. There were also scathing condemnations of their late husbands' decisions, and odd marriage proposals from dysfunctional men they had never met. Hollywood came calling; what about a film version of the story?

In her own journey, Betty reached an unexpected turning point on October 11, 1956.

"Marj just came on the radio and asked me to go to New York to help on Abe's book. Lord—what shall I do?"

What Betty Elliot called "Abe's book" was the story of the five martyred missionaries; the book that would come to be known as

Through Gates of Splendor. Abe Van Der Puy, Ecuador field director for the World Radio Missionary Fellowship, had sent out the press releases that first reported the missing missionaries, the search efforts, and the discovery of their bodies. The widows had also given Abe their husbands' journals and notes, so he had an account of their plans to reach the Waodani. He had written much of a manuscript about the men. *Reader's Digest,* which appeared in at least 10 million American homes every month—the greatest circulation of any magazine in the country at the time—wanted to publish the story. Since Abe's manuscript lacked zip and adventure, an *RD* editor named Clarence Hall agreed to serve as ghostwriter. He took Abe's notes and materials, and wrote the *Reader's Digest* "condensed book" that appeared in the August 1956 issue of the magazine.

Now it was time for the actual book by the same title. "Through Gates of Splendor" was drawn from the hymn the five missionaries had sung the night before they went to the Waodani. The fourth verse evoked the image of "gates of pearly splendor," through which victorious servants of God would pass to spend "endless days" with Christ.

Abe Van Der Puy was a great Christian leader, but—by his own admission—was not a great writer. The missionaries all knew that Betty Elliot was bookish, literary, and had had a front-row seat for all of the story's inherent drama. She might well be the best person to tell it.

Marj Saint, whose family had been close friends with the Van Der Puys for years, contacted Betty on Abe's behalf.

Betty, being Betty, made a list of pros and cons about the possibility of leaving her work in Ecuador to take on the writing project in New York.

On the positive side, she noted that Abe had said he needed her help, that she could send her Quichua students to another school where "they would get a better [education] anyway than from me," that other missionaries were willing to come and take over her other work, that her parents wanted to see her, that money was available for travel and expenses.

The cons: was she leaving work undone in Shandia? Was this the time for a furlough? Those who were taking her place didn't know Quichua, only Spanish. Last, she was worried about her own pride, that going to the U.S. at this point, and for such a job, would cause people to say "flattering things" to her.

She prayed about it all. Then the personal paper trail gets much more sparse. Over the rest of 1956, there are few entries in Betty's journal, mostly jottings that show that yes, she decided to "help with Abe's book."

In the late fall, she made her way, with twenty-one-month-old Val, to her parents' home in New Jersey. She realized quickly she "could not possibly settle down in the U.S. It holds nothing for me." Leaving Val in her parents' care, she took the train to New York.

Betty arrived at Harper & Brothers, the publisher that had flown her to the U.S. Betty thought she was going to help with the final editing of Abe's manuscript. Instead, as she arrived at Harper's offices, she met a dark-haired, large-nosed editor named Mel Arnold. An omnivorous reader and accomplished editor, Arnold had published the works of humanitarian Albert Schweitzer and would later also serve as editor for Dr. Martin Luther King Jr. (Both were Nobel Peace Prize recipients.)

And now, here was Betty Elliot. Mel Arnold pointed her to a typewriter.

"Write something," he said.

"What?" asked Betty.

"Anything will do," said Mel.

So Betty obligingly sat down, and wrote about a colorful bus trip toward a jungle village in Ecuador.

Mel read it . . . and grinned. Betty was hired.

She spent long days writing in a New York hotel room, wrestling with the constant pain, joy, despair, and fatigue that every writer knows. She wrangled with editors and was hosted at literary dinners in Greenwich Village with "men in turtle-necks, women in black cotton stockings and straight hair . . . reverse snobs." There were visits to art galleries, cocktail parties, movie recommendations—"Oh, Betty, be sure to see 'Lust for Life,' the movie on Van Gogh!"—in short, Betty had entered a world as foreign to a missionary from Ecuador as the Elliots' jungle mission station would be to the Greenwich Village beatniks of the day.

Soon Betty was churning out thousands of words each day. "Boy, you're really rolling," Mel would tell her. "The impact of this . . . is— well, like a ton of bricks." "My eyes were moist," he'd continue, "and I'm a tough guy . . . You must have worked all night!" "The opening chapter . . . a '*tour de force.*'"

"Lord," Betty exulted in her journal. "Bouquets for Thee!"

Sometimes the bouquets wilted. "Harper asked me to rewrite," she wrote the week before Christmas, after she'd gotten a sizeable chunk of the story done. "Terrific blow, after all the build-up they'd given me." The copy editor had read the manuscript and declared it "totally unpublishable." She wanted a complete reorganization, deletion of many diary quotes, less background on the men, more description, more of the wives' stories, and more dialogue.

"Lord," Betty moaned in her journal. "You've got to do it from here on in. I'm finished."

Any writer can identify with her despair. But she would finish. Eventually. Cornell Capa, the *Life* magazine photographer who had covered the missionaries' deaths, proved to be a stalwart friend. No stranger to creative angst, he stood behind her while she typed, cheered her on, and affirmed her writing gifts.

Betty spent Christmas with Valerie and her parents back at Birdsong, remembering the previous year when she and Jim had celebrated Christ's birth with Ed and Marilou McCully and Pete and Olive Fleming, laughing until they cried, singing around the little bamboo Christmas tree, deep in the jungle of Ecuador.

She finished off her journal with these words: "1/1/57, 1:15 a.m. Nineteen fifty-six, the year in which dear Jim met Jesus Christ face to face, is now history. I was reluctant to relinquish it, for I was with him one day of 1956. Lord, I bless the hand that guided."

CHAPTER 25

A Blank Wall

"To take you to His end by the way that you know
would profit you little. He chooses for you a way you
know not, that you may be compelled into a thousand
intercourses with Himself which will make the journey
forever memorable to Him and to you."
—C. G. Moore

*B*etty Elliot returned to Ecuador on January 15, 1957. *Through Gates*
of Splendor had not yet been printed. Its newly-minted author—who,
after its release, would be known to the world as *Elisabeth* Elliot—and
toddler Valerie settled back into their home at the mission station in
Shandia. A missionary friend and his family had lived and worked
there during Betty's absence.

New York had been a literary adventure, but its effects evaporated
quickly. "I belong in the jungle, I know," Betty wrote confidently in
her journal. Beyond that one certainty, however, the future was "a
blank wall."

The Quichua community at Shandia had grown well while she was
gone. Two days after her return, seventeen new believers—their names
carefully listed in Betty's journal—were baptized by their Quichua
leaders, Mariano, Gervacio, Elias, and Venancio. Jim had trained
these men. His hope that they would lead a self-sustaining church
community had become a reality. The Indian Christians, sobered
and galvanized by the deaths of the five U.S. missionaries, had felt a
new sense of urgency in their own responsibility to disciple Quichuan
believers, so the gospel could spread further among their people.
(Venancio would faithfully lead the church in Shandia for years, a
friend of the Elliot family for the rest of Betty's life.)

If the state of the church was pleasing to Betty, the state of her home was not. She sadly noted in her journal that the family who'd lived there while she was in the U.S. had stopped up her plumbing, broken her lawn mower, torn her shower curtain, and broken her toilet seat. The kitchen was "filthy," the sheets and towels all stained and yellow. Now, as she and Valerie settled in, the four other children tracked mud all over newly washed clothes, plucked and crushed Betty's tender new flower buds, and industriously poured dirt into the home's water tanks. At breakfast the father would sit at the table and "clean his ears with a bobby pin, examining minutely the findings."

Betty and the other mom shared cooking duties; evidently the artful arrangement of cuisine that Betty had learned at HDA was not the other mother's gastronomical style. "Oh," Betty moaned, "food must always be prepared in huge, greasy, disgusting quantities." Lunch was served an hour late, with the "beef and brownies raw." Pots burned, trash overflowed, chaos reigned.

Betty was undone.

"Is it wrong for me to be thus revolted?" she wondered. Was she just being snobbish? She had lived in all kinds of accommodations over the years, with all kinds of different roommates. But the muddled disarray now plaguing the home that Jim had so carefully built pushed her over the edge. Her deep-seated love of tidiness pre-dated the Marie Kondos of the world, but it's fair to say that someone else's underwear tossed in the corner of the shared bathroom just did not "spark joy" for Elisabeth Elliot. A product of her own pristine home of origin, she despised disorder and what she considered slothfulness. Even a leaf-hut in the jungle could be a place of beauty, she thought, as could any home. It wasn't a matter of money, but of a mind-set of discipline and creativity in one's habitat.

At any rate, seeing her own home run in a manner not of her choosing brought Betty to a low place that far more severe tests had not. "Why am I made thus?" she mourned. "Intense, sensitive, possessive—why should I care so deeply? Oh that the Will should be all I care for!"

It was not only devastating to Betty to see "the ruin of the lovely things Jim made." She hit the wall one evening when she heard her missionary friends discussing a garishly-illustrated children's book.

"I am crying," she reported to her journal, jotting the conversation she'd just heard. "Just came from [where] [the couple] were discussing art and literature. 'Let the kids have it (a [poor]-quality 'Christian' book of pure trash in art and content) if it gives them pleasure.'

"'As far as the art-work goes—the kids don't know the difference . . .'

"'They'll learn to recognize beauty in time—just let the majority of what they see be good.'"

Many of us wouldn't have thought too hard about such an exchange. But the casual exposure of God's children to inferior, tacky, or sentimental religious illustrations ripped at the very heart of Betty Elliot's core assumptions about art, beauty, and order in the universe. Later, in the privacy of her journal, she erupted—a Vesuvius of artistic loneliness.

"Oh God—God!! We are poles, poles POLES apart. I said nothing. What can one say to such? Two people with no idea of beauty. And the loneliness—oh the utter, vacuous, vast, inconsolable irremediable loneliness of my position! It was too great. I had to . . . wail in misery. I literally wailed. I could not help myself. And how can my child be reared in this atmosphere? Oh Lord—take me out of here."

Had domestic disorder and inferior art accomplished what the brutal Waodani and the horrific death of her husband could not; sending the endlessly stalwart Elisabeth Elliot fleeing madly for civilization?

No.

In the end, Betty followed her usual directive, long learned from Amy Carmichael. *In acceptance lieth peace.* She decided to accept the situation. She thought about already having to relinquish Jim, as well as her dreams for their future together. She decided to give over the house to the missionary family, and move elsewhere. Once she'd made this decision, still wondering if she was being a bit of a snob, she found herself reading in Jeremiah, ". . . the delicately bred I will destroy, and . . . *their houses shall be turned over to others.*"[1]

She saw herself in Jeremiah's description. Well, so much for the "delicately bred."

She tortured herself further by reading 1 Corinthians 13. Love is not jealous . . . boastful . . . arrogant . . . rude . . . irritable . . . resentful.

She sighed. "I was all of these today."

In the midst of Betty's various trials—major, minor, domestic, and otherwise—*Life* magazine photographer Cornell Capa arrived in Ecuador. During his trip to the Amazon for his *Life* magazine assignment in January 1956, Capa had discovered a subculture he knew little about. A Hungarian Jew, Capa later called Christian outreach work "a totally unfamiliar world."[2] The slain missionaries' faith—and the continued conviction of the widows—both mystified and intrigued him. Capa had consumed Jim Elliot's journals and asked a thousand questions. "You could never convert me with [a Christian book]," he said, "but you could with the diaries of those men."[3] He saw these strange missionary creatures with profound human empathy.

Capa's images "communicated complex emotions about both the heroism and the humanity of the five families and other evangelical missionaries in Ecuador. The people in his photographs were not the repressed, two-dimension figures of the fundamentalist missionary stereotype. They were idealistic young men and women facing tragedy with dignity, deep feeling, and faith. Pictures of the search party showed missionaries willing to risk their lives to help—and as it turned out, to bury—their friends."[4]

And in Betty Elliot, Cornell Capa had found a well-read kindred spirit who articulated Christian faith in ways that were intellectually compelling. He was anxious for *Life* to do a follow-up story about the widows and their continued work in the jungle.

Cornell Capa was born in Hungary in 1918. While studying in Paris to become a doctor in the 1930s, he began developing film for his older brother, Robert. Robert would become world-famous for his dramatic photos taken during the Spanish Civil War, the Allies' invasion of France on D-Day, and his early shots of the developing conflict in Vietnam. Capa, too, fell in love with film, and abandoned his medical studies. He was hired by *Life* magazine after serving in World War II in a U.S. Air Force photo intelligence unit. His brother's career as a war photographer was already well-established. Capa determined that he would be "a photographer for peace."[5] His brilliant use of light, shadow, and poignant detail created photos that celebrated what he called "genuine human feeling"—the commonalities that draw people together across cultures and life experiences.

Mr. Capa "often quoted the words of the photographer Lewis Hine: 'There are two things I wanted to do. I wanted to show the things that needed to be corrected. And I wanted to show the things that needed to be appreciated.'"[6]

He photographed John F. Kennedy's presidential campaign and first 100 days of office (Jacqueline Kennedy would become a friend and fan), Robert Kennedy, the 1967 Six-Day War, Bolshoi ballerinas, political dissidents in Nicaragua, Juan Peron's regime in Argentina, Russian Orthodox priests in Soviet Russia . . . and Elisabeth Elliot and her fellow missionaries among Indian tribes in Ecuador.[7]

When the hearty, dark-haired Capa showed up in Shandia in the spring of 1957, he shot hundreds of rolls of film. He taught his friend Betty to do the same, defying her tendency toward frugality in that pre-digital age. "Film is nothing!" he'd say, waving his hands dismissively. "Use it!" He challenged her to see, to truly *see*, the beauties in the ordinary people and settings around her. Though the camera was just a tool, he knew, he loved its power to "provoke discussion, awaken conscience, evoke sympathy, spotlight human misery and joy

which otherwise would pass unseen, un-understood and unnoticed."[8]
Or, as Betty described it, "Capa sees Truth, he attempts to capture it.
The camera is the extension of his eye. What he freezes in that moment
is a statement about life."[9]

Betty was an apt pupil. Her father's early training in noticing
details in everything from birds to church visitors had taught her to
observe well. Capa cheered Betty on in her photography in the same
way he'd encouraged her not to give up during her frustrating days of
writing *Through Gates of Splendor* in Manhattan in late 1956. He
was not put off, as were some men of the time, by her independence,
stubbornness, and resolve. He appreciated her spirit . . . and he fell just
a little bit in love with her.

Betty the photographer, 1958

"You did a hell of a good job on the book," he told her. His gruff
praise meant more to her than the platitudes of all the Christians
who'd read *Through Gates of Splendor*'s manuscript in process and
told her it was "inspiring" or that it had really blessed their souls. She
talked with him long and late into the nights about Christ.

"An amazing man, really," she wrote in her journal. "Oh, if only
he would believe all he knows by now!" Capa had an answer for that.
"I believe," he told her. "I do not accept."

Capa headed back to New York. "He is a real friend, and I felt a sense of loss at his going," wrote Betty. "The Lord knew his visit was what I needed. God give him faith."

In spite of Capa's kudos, however, Betty feared that *Through Gates of Splendor* would be an enormous failure. The book was to be released in two months. "Shall I seriously take up writing?" she wondered. "Should I go to the Waodani? Should I remain here?"

Even as she jotted such questions in her journal, and reassured herself that "my Father knows exactly what He will do," there was no question that Betty Elliot yearned to go to the Waodani. She knew that public opinion would be severely critical of any advances toward the tribe. She knew that any actual contact with the Waodani would require miracles.

"Why not expect them, then?" she wrote. She had placed herself—and Val—in God's hands. She believed He used "weak things" to accomplish His purposes. "Val and I would qualify!" She believed that God had a plan for the Waodani that He intended to accomplish, and she knew that her longing and concern for the tribe grew heavier every day.

In mid-April of '57, MAF pilot Johnny Keenan flew Betty over Waodani territory as he made one of the standard gift drops that he'd continued since Nate Saint and the others were killed. She could hardly bear just *seeing* the tribe from above rather than being with them on the ground. "It is not possible to put on paper what this <u>sight</u> of the Waodani, in living flesh and blood, has done to me," she wrote in her journal. "I <u>long</u> to get to them." She was very disappointed, she said, that they didn't have to make a forced landing in Waodani territory. It's unlikely that pilot Johnny Keenan felt the same way.

Christians around the world, awakened to the situation, prayed regularly for the tribe and eagerly awaited the next chapter in the dramatic story.* When would this unreached people group hear the hope

---

*People have told it and retold the missionaries' story for generations. Some have used it to fit their own agenda. Back in the fifties (in the post-World War II mindset) it was often presented in terms that now curdle our ears, contrasting the jungle "savages" with the "cream of America's youth" who launched their own top-secret D-day invasion, and died on the beach. Many have used it as a "from tragedy to triumph" tale, glossing over the pain to trumpet the glorious way God neatly used the deaths of five men to save an entire tribe, then tie it up with a Christian bow, caricaturing both the missionaries and the Waodani. Others who are hostile to missions use it to demonize conspiracy collusions of imperialistic missionaries with oil companies, the CIA, and the American government, to the eventual ruination of an indigenous people group. Still others shame the five missionaries as impetuous and ill prepared for their mission. Some show the neat

and love of the gospel? When would they know that they didn't have to live and die by the spear?

This widespread anticipation—and expectation—may well have triggered some of the more unfortunate aspects of the mission to reach the Waodani. Corrupted motives mixed in with the high calling to bring the gospel to the tribe, as if the Waodani were a prize to be won . . . and the mission agency associated with that "success" would reap some really great PR.

Betty Elliot was not a public relations-minded person. She cared little about presenting a good face to the public—or to people in private, for that matter—or parlaying a dramatic missionary story into increased donor dollars. Betty was possessed by a different type of passion. Some—including worried loved ones within her own family—accused her of being suicidal. Certainly she wouldn't have minded if she did die, but she was plainly compelled by the belief that God really was calling her to the tribe.

The key element necessary to go to the Waodani—beyond the will of God and a few miracles—was the ability to communicate in their language. Betty was an extraordinarily gifted linguist—all she needed was an informant. Dayuma had given language information to the five missionaries before their death, and was the only available candidate.

The only problem was that she *wasn't* readily available. Access to Dayuma typically meant passing through her gatekeeper, Rachel Saint. And that gate was not often open.

---

cause-and-effect of the five men's deaths and the immediate upsurge in young people signing up to go to the mission field. Some tell the story as if Jim Elliot was the heroic leader of a group of four other nameless colleagues. Some make the story all about Dayuma, the Waodani woman who had left the tribe in her early teens; the missionaries were killed because the Waodani thought they had eaten Dayuma. Others put the whole story in a blender, mixing up the characters and wondering why the missionaries didn't just drop gospel tracts from their airplane to the illiterate jungle people below.

CHAPTER 26

"The Eyes of the World Are on That Tribe"

"Though everything without fall into confusion,
and though thy body be in pain and suffering, and thy soul
in desolation and distress, yet let thy spirit be unmoved
by it all, placid and serene, delighted in and with its God
inwardly, and with His good pleasure outwardly."
—Gerhard Tersteegen

"I read somewhere that anyone who is
not confused is very badly informed."
—Betty Elliot

*R*achel Saint had felt a strong connection to the Waodani for years, ever since she had her "vision" of "brown-skinned people in a jungle" decades earlier. She expressed anger rather than sadness when she heard of her brother's death—the five missionaries should not have kept her in the dark about their plans to reach the tribe.[1] Now she could not help but feel that the Waodani, long-promised by God, were hers, and she was theirs; it was just a matter of getting to them.

Rachel had spent months with Dayuma at the hacienda where she worked. Though she and Dayuma shared no common language—Rachel did not speak Quichua, and Dayuma did not speak Spanish or English—Rachel had slowly learned bits and pieces of the Waodani tongue from the young woman.

In March 1956, Rachel left the hacienda to attend a conference. Another missionary arranged (without Rachel's knowledge) for

Betty Elliot to spend several days with Dayuma. (This understandably would not improve relations with Rachel.) Betty's knowledge of Quichua and her natural gifts enabled her to learn much more in a few days than Rachel had learned in months.

Betty later traveled to Shell to meet with Rachel about translation issues and their common dream of going to the Waodani. Though Rachel later commented that "it gave us both the first opportunity to air out a lot of misunderstandings."[2] Betty noted in her own journal that Rachel had not been particularly encouraging. "[Went to] Shell to talk to Rachel. . . . No signs of willingness to cooperate. . . . This seems tragic to me—when we can have fellowship in Christ, and are equally burdened for the Waodani—O Thou who are the Wonderful Counsellor—show the solution. Smash the barriers."

For her part, Rachel wrote, "The up-shot was she hoped we could have fellowship with each other even if we do not agree about mission policies."[3]

Regarding those policies, in early 1955 Betty had written to her parents, ". . . having observed Wycliffe methods here, I could very seriously question the wisdom of ever becoming connected with them. They go to extremes in trying to make the government think they are not 'evangelicals' but purely technicians. They fool no one, but do a lot to destroy fellowship among the missionaries. It is really sad. Nate Saint says he can't see how Rachel can conscientiously continue with them."[4]

It's important to note that the Wycliffe and SIL organizations today are not the same as what Betty Elliot experienced in the 1950s, when Cameron Townsend (colorful founder of both Wycliffe Bible Translators and the Summer Institute of Linguistics) shaped the narrative of both organizations in Ecuador.

Known as "Uncle Cam," Cameron Townsend was a legendary, unconventional, and fairly inexorable figure in Latin American missionary work. As a young man Cameron had gone to Guatemala in 1917, anxious to spread God's Word by selling Spanish Bibles. He was shocked to discover that people in the area spoke not Spanish, but *Cakchiquel* . . . and Bibles in that unwritten language just did not exist. Cameron began to realize the enormous diversity of people groups who had no Bible in their mother tongue. He knew that such translation was the key to indigenous peoples understanding the gospel and forming growing churches of their own.

In 1934 he started the Summer Institute of Linguistics (where young Betty Howard studied after her graduation from Wheaton), which equipped students to translate the Bible into previously unwritten languages, forging the way for a new kind of missionary:

the translator-linguist. The work continued to grow, and in 1942 Cameron officially founded SIL's companion organization, Wycliffe Bible Translators, to promote and support this scientific linguistic work.

There is much more that could be said about the various political, social, and religious complexities of the intertwined organizations in the environment of 1950s' Ecuador. But what is germane to our story is that Rachel Saint was an SIL linguist, and Betty Elliot and others were under the auspices of other missions agencies.

At the best of times the various mission entities worked with great unity and mutual cooperation. At the worst . . . things could get territorial. Now that the Waodani story had unleashed its sensational response around the world, thousands of Christians were praying for the tribe. They were anxious to hear the next chapter in the story, and Cameron Townsend saw a great opportunity. "[T]he controversial, entrepreneurial genius . . . viewed public interest in the Waodani among Americans at home as a sign from God that this tribe could be a potentially powerful public relations tool on behalf of Bible translation."[5]

In other words, if the Waodani could be "won for Christ," Wycliffe and SIL would be seen as winners as well. As the "prize" of first successful contact with the famous Waodani hung just out of reach, tensions between the various missions groups rose.

Meanwhile, Dayuma had been slowly learning Bible stories and the gospel message from Rachel Saint. She would become the "first Waodani convert," an unlikely Christian celebrity. And in a public relations move that is rather hard to conceive of today, Cameron Townsend arranged for Rachel and Dayuma to visit the United States and to appear on the then-popular television show *This Is Your Life*.

This Is Your Life was a relentlessly upbeat weekly documentary— perhaps the very first "reality" TV show. It was broadcast on NBC from 1952 to 1961. Its cheerful host, Ralph Edwards, would feature both celebrities and ordinary people who'd done something noteworthy, "surprising" them on his live show with significant guests from their lives, who would in turn tell tales of their worthy deeds. *Time* magazine once called *This Is Your Life* "the most sickeningly sentimental show on the air,"[6] but perhaps *Time* was just being snarky. Mainstream audiences loved it.

Rachel and Dayuma made their way to Ralph Edwards' Los Angeles studio, somehow thinking they were merely going to a meeting. Suddenly they found themselves on live television, with soaring theme music and a set decorated to look like Hollywood's idea of the Amazonian jungle. Wearing a Sunday dress and a hat with netting, clutching a pair of three-quarter-length gloves and a white handbag, 42-year-old Rachel perched on a sofa, a mystified Dayuma by her side, as Ralph Edwards intoned his trademark introduction . . . "Rachel Saint of Pennsylvania, Peru, and Ecuador, *this is your life!*"

As the theme music swelled, Ralph Edwards heralded Rachel for her missionary work among various tribes, her study of the Waodani language, and the news that she was planning to go to the infamous Waodani "savages," the "hardest assignment" she could have chosen. He then welcomed missionary Loretta Anderson, with whom Rachel had worked in Peru for six months. Anderson served as the lead-up to exotic guest Chief Tariri of Peru's headhunting Shapra tribe.

Jungle drums beat in the background. Loretta Anderson trans-lated as the chief gave testimony to his faith in Christ, by which the viewer was made to understand that he had given up his headhunting ways. Guest Carlos Sevilla, owner of the hacienda where Dayuma had worked for years, also appeared on camera; Dayuma shared her story. The audience clapped wildly, with most of the non-English-speaking on-stage guests demonstrating a cheerful composure regarding their strange surroundings.

The show was a hit, seen by thirty million viewers. Thanks to Cameron Townsend's planning, Rachel and Dayuma also appeared at a Billy Graham crusade in New York City, where Dayuma told a brief Bible story in the Waodani language, and Rachel spoke of her desire to translate the entire Bible into that as-yet unknown tongue. Despite Dayuma's susceptibility to numerous illnesses—coming from her isolation in the rainforest, she had little immunity—she and Rachel stayed in the U.S. from May 1957 through May 1958. Shortly before they returned to Ecuador, Rachel and Dayuma traveled to Wheaton College, where Dayuma was formally baptized by Wheaton President Edman. Photos of the smiling, white-robed Dayuma, the "first convert from the murderous Waodani tribe," flooded Christian media.

Meanwhile, Betty Elliot lived far from the limelight. She plugged along in her jungle life, delivering babies, working with an encephalitis case, teaching classes, taking care of Valerie, and musing as the silver moon rose over the swaying banana trees, praying for God to lead her where He wanted her to go.

"Evening falls over the jungle—the river lies apparently quiet along white beaches, luminous in the full moonlight. . . . Here I am, alone. . . . His hand brought me here. Yet there is often a sense of wondering at His purposes. . . .

"I looked at my face in the mirror tonight, by electric light. Realized how very long it's been since I did that. When I comb my hair in the morning, I do not even glance at my face. It seemed to me to have changed a great deal from what I remembered—dull and colorless, far too stern. I thought perhaps it is not good for me to be alone—but God has arranged it thus, so it must be.

"Time seems to carry me farther and farther from Jim. Yet in reality, each evening marks another day nearer to him. The longing is very great."

She continued to dream of Jim constantly. "Sex hunger is overwhelming very often. O Lord—Thou knowest <u>all</u>. How long?

"Evening (and a full-moon-lit one at that) I sit at my desk . . . I realize I am shivering and my flesh is all goosed. If I had Jim here, he would get into bed, warm it, and then take me beside him, warming me with his great strong arms, huge chest and thick thighs . . . Oh, it was so easy then, so simple, so lovely. And now."

"My God! How can this go on? This desperate wanting, aching desire, only to be with him, to share one single thought, to touch his forehead, to know his love as I once knew it. Dreaming night and day . . .

"And the world looks at us and says, 'She seems in excellent spirits,' 'Those widows carry on wonderfully,' etc.

"My God, when will it end?"

It was a poignant, but rhetorical, question. She knew when it would end. She jotted the answer, from Psalm 27:13–14:

> "I believe that I shall see
> The goodness of the Lord
> In the land of the living
> Wait for the Lord."

So . . . because she was Elisabeth Elliot . . . she moved on from her feelings. She mused about how the apostle Paul was right, that a married women was more concerned with her husband, but "the widow is given a higher privilege—to serve Christ, and concentrate solely on that. My Father—help me to do this. Give determination."

Betty had come to the belief that widows in fact should not marry again, so as to serve God without distraction. She pasted a relevant *Time* magazine article into her journal. The article, from September 30, 1957, reports that the Catholic pope affirmed that while second marriages by widows were not wrong, "it is preferable that they not marry."

"Even Pope Pius XII sees my point," she wrote, encouraged that the pontiff had been enlightened enough to agree with her.

Meanwhile she chafed at some of the superficial preoccupations of conventional Protestant Christianity. A September 1957 issue of the popular *Moody Monthly* magazine got the full-on Betty Elliot critique:

> The advertisements simply negate all that we believe as Christians. By reading them one discovers what *trifles* interest us . . . lightweight aluminum communion sets . . . tiny TV salt and pepper set . . . keepsake plates—[a] "dignified way to raise money" . . . "Lose weight the Sereno-Safe Way!" . . . "How a little cash, a little time, a little course are really the only secrets to doing the work of the Kingdom in an effective way!" . . . "Follow-up made easy" . . . "How to be money-wise and Christian too!"

Betty mourned over that last phrase—which oddly inferred that being money-wise was not ordinarily associated with being a Christian. She mourned also as she watched her daughter run after one of the other missionary men when he returned home after a long trip. His kids clustered around him, and little Val joined the gang, calling out, "Daddy! Daddy!"

"Jim will NEVER again come home," Betty wrote. "O God—put Thou my tears (which I don't shed) into Thy bottle.

"What is suffering, after all?" she mused. "Are there any limits to human suffering?" She thought not. "I simply go on . . . and on . . . 'standing' things which I couldn't possibly stand."

Suffering would be one of the hallmark themes of her life. Now, chafing, lonely, and longing for action among the Waodani, she sat in the jungle, a soldier awaiting divine orders that just did not come.

In October, there was news from the outside world. Contrary to Betty's dim expectations, *Through Gates of Splendor*, was an enormous success. It topped the bestseller lists. Reviewers loved it. Readers bought it for their friends. Betty wrote in her journal that individual sales meant that "more than a quarter of a million dollars"—a huge sum to her frugal 1950s' mind—"has been spent by the public in buying it–quite frightening." By year's end, it would sell more than 175,000 copies. One reviewer called it "the leading missionary book of this generation."[7]

At about the same time author Elisabeth Elliot was receiving acclamation in the U.S., jungle missionary Betty Elliot was on the brink—though she did not know it—of her long-sought adventure with the Waodani.

The tribe's worldwide notoriety had made the eastern jungle of Ecuador a destination for curious Christians who wanted to see where the missionary martyrs were buried, tourists who wanted to take pictures of naked tribal people, and unhelpful individuals who thought God had told them to come and help.

Hobey Lowrance, the senior Missionary Aviation Fellowship pilot who had taken Nate Saint's place, reported to his boss about the number of "outsiders" who were appearing in Shell, wanting to be flown to Waodani territory. (Yes, this was the same Hobey who had been driving the car that stalled on the railroad tracks back in 1948, almost killing himself, Jim Elliot, and their other friends. If that had happened, this would be a much shorter book. At any rate, once he'd successfully survived college, Hobey had joined MAF.)

"Seems the whole world wants to horn in," he observed. There was an unethical journalist from Miami who'd been flitting about. There were two Roman Catholic priests who didn't know why there was so much publicity: they claimed they had in fact "'Christianized' the Waodani 40 years ago."[8] A family member of one of the five missionaries wanted to go live on the beach where his loved one was killed. Then there was a Canadian psychologist named Robert Tremblay. He wanted to reach the Waodani with the gospel, but apparently did not know it himself. He would wander in and out of the Waodani story until his precipitous departure during the summer of 1958. In Hobey's blunt analysis, "The danger is that he apparently is a bit off his rocker, plus having domestic troubles, so [he] feels he has nothing to lose."[9]

Like Betty Elliot and Rachel Saint, long-term missionary Wilfred Tidmarsh longed to connect with the tribe. He and his Quichua workers had built a bamboo hut at a river junction not far from a Waodani settlement. They cleared jungle for a nearby airstrip; Dr. Tidmarsh was anxious to cultivate contact with the Waodani, right at their own front door.

Fortunately, Dr. Tidmarsh was away when the Waodani came knocking at *his* front door. They sacked his hut, scattered his clothes, medicines, and language files, tore up his paper money, and took his machetes and cooking pots. They pulled the door off its flimsy hinges and left two crossed spears blocking the opening.

Many of the missionaries in the area took the staged message as a sign from God to pull back, reassess, and wait. In her journal, Betty wondered just what the ransacking meant, but the tribal hostility didn't change her intentions. Now writing her second book, Jim Elliot's biography, *Shadow of the Almighty*, she was immersed in her late husband's powerful letters and old journal entries. As she captured Jim's life story on paper, her own desire to go to the Waodani intensified.

After the attack on Dr. Tidmarsh's hut, SIL's Cameron Townsend wrote the good doctor a cautionary letter. "The next move to the Waodani must be a fruitful move. The eyes of the world are upon that tribe. The stage has been set through the sacrifice of five missionaries, the extraordinary coverage given that heroic effort by the secular press and now Betty Elliot's inspiring book [*Through Gates of Splendor*], for the greatest demonstration in history of the power of the Gospel in the savage heart."[10]

If given to the type of sensationalism Betty despised, Cameron Townsend was genuinely convinced that the power of that gospel came through the Word of God, translated into indigenous people's own vernacular. He urged Wilfred Tidmarsh—and others—to wait until "salvation verses and one of the Gospels in Waodani" were available.

Townsend went further than just counseling caution, however. If Dr. Tidmarsh continued to try to connect with the tribe, Townsend said he would instruct his SIL people who had access to Waodani linguistic data (and Dayuma) not to cooperate with other missions entities.[11]

Appalled, Dr. Tidmarsh shared that inflammatory letter with friends. Hobey Lowrance gave his unvarnished paraphrase of what it seemed like Uncle Cam was saying: "We [SIL] are the ones to do the job . . . when we've written the language and translated the Gospel, we'll call you. May be two years, maybe more. We have the only Waodani informant . . . you'd better play ball with us, or you'll get *nothing* more."[12]

Betty Elliot seethed in her journal on November 6, 1957, "A letter from Cam Townsend practically <u>commands</u> Dr. T. to suspend operations. Townsend has ordered all <u>his</u> 'missionaries' to refuse any further help to Dr. T. linguistically. Says Rachel will soon have Scriptures in Waodani language!!! Quote: 'Wait till then—Don't be a soldier without a sword, brother.'"

Townsend was a visionary who saw great things ahead—the Scriptures would "soon" be available in the Waodani language. He assumed that Rachel Saint was more successful in her translation work than she actually was.

The Waodani New Testament would not actually be completed until 1992—35 years later. Translators Catherine Peeke, who worked full-time with the Waodani for many years, her coworker German linguist Rosi Jung, and about twelve Waodani helpers would accomplish the huge task of rendering the New Testament into this very difficult tongue.

But even without that foreknowledge, back in 1957 Betty and others felt that Cameron Townsend was claiming authority over matters that just did not belong to him.

Betty concluded her journal entry,

"My God—who does he think he is?"

CHAPTER 27

"If They Killed Me,
Better Still"

"The Waodani are a constant weight to me. Who is to go, and when? . . . What am I waiting for? Sometimes temptation is strong to pick up Valerie, a Bible, pencil and paper, and start walking. I don't do it. Why? Either because I am afraid of them, afraid of public opinion, or afraid I'd be disobeying the Lord. I don't know my own heart well enough to tell which it is. But I am praying, 'Here am I, Lord. SEND ME . . . if I were successful, nothing could make me happier on earth. If they killed me, better still!"[1]
—Betty Elliot, letter to parents, 1957

About a week after Betty Elliot steamed in her journal about road-blocks to the Waodani, the story took an abrupt turn.

At about six o'clock in the morning of November 13, 1957, sev-eral Waodani women, identifiable by their characteristic haircuts, ear holes, and nudity, emerged from the jungle near a small cluster of Quichua houses on the Oglan River. The surprised Quichuas gave them food and clothes. Though the Indians could not understand one another, it seemed that the Waodani women might hang around for a while. A Quichua man named Dario Santi took them into his home, which was soon surrounded by curious neighbors.

Two Quichua men ran several hours through the jungle to Dr. Tidmarsh's home in Arajuno. Betty Elliot "happened" to be visiting there with the doctor's wife while he was away. The men gasped out the story to Betty, whose heart pounded wildly. Could it be? Was God opening a door to the tribe?

Gwen Tidmarsh immediately offered to take care of little Valerie; Betty should *go* to these unexpectedly available Waodani women. In about seven minutes, Betty packed up a carrying net, stuffing in a toothbrush, a few pieces of clothing and her essentials—camera, snake-bite kit, language notebooks, pens, and paper—and hit the trail.

She now had no doubt as to God's leading. After all, she thought, God had led her to visit Arajuno when she did. He had seen to it that the good Dr. Tidmarsh was elsewhere. "When the word came, my unhesitating decision was to come at once. Gwen concurred; this fulfilled what I have been sure of all along: when the time came to <u>do</u> something, it would be <u>incontestably evident</u> to the one who was to do it."[2]

When Betty arrived at the Quichua settlement at about five o'clock in the afternoon, the Waodani women were sitting on a rough wooden bench. One was unmistakably the older woman who had visited with Jim and his fellow missionaries at Palm Beach, two days before the men were killed. Betty recognized her torn right ear from the photos recovered from Nate Saint's camera. Her name was Mintaka.

The other woman was Mangamu. She held tight to the hand of a Quichua girl, but showed no fear when Betty arrived. The Quichuas gave them homemade cigarettes (for which the Waodani did not register a whole lot of enthusiasm). They listened to the ticking of Betty's watch, and watched with good-natured patience as Betty tried to teach them to whistle. One held a Quichua child in her lap, running her fingers through the little girl's hair. The two grinned broadly when Betty and the others sang Quichua songs.

As evening fell on the strange gathering, the women all went to bed—sharing a cramped, bamboo-walled room. Mintaka started singing—or crying, it was hard to tell—a single, nasal note, with rhythmic tones. No words.

The Quichua men had weapons ready, should other Waodani attack. Most thought, however, that since they were in Quichua, rather than Waodani territory, they should be safe. Meanwhile, Betty felt stunned that she was with people who *knew* what had actually happened to her husband and friends. "To think that these girls could tell me what happened to Jim and WHY! (From their viewpoint, of course.)"

She spent the next few days taking hundreds of pictures and making copious notes about Mintaka and Mangamu's strange language. She drew pictures of the shape of their teeth, noting the positions of their tongues as they talked. The opportunity to hear the Waodani language pouring out in rich torrents was overwhelming, confusing, and exhilarating, all at once.

Dr. Tidmarsh arrived, bringing a tape recorder so Betty could record language data. As they talked privately about the possible threat of attack, he told her, "'Oh, but we don't consider the possibility of being killed!'"

"How ridiculous," Betty thought. "Nothing is a clearer possibility. But this, too, is in God's hands."

The MAF plane dropped in supplies; Betty lanced a boil and applied an antibiotic on one of the Waodani women's buttocks, wondering if she was the first "foreigner" to administer medical care to a Waodani. The women constantly told unintelligible stories illustrated with gestures portraying spearings and terror. They spoke constantly of a killer named "Moipa." Most evenings Mintaka would half-cry, half-sing her nasal, one-note song that went on for hundreds of repetitive stanzas.

Convinced that she should spend as much time as possible with these Waodani women, Betty made her way back to the mission outpost to get her daughter and more supplies for the long run. While there, she poured out her heart in her journal:

> "Once more I am nearly overwhelmed with the knowledge that this God is the Lord." After all, the Lord did "strange, terrible things" in the Old Testament to show that He was sovereign. "He is still doing them—and very wonderful things. He made two Waodani appear, He allowed me . . . to meet them!"

Betty gathered up everything she could think of for an indefinite stay on the banks of the Curaray, near where the Waodani women had come out of the jungle. This was Quichua territory, of course, but close to Waodani lands. Betty's fellow widows Marilou McCully and Barbara Youderian helped her pack for this unprecedented opportunity to live with the two Waodani women and learn their language. "Marilou and Barbara are here too—everyone highly excited."

Still, Betty felt the weight of the task ahead. She meditated on Scripture. She remembered the words of great old hymns. She yielded herself to the will of the Father.

Then she packed up Valerie, now almost three, in a little carrying chair designed by her Quichua friend Fermin. He carried Val up and down the steep trails as Betty lugged language and recording equipment. They arrived back in the Quichua settlement on November 22, 1957 and went to sleep to the sound of Mintaka and her one-note song.

The next morning, all the Quichua men had gone out hunting. Betty was in the river with the two Waodani women, bathing Valerie and washing clothes. Suddenly there was a cry from the shore, with much confusion: "WAODANI!"

Betty had just washed and rinsed her hair. She grabbed up little Val (who was naked) and ran streaming through the shallow water to the beach. Quichua men came running, gasping out the story. A man named Honorario and his young wife, Maruja, had headed downriver in their canoe that morning.

The Waodani had evidently spied out the scene the day before, intent on abducting the fourteen-year-old Maruja. They waited downriver when the couple got in their canoe. As it approached, the Waodani mowed down Honorario with a volley of spears, and killed his hunting dog. They took Maruja captive, and slipped back into their own territory, leaving twenty-two lances in Honorario's broken body.

The Quichuas brought back some of the spears. Betty saw that one had been wrapped with a page of Scripture with a heading that read, ironically, "the sufferings of Paul as an apostle," tied to the lance with red threads. Evidently the Waodani had torn pages from the Bible they'd stolen from Dr. Tidmarsh's hut. Some of the other lances were "decorated" with feathers, woven thongs, and fresh green leaves. All were clotted with blood.

Even as Valerie, unfazed by the chaos of the morning, played with a washbasin, putting it on her head—"hat, Mama!"—Betty could not help but think of Jim's grim death. These Waodani and their spears; the casual theft of human lives: would it ever end?

"I would like to 'fly away and be at rest,'" Betty wrote in her journal, even as the Quichua death wail floated up from their camp and Honorario's body (the spears removed) lay wrapped in a bloody shroud.

Yes, Betty knew that her hero Amy Carmichael had called the missionary life "a chance to die," but Betty had had enough of death. She wanted to "[g]et out and completely away from the Waodani and all that they mean. I've felt like this several times in my missionary life—when they killed Macario [her Colorado language informant], when Senora Maruja died [in childbirth, among the Colorados], when I've had to bid Jim goodbye, and when I had to return to Shandia after Jim died."

"I could almost say I've had <u>enough</u> of these Waodani, and wish God would take me away," she concluded.

But.

For Betty Elliot, there was always that "but." *I feel this . . . but I will do His will, not my own.*

Mourners sit with Honorario's body

"But if God wants me to stay," she concluded, still thinking of those bloody lances, "He will give me grace to remain here . . . by His grace I will do all that He intends for me to do to reach them."[3]

Poised to realize her dream of perhaps walking into Waodani territory, thwarted by fresh violence on this same Curaray River where Jim had died, Betty Elliot did not know what God specifically wanted her to do. It was an almost unbearable time of waiting, yet again, full of the questions that had filled her mind for the past year.

Why would God stymie work designed to extend His kingdom? Would she ever stop yearning for Jim? Would she ever have a proper cup of tea and a silver butter knife again? Would she ever learn the impossible language of the Waodani? Would God ever allow her to go to them, or was Honorario's killing a clear sign from Him to back off? And if she did go to the tribe, would they kill her immediately? Or would they wait a while?

In the midst of all the questions, she jotted one last thought in her journal: "When I felt . . . that someone was going to pay a price for the Waodani, I'd no idea how soon my bill would arrive!

"And I don't think for a minute that it's all paid."

CHAPTER 28

A Missionary Hag

"I could say glibly to these terrified women,
'God will protect us.'
But I have no guarantee that He will!
He did not protect Jim et al., or [Honorario] today.
That in no way shakes my <u>trust</u>*."*
—Betty Elliot journal

After Honorario's bloody killing on the Curaray River, Betty and the two Waodani women, Mangamu and Mintaka—whom Betty called M and M—returned to the mission station in Shandia. There Betty continued to work with the Quichua church and school; she spent the balance of her time studying the tribal women's language and pleading with God to show her when, where, and how to go to the Waodani.

The two Waodani women called Betty Elliot "Gikari." What did it mean? she wondered. Skinny? Pale? Tall? Foreigner? Idiot?

It probably meant "idiot," she decided. She felt like an idiot most of the time. No matter how much she listened, recorded, transcribed, and prayed, the Waodani language was a mystery. She would understand rudimentary vocabulary, congratulate herself, and then be confronted with a torrent of intelligible verbiage that sent her spinning back into despair. Mintaka helpfully observed that she could not understand them—or "hear" them—because Betty's hair covered her ears. "You must cut it like ours," she told Betty. (Betty, perhaps concerned about her mother's intimate interest in her jungle hairdos, refrained from doing so.)

For her part, Valerie seemed to be picking up the language just fine, though she'd cheerfully mix Quichua, English, and Waodani into her own happy prattle. A skillful mimic like her mother, she could duplicate poor Mangamu's endless tonal crying song perfectly, so much so that even Mangamu would laugh when Val would "sing."

Elisabeth was now thirty-one years old. She'd been a dutiful daughter, an avid student, a loving wife and mother, a dedicated missionary. She had not held back the most precious thing in her life—Jim. She'd publicly analyzed and reported the story of his destruction when she'd agreed to write *Through Gates of Splendor*. She'd succeeded in the Manhattan literary world, with its unyielding tyranny of editors and deadlines, and returned to the wilds of Ecuador with her small blonde Jim-child. She had run through the Amazon jungle like Wonder Woman to save women in childbirth, medical supplies on her back. She had comforted those who were dying. She had lanced boils, delivered babies, and given shots. Yes, she missed the niceties of civilized life, but she had thrown herself into everything God brought her way. She'd felt confusion, despair, tedium . . . but in every instance she obeyed what she discerned to be God's will.

Elisabeth Elliot's father trained her to *observe* when she was young, but her keen eye saw more than birds, natural beauty, and church visitors. She saw what was *right*. She had a linguist's ear for inflection, meaning, and deception. She grew up in a black-and-white world where the wages of sloth was dust and a poorly sharpened pencil badly missed the point. She gloried in the great hymns of the faith—all five verses. She wrote dutifully, reams of journal pages, forests of correspondence. Her schooling had trained and equipped her to go forth in victory for the Lord. Yes, she knew the road could end in death. She had heard martyrs' stories from the time she was a child. It was almost no surprise that her husband became one . . . or that she might well embrace a similar fate.

But if the Betty Elliot of her college days had been a refrigerated rose, cerebral, untouched, and dutiful, the Betty Elliot who now chafed to go to the Waodani was passionate, open, ready to engage, and seasoned. Earlier in her life she'd had a tidy confidence that God's will likely matched the will of her family, school, and faith community. She absorbed with great alacrity everything that Hampden DuBose Academy, Wheaton College, and her parents and loved ones had taught her. She certainly didn't swallow it all; she'd always been a critical thinker.

But now, something new was emerging. The utter loneliness caused by Jim's death, and the responses of some who wanted to manage the missionary martyr narrative for their own purposes, created a deeper, more complex Betty, one who was willing to call things as she saw them—not as they were "supposed" to be. She was still dutiful, responsible, and self-disciplined. But she had seen Noah's naked backside, so to speak, and she was not willing to deny that sometimes even religious leaders, like the fictitious emperor in the children's story, wore no clothes.

Betty chafed at the disparity between what she saw in the gospel and what she saw in the organized church. She wasn't afraid to ask real questions. She was quick to pick up the scent of hypocrisy and legalism, but she always applied such analysis to herself first. She wasn't a cynic, hardened into denying the existence of truth. She was, if you will, a realist. She believed in the Real, the absolute of the God who *is*. She questioned what was done in His name, the fake trappings she saw, all too plentifully, in the missionary world in which she lived. She would continue to ask questions, seeking to discern the Real from the false fluff, for decades to come . . . until such questions were crushed by the heavy yoke she had chosen for herself to bear.

In early 1958 Betty wrote in her journal about the words of a friend whom she considered a "model missionary."

"I think it must take a person about ten years to get over a Bible School education," the friend had written. "I am still recovering, all appreciation and thanksgiving for all that I learned, of course. But there's a great undoing process too, learning to look to Him and follow Him irrespective of what the Christian brethren say . . . I myself do so much of this business of imposing standards on the outside that did not really come from the heart when . . . It breeds hypocrisy, as I can't help feeling that many . . . students have had terrible fights with hypocrisy and legalism after finishing there, for so many things were imposed from the outside that had not been worked into the heart by the Holy Spirit. For this reason, I am anxious for the people here [new believers], that every move they make comes from the heart and not from a legally imposed set of rules."

Betty felt some of the same frustrations. A journalist from a religious periodical called *Christian Life* published a misleading story after promising her he would not release it without her permission. Betty mourned that the outside world sometimes deals more straightforwardly than did fellow believers. "I would far rather be identified with *Life* than with *Christian Life*," she wrote to her parents.[1]

Betty occasionally attended a Thursday night Bible study for gringos at one of the other mission stations. She watched as the missionaries and staff filed in and took their seats; compliantly reading and responding to the assignment for the evening, plodding through the study sheets provided. The proceedings seemed diffident, dutiful, and fairly deadly.

"Discussion" consisted of "the old Bible School line . . . the stock answers, the accepted interpretations," unexamined in the ten or fifteen years since they first started giving such answers while in school. "It is disheartening," thought Betty. "God have mercy upon us and incline our hearts to keep Thy law—then maybe we'll learn something."

Around the same time, she listened to a veteran missionary deliver an error-riddled sermon in the Quichua language. The Indians listened politely, though she had heard them privately mock the preacher's fractured speech. His simplistic, behavior-focused *content*, however, was what really curdled Betty's spirit. "Oh, what are we teaching?" she moaned in her journal. Was it "TRUE?" Or was it opinion, accepted social mores, or something worse?

She noted how Wilfred Tidmarsh had written possessively about M and M as "*our* Waodani women.'" (The italics were his.) "God preserve me from such a spirit. They are Thine, the word is Thine, I am Thine."

". . . Do with them, and with me (and with T.!) as Thou wilt," she continued, quoting from the Anglican prayer, the "Southwell Litany." "Preserve me 'from all harms and hindrances of offensive manners and self-assertion . . . from overwhelming love of our own ideas and blindness to the value of other . . . from all jealousy . . . from the retort of irritation and the taunt of sarcasm . . . from all arrogance in dealings with all men . . . Chiefly, O Lord, we pray Thee, give us knowledge of Thee, to see Thee in all Thy works . . . to hear and know Thy call.'

"[I'm] conscious of a great change in my mode of thinking," she observed a few pages later. "Brought to essentials more than ever, forced there from the eternal, which affects the internal. Trying to make living simpler than ever: no napkins, no serving dishes, no butter plate, nothing to iron at all, no cleaning to do . . . no socks, one dish per meal, no desserts. Today I suddenly thought what a hag I must look—no shoes on, hair perfectly straight, no belt on, not even a brassiere! I would not think of going this way were there a single soul who'd notice it. But there's not. Days go by now without my hearing one word of English, except Valerie's.

"And what has all this taught me? 'The things which are not seen are eternal.' I thought I knew this and practiced on it before. But I have been stripped of even more lately—things others could never realize. God knows I <u>love</u> to dress nicely, to have a spacious, clean, well-furnished, tasteful home; to have nice (nicer than necessary, I mean) food and table appointments. And He says to me, 'Lovest Thou Me more than these?' And I answer, 'Thou knowest all things . . . Thou knowest no other motive could suffice.' Only bring Thy light, Lord, to the Waodani! Let me not shrink from anything that might contribute in the long run to that end."

Certainly this wasn't a new Betty; it was an older Betty—one who didn't much like easy or formulaic answers and was ready to ignore the many voices sending counsel her way, in favor of the one Voice only she could discern for herself. As always, the key question for her was, when was it time to go to the Waodani, how should she proceed?

In the spring of '58, the mentally unstable Canadian Robert Tremblay continued to threaten the situation. Betty heard through the jungle grapevine that Tremblay was coming to her home with two Ecuadorian soldiers to rescue Mintaka and Mangamu. (He spread word that he had flown over Shandia and the two Waodani women had made wild gestures toward his low-flying plane, begging for rescue.)

This was "too much for even gullible Ecuadorians to swallow," Betty humphed in her journal. The governor for the region asked her to bring the two women to Tena, the provincial capital; there she obtained citizenship papers for them, asserting their right to travel and live outside of Waodani lands.[2]

Then there was a bit of respite; Betty read a local newspaper article that announced that the unbalanced Dr. Tremblay was leaving Ecuador and giving up on his Waodani project, for "lack of cooperation." She assumed the last phrase applied to her, and breathed with relief that he would be out of the picture; his agitations of the Waodani had imperiled the entire missionary community.

Every week's mail brought grab-bags of lofty sentiments and strange requests from the U.S. and beyond. Things such as:

> A helpful suggestion from a sister in Toronto that the missionaries drop picture-rolls to the Waodani, depicting the story of salvation.

> A woman from Texas wrote to encourage Betty that "Mrs. So-and-So, 'one of our finest and most brilliant women,' offered a beautiful prayer for [Betty] in a recent meeting."

> An international ministry in Singapore requested that Betty record a taped message to reach "'125 of Asia's sharpest Christian teen-agers . . . the cream of Asia's youth'. . ." "'We want you to provide the 'spark' to cause the youngsters to surrender and to GO.'"

> A Christian university announced its plans to offer the five missionary widows honorary doctorates.[3]

> On a humbler note, a U.S. farmer wrote, "We've named our five cows after you five dear girls, and pray for you as we milk them each day."

"Lord, untangle it all!" wrote Betty.

Meanwhile, Marj Saint and Sam Saint, Nate's brother, wanted Betty to write Nate's biography. She felt she should press on in her work with M and M . . . although she couldn't help wondering—why even learn the language of a disappearing people group? "I am a complete failure. I'm living half gringo, half Indian, trying to please these Waodani women," who more often than not would just look at her with a dismissive, characteristic Indian "bah!" and turn away.

Perhaps the growing tension was taking its toll; Betty's subconscious took some imaginative turns. "Dreamed last night that [one of the other missionary wives in Ecuador, not one of the five widows] shot and killed [her husband] in front of my eyes. He cried out, 'Oh, but it's so <u>hard</u> to die!' And fell headlong with a terrible crash. [The wife] quietly replaced the pistol in her apron pocket and carried him out of the room."

In another vivid dream, she "lay on Jim's chest in bed, thought 'Oh, thanks Lord! If you'll just let me do this <u>once</u> in a while, I'll be able to carry on. This is what I <u>need</u>.' And Jim was so tender—I long for the shelter, haven of his love. O God—it still is my Desired Haven. I cannot stop loving and longing with all of my heart. Oh, what a punishment Thou has meted to me for my failures."

Did Betty really believe that God had taken Jim because of all her failures? It's doubtful. Her theology was stronger than that. But the comment shows how deeply she mourned her own failings.

"It is a relief and joy when little Val appears—her head in a little white cap (she still has ring worm), a yellow nightgown, showing only her dainty little ankles and feet. From a human standpoint it seems she is what makes life livable."

Still, Val could make life a riddle as puzzling as the Waodani. She called to Betty one day as she played outside their little house.

"The bugs are biting me," she told her mother.

"Then come inside," responded Betty.

Val: "Why?"

Betty: "So the bugs won't bite you."

Val: "Why?"

Betty: "Don't say, why."

Val: "But I need to say why."

Betty: "No, you don't need to say why."

Val: "Why?"

CHAPTER 29

"To Hell with My Zeal!"

"Dying, crying, I came; dying, burying, crying, I hid.
I hid burying, crying, saying 'You are going to die.'
Children grow up and die. Children grow up and die."
—Betty Elliot's January 1958 translation,
Mangamu's account of inter-tribal killings

In early May, Betty took M and M on a bus, jeep, and train trip to the coastal city of Guayaquil, thinking that they should at least have some idea of the complexities and scope of the outside world beyond the jungle. The women giggled as they wore warm "snugglies" under their borrowed clothes, noting the cold at the twelve-thousand-foot pass through the Andes on their way to the coastal plain. They weren't particularly impressed with modern buildings, cars, streets, or neon lights, but the huge stacks of bananas at the outdoor market got a nod, as well as the crabs and crayfish at the seafood market. Betty bought a selection, which the two women loosed under the bed in their sleeping room, except for the ones they cooked on a kerosene flame for immediate consumption.

Betty asked the women dozens of questions about the local flora and fauna, her ever-present language notebook in her lap. They gave her a similar word for most of the sights she'd pointed out: snow-capped mountains, goats, sheep, and rabbits. Careful checking by our diligent linguist led to the discovery that the word M and M used simply meant, "Who knows *what* it is?"[1]

M and M reassured Betty regarding their intentions on returning to their tribe, and reaffirmed that Betty would be safe with them: "We will go in the airplane to the doctor's house. From there we will go on foot. We know the trail. We will carry Valerie. We will live with

201

Gikita, he will fish for us and bring us meat from the forest. We will have a good house. . . . There will be plenty of plaintain and manioc, but if you want to, the plane can drop your food for you. We will help you pick it up. You will be able to see our children. They will love you and Valerie. You will take your [injection] needle and help the sick people. We will live well."[2]

"But they will spear us, won't they?" asked Betty.

"It is the downriver ones who spear. They are far away," the women responded.

"But they speared my husband. They will spear us."

"Gikari! Your husband was a man. You are a woman."

"What about [others]? Won't they spear me?" Betty asked.

"[They] are our kinsmen! We will say, 'Here is our mother. We love her. She is good.'"[3]

In late May, Rachel Saint and the celebrated "first Waodani convert," Dayuma, made their long-awaited return to Ecuador after almost a year in the United States. The peripatetic Cornell Capa arrived in Ecuador at the same time; this reunion between Dayuma and her two long-lost Waodani relatives who were living with Betty was bound to make great photos for *Life* magazine.

Rachel invited Betty and M and M to the SIL base in Limon Cocha—a plane-hop from where they'd been staying in Shandia. She and Dayuma were waiting as Betty and the two Waodani women touched down on the runway.

Dayuma approached the plane (Betty said later) "dressed fit to kill in [a] wide, long cotton skirt, blue satiny blouse, suede shoes, and a rhinestone necklace!" (In her journal, Rachel had written of Dayuma's elaborate, Quichua-influenced costume in light of meeting her fellow Waodani tribeswomen, "There was nothing I could do about it. She was as high as a kite with anticipation and excitement.")[4]

It was not exactly the long-awaited reunion with a beloved relative that Westerners would expect.

"That's Dayuma," Mintaka grunted, scratching her armpit.

They emerged from the plane; Mangamu immediately launched into a long, anguished tirade of everything that had happened in the tribe since Dayuma's departure as a young girl, including the deaths of various family members.

Dayuma burst into tears. She had heard this news from other sources, but now to hear it firsthand was overwhelming. Mangamu spared no gory detail of the murders. Dr. Tidmarsh, on hand to record the historic meeting, set his tape recorder aside. Cornell Capa stopped snapping photos.

Everyone regrouped, eventually settling into various huts and lodgings at the SIL base. The balance of the summer passed as Betty, Rachel, and the three Waodani women settled into some sort of uneasy domesticity, even as they considered and reconsidered the best plan for going to the tribe. The two American missionaries both wanted to capture as much language data as possible, but in this, as well as the overarching understanding of God's plan for the Waodani, they had vastly different ideas.

Valerie, M and M, and Cornell Capa

One morning Betty read the familiar verse in Scripture, "If two of you agree on earth about anything they ask, it will be done for them by my Father in heaven. For where two or three are gathered in my name, there am I in the midst of them" (Matt. 18:19–21 RSV). "I mentioned it to R.," she noted in her journal, "and said, 'We are agreed, aren't we, that this is what we ought to prepare for?' Answer: 'Well, it's certainly been my goal long before you ever thought of it.'

"So I am not sure what her attitude is about my going," Betty wrote mildly. "I am counting on the Lord to direct in every detail." She was "willing to do all in my power to promote cooperation between Rachel and me."

As Betty would observe many times over the coming years, she and Rachel were two people whose personalities, perceptions, and inclinations could not have been more different. At the same time, they were both courageous, stubborn, and absolutely committed to doing what they believed God was telling them to do.

Rachel evidently viewed Betty as culturally insensitive. Rachel wrote, "She doesn't have much time for observing other people's way of life anyway. I have lived with Latins too long not to know you have to consider them, and their different ways."[5]

Betty, meanwhile, mourned over Rachel's language analysis. The one thing that might have united the two women—a common desire to translate the Waodani language—was as thorny a coil of barbed-wire barrier as everything else in their relationship. They did not use the same techniques, processed verb conjugations differently, and despaired at each other's interpretation of suffixes, verb forms, and life in general.

Rachel focused on the always-volatile Dayuma. She wrote in her journal, "We have had days of conflict. D's nerves are at the breaking point. B. talks to her, tells me what the plan is . . . and if I even ask a question D. flares, gets mad, yells at me, screams, exaggerates, and says she will go with [Betty], that I am afraid, etc. . . ." If anything did not please Dayuma, "she hits the thatch—is furious, actually and the thing is anything but in the Spirit. . . . Of one thing I am sure, there can be no blessing and no victory with this kind of spirit. May Jesus help me to teach her His Victory over the very thing that has made the tribe the killers that they are. . . . B. day by day gets meaning from D that she was not able to get from her two and I try day by day to understand more—and D is in this new role of taking it out on me as against everyone else. Biggest hindering factor I see is Dayuma's mad spirit—that of not being quietly led by His Spirit and playing us against each other."[6]

Dayuma often cried herself to sleep, and woke in a less than tender mood. Rachel wrote on August 3, "D started fussing and shouting around, I told her to . . . go—without breakfast (which she had said she wasn't going to eat)—that I wasn't going to cook . . . if we weren't going to live as a family the way the Lord told us too. [sic.] Then I dragged her in by the hair—not too much protest."[7]

After this unconventional conflict resolution, they ate breakfast, and Rachel reported that Dayuma and the two other Waodani women went off fishing for the day, returning at sunset "all sweetened up" by the fish that they had caught.

It was a strange summer. Cameron Townsend often weighed in with opinions, as did Grady Parrott of Missionary Aviation Fellowship. Betty, desperately seeking to capture the Waodani language, dogged Rachel about verb forms and other technicalities. Dayuma sometimes sweetly served as a human bridge between cultures for the sake of the gospel, and sometimes blew up in wild rages. Rachel prayed for God's help, dragged Dayuma around by her hair (or occasionally Dayuma dragged *her*), and puzzled over the strange complexities of Betty Elliot, even as Betty pondered the same about Rachel Saint.

They each considered the other a far more foreign culture than the exotic, Stone-age Waodani women with whom they now lived.

Meanwhile, Betty would write in letters home such things as "It makes no difference to me if I am killed or not killed" . . . "I WOULD NEVER GO BECAUSE IT'S SAFE, BUT BECAUSE IT'S APPOINTED." . . . "I cannot be moved by your tears . . . I suppose if Valerie survives she would be my only legal heir, right? Dad, I've written out what is to be done with my money. . . . Mother, I don't mean to sound callous . . ."[8]

Betty would nonchalantly combine such life-and-death matters with jungle observations, such as bird watching details for her ornithologist father, "Dad, you'd go crazy here. The birds! . . . Huge red-crested ones the size of a vulture; tiny yellow ones as brilliant as sunlight, it seemed; vivid blue and red ones; great orioles, with hanging nests as big as grapefruit; flashing flocks of parrots and toucans. We saw a large red monkey swinging in a high tree nearby, and later several vultures resting on what we took to be a log at first. It then proved to be a dead alligator, probably 10 or 12 feet long, lying with its swollen feet in the air. The stench was ripe, to say the least."[9]

Around this time, the locally infamous Dr. Tremblay reappeared in the story. The missionaries heard rumors about him raging through the jungle; that he had a submachine gun, that he had threatened to shoot down any missionary planes dropping gifts for the Waodani. He hired four Quichuas to take him down the Curaray, to a bend in the river about a mile past "Palm Beach," where the missionaries had been killed. He camped there for a few weeks, then sent the Quichuas home and relocated to a deserted Wao clearing.

Choosing the sturdiest of the homes, he barricaded himself inside, shooting wildly into the clearing and surrounding jungle every night. Waodani in the area, entertained by this strange intruder's behavior, monitored his movements for several weeks. Because of his matted blond hair, they'd taken to calling him *"Kogincoo,"* their word for a local breed of light, hairy jungle monkey.[10]

Finally the Waodani heard what would be the last gunshot from old Kogincoo. Silence. The next morning, two women peered into the house through a crack in the fronds. They saw Tremblay sprawled on the floor next to one of his guns, a pair of old trousers partially over his head, his brains blown out of one ear. His mental challenges, perhaps a form of what's now known as PTSD, had led to his suicide.

The subsequent story (told and retold among the Waodani) went something like this. The Waodani rummaged through Tremblay's possessions, then pulled his body out of the house and used it for spearing practice. Two men repeatedly speared the neck until the head was nearly severed. They pulled a ring from Tremblay's rotting finger and made a necklace out of his teeth.[11]

Betty Elliot sent a prayer letter home to her supporters dated July 23, 1958. It was a sanitized version of the waiting game in Limon Cocha and of Tremblay's death; the great challenges of the Waodani language, and the role of Dayuma, M, and M as, perhaps, God's plan to "bridge the gulf fixed between us and the tribe."[12]

The only hint of the swirling turmoil of her days was in the old hymn she chose to include at the bottom of her polite letter.

> *"'Twas He who taught me thus to pray*
> *And He I know has answered prayer,*
> *But it has been in such a way*
> *As almost drove me to despair."*

Perhaps Betty was thinking of the "verdict" Cameron Townsend had now given: if Betty were to go into Waodani territory with M and M, Dayuma would not be allowed to go. If Betty would agree not to go to the Waodani, then Townsend would consider giving permission for Dayuma to do so.

Meanwhile Wilfred Tidmarsh had written to Betty that he was sure that it was not the right time for her to go into Waodani territory. (He also refused to share Waodani language data Rachel had given him, as she'd instructed him not to share it with Betty.) Voices all around her, as if from a great distance, pled, dissuaded, argued, and reasoned.

Letters arrived regularly from Jim's mother. "Mom Elliot [is] pleading with me not to go. 'Can't you see this Betty? Let's not get carried away . . . your zeal is wonderful . . . but it would be foolish . . . etc. etc.'

"To hell with my 'zeal,'" Betty exploded in her journal. If this mission was a matter of her own fervor, she would quit right now, pack it all up, and return to the States for a nice, long furlough. It was not "admirable missionary zeal" that spurred her, nor desire. "And as for my going to the Waodani because I 'long' to—!!!! I can never forget those days on the Curaray. The romance collapsed entirely."

Yes, the Curaray River, where Jim's savaged corpse had lodged. The Curaray, where, the Waodani had attacked and she had stared at Honorario's blood on the dripping spears. She remembered the horrible, primal lurch in her heart as the Quichuas screamed and she grabbed little, naked Valerie from the river. She had felt then that she didn't care if she ever went to the Waodani or ever heard their name again.

No, it was something beyond duty or misty-eyed missionary visions that spurred Betty straight toward the Waodani. "All I want is what You want," she wrote in a prayer in her journal. "I've sung it in tear-jerking missionary meetings, but I write it here with all of my heart—'Where He leads me, I will follow.'"

The Waodani women were restless. M and M had told their people that if they didn't return to the tribe by the time the *kapok* (a tropical tree) was ripe, that meant they were dead. Given the tribe's tendency toward revenge, it was in everyone's best interest for the two Waodani women to get back home and show their relatives that they were alive and well. Dayuma, meanwhile, could be firmly relied on to be unpredictable, her natural personality exacerbated by her sorrow over her brothers' deaths and her excitement about seeing her people again. A savvy manipulator, she constantly stirred up trouble by playing Betty and Rachel against each other.

But Dayuma was central to the plan. Since she had learned the basics of the gospel story and other Bible stories from Rachel, she was the intercultural broker who could connect the white "foreigners," or *cowodi*, with the tribe. Because of this, Wycliffe's Cameron Townsend wanted the little group to wait. Wait until Dayuma was better schooled in her knowledge of the Bible. Wait until M and M became Christians themselves. Wait until the missionaries were equipped with at least a partial written translation of the New Testament in the Waodani tongue.

So that late summer of 1958 swirled on, half drama, half comedy, a mix of strong, very different personalities and opinions all presumably pointing toward the same goal—waiting, waiting, for some kind of resolution.*

By August 22, it appeared that M and M had changed their minds about Betty going with them to the tribe. There were concerns, all shrouded in various types of fog; language issues as well as the delicate balance of relationships between Rachel, Dayuma, and Betty. For one, Betty was told that the women felt that the Waodani would expect

---

*Rachel Saint was constrained by Wycliffe. As an independent missionary under the Plymouth Brethren, Betty was more of a free agent. If she went to the tribe, she'd need air support in terms of supplies flown in for herself and Valerie. This would fall to Missionary Aviation Fellowship, which was concerned for her safety.

revenge for the death of the unbalanced Dr. Tremblay, even though he had taken his own life, and that they somehow thought Betty was Tremblay's *wife*.

The key stress, however, was the relationships between Americans, not the Waodani. "If you go down there to the Curaray, thinking M and M want you to go, you are miserably mistaken," Rachel told Betty (as recorded in Betty's journal).

"Listen, Betty," she continued, "this isn't just child's play. They're killers."

To this, an incredulous Betty wrote in her journal, "My thought was to answer, 'I should think it would not be necessary to remind you, Rachel, that I lost my husband. I know they are killers.' My answer: none."

It was excruciating. Betty felt that perhaps she was experiencing the same dark torment of soul that had so plagued Jim just before his entrance into Waodani territory. The Waodani women constantly changed their minds about their plans to return to the tribe, as well as their perspective on whether their people would welcome them or kill them.

In despair over the constantly shifting state of affairs, Betty constantly threw herself on the fact that God's character did not shift. "He is my Rock. It is on Him I count, not on the purity of my own heart . . . His promises depend on His character, NOT MINE. This is the only foundation for faith."

A few days later, on September 3, 1958, the clouds of confusion finally cleared. Dayuma, Mangamu, and Mintaka decided to go back to the tribe. They would tell their people about the missionaries, and then they'd come back out of the jungle to get Betty and the rest.

Mintaka, Mangamu, Dayuma, Betty, Valerie, several Quichua helpers, three dogs, one cat, one parrot, and assorted cargo were flown to Arajuno, at the edge of Waodani territory. From there M and M and Dayuma would visit the tribe; Betty would wait at Dr. Tidmarsh's house for their return.

An hour after they arrived, the three Waodani women walked the long path toward their people, soon disappearing from sight. They might as well have gone to the dark side of the moon.

Would they ever walk out again? Would they be killed? No one knew.

A week later MAF pilot Dan Derr flew Betty over the known Waodani settlement. She and the three women had made plans that they would be on the lookout for her. When they saw the missionary plane, they would signal from the ground that all was well. There was no sign of them.

Dr. Tidmarsh and a colleague, a medical doctor, were working on the airstrip near Dr. Tidmarsh's house. They discovered distinctive Waodani footprints in the area. The next afternoon the two men were outside when they heard a terrible scream coming from the jungle on the Waodani side of the river. The doctor called it a "terminal" cry. The next day Dr. Tidmarsh saw vultures hovering near the river. His hypothesis? That Dayuma had been on her way out of the jungle, was tracked, hacked, and killed.

Waiting. On Wednesday, September 24, Marj Saint came to stay with Betty Elliot so she would not be alone while Dr. Tidmarsh and his wife traveled to Quito for some routine medical work. That night, Betty prayed, "Lord, if those women are still alive, let them come while Marj is here."

The next morning, as Betty hung clothes out on the outside line to dry, several young Quichua men arrived. "Good morning!" said Betty. She clipped a small dress of Valerie's onto the clothesline. "Why have you come?"

"For nothing," they replied.

Betty was wild for news. "Well, don't you know anything about the Waodani women?" she asked.

The men looked up at the sky. "Oh, yes," one replied. He shrugged and looked at his friends. "They came out."

Betty nearly died, right there at the clothesline. The man went on to casually inform her that the women were now just a short distance down the trail, bathing.

Betty ran for Marj Saint and her camera, grabbed Val, and just as they breathlessly reached the end of the airstrip they heard a voice singing, of all things, "Yes, Jesus loves me," in English! It was Dayuma. There was a rustle in the reeds and leaves at the edge of the forest, then the women broke out of the high bush, moving straight toward them. It was a whole group: Dayuma, M and M, four other Waodani women, one carrying a baby, and two boys. They were coming with the invitation Betty Elliot had desired above anything else on earth: an offer for Betty, Valerie, and Rachel Saint to come and live with the Waodani tribe.

CHAPTER 30

Child Lives among Her
Father's Killers

"If a duty is clear, the dangers surrounding it are irrelevant."
—Elisabeth Elliot

CHILD AMONG HER FATHER'S KILLERS:
MISSIONARIES LIVE WITH WAODANI
—*Life* magazine headline, November 24, 1958

The missionary network buzzed with the news. Thousands of Christians in the U.S. and elsewhere prayed that the invitation for "foreigners" to actually live with the Waodani might be the long-awaited breakthrough to bring the gospel to the infamous tribe. In spite of many complications, the various mission agencies involved gradually swung into action. Cameron Townsend gave his permission for Wycliffe worker Rachel Saint to go to the tribe; Missionary Aviation Fellowship would support Betty, Rachel, and Val with supplies as needed. The Waodani would speak for themselves . . . though few understood, really, what they were saying.

On Monday, October 6, Betty, Val, Rachel, Dayuma, the Waodani women, and five Quichua men carrying three-year-old Val and the missionaries' gear—recording equipment, notebooks, cameras, film, paper, and supplies—hit the trail. (Betty had reluctantly left her tea kettle behind.) It turned out that one of the women who'd come out of the forest was in fact Maruja, the young girl who'd been abducted by the Waodani a year earlier after they killed her husband, Honorario. "In my opinion," she told Betty cheerfully, "you'll soon be eaten by vultures." Maruja went on to share that she expected the Waodani to kill the Americans unless she returned with them—so Betty and Rachel should give her money to do so. They declined the deal. Maruja accompanied the group anyway.

It took three days of hard trekking, climbing, and canoeing. The Indians fished and hunted along the way, and Betty began to get to know who was who—including Ipa, the young mother in the group. At one "campsite," Betty wrote, "We had a good swim while the men set up the tall razor grass stalks for our sleeping huts. As I write by firelight, sitting on the sand, little Val is singing 'Jesus loves me' at the top of her healthy lungs—lying all by herself on some banana leaves in the shelter a few yards away. And by my side sits sweet-faced Ipa, nursing her son. I showed her Jim's picture, pasted in the front of my diary. Her husband killed mine, and I love her."

(As she would later discover, Betty was dealing with incorrect information. Ipa's husband had not been part of the group that killed the five North Americans. Betty would hear various accounts of the killings as her understanding of the Waodani language grew. The main impetus—she understood from Dayuma—was Nenkiwi's lie. The Americans were killed "for nothing.")[1]

The group arrived at their destination the next day. It was October 8, 1958: "Jim's thirty-first birthday, our fifth wedding anniversary—and today I met one of my husband's killers. Kimu, Mangamu's brother . . . welcomed us with [a] calm smile . . . Valerie stared and stared at Kimu and said, "He looks like a daddy. Is he my daddy?"

At that pivotal moment, Betty realized that the dreaded Waodani, whose very name personified *death* to her, were just human beings to her small daughter. Valerie had grown up among Indians. These Indians didn't happen to be wearing clothes, but such things were immaterial to Val. She saw Kimu, a muscular, vibrant young man, and associated him in her mind with her own strong, young father whom she'd never really known. She was comfortable, and content.

From that point on, Betty Elliot's diary from these early days among the tribe reads like a novel form of alternative literature. She was living in a world where the "normal" standards of relationship or interaction just did not apply. Killers and their victims' loved ones normally do not live, eat, and sleep in community. Clothed people and nudists don't usually mingle. "Savages" and "civilized," or "pagans" and Christians . . . the usual, conventional dichotomies just weren't in play in that remote clearing in the Amazon rainforest, circa October 1958.

Friends

Given their volatility, Betty had no particular reason to assume that the tribe would not kill her. Nor did she have any particular reason to assume that they would. Given the violent loss of her husband, she knew that God's *physical* protection was not assured. But her raw reactions came neither from the experiences of the past nor grim possibilities in the future. She was living in the moment, and the clearest emotion that rises from the pages of her closely written notebook is a sense of *wonder. How in the world could God cause such things to be?*

After all of the prayer, planning, and anguish, here she was, simply *living* among the dreaded Waodani. It was remarkably ordinary. Her daughter played in the clear-running stream and slept on a few split bamboo logs while Betty dozed Waodani style in a hammock above her. They ate whatever the Waodani ate . . . a monkey arm—its fingers clenched and black, roasted in the fire—wild turkey, or a fish or bird. The little missionary airplane dropped occasional food and mail . . . milk for Valerie, instant coffee for Betty and Rachel.

Betty among the Waodani

At night everyone would stoke their fires. The Waodani would sit in the clearing, motionless, eyes fixed ahead, fists clasped in front of their chests as they sang a curiously hypnotic, "hard, nasal tone—in three parts, a single C-minor chord, unvaried through literally hundreds of repetitions of a seven-beat phrase."

During the days the men would hunt for wild boar, monkey, toucan, whatever they could find. Sometimes other Waodani would arrive from the main settlement deeper in the jungle. Betty began to learn different personalities, and to absorb pieces of the story that had taken her husband's life. She'd watch Dyuwi, or Mincaye, or Kimu hard at work during the day, cutting trees down with an axe to make a clearing for the missionary plane to land.

"Mincaye[2] . . . is a taller, lean, very muscular man, and the grace of his body as he swings the axe (very expertly) is wonderful to watch. He has a lovely, wide smile, even white teeth.

"I am supremely happy—just being in the place to which the Lord has brought me. I cannot help thinking constantly . . . if only! 1) these men had known what Jim had come for and how he loved them 2) he could be here with me sharing in all this which he hoped for. But there will be abundant reason revealed when the time comes, and I believe that."

On their first Sunday in the camp, Dayuma had everyone gather in one of the larger, unfinished houses so she could tell them a Bible story. They were obedient to this unheard-of concept, and sat where she told them . . . but the idea of everyone having to pay attention to *one* person was totally foreign. Any number of side conversations sprung up at once. "She told them to listen . . . they meekly shut up."

Still, Dawa searched her ribs for chiggers, Mangamu picked her little son's teeth with a stick. Uba inspected the foot fungus of her daughter and shared it with her neighbor. Gikita and Kumi watched the birds, commenting on their flight.

When it came time to pray, M and M helpfully informed the other Waodani that this meant it was time to "go to sleep." There was a fair amount of "giggling as the new ones checked to see just how this was done. The three men put hands over their faces. All were silent through D's long, long, long monotone. "She prayed for everyone from here to [New Jersey]," Betty observed dryly.

That same morning Betty watched Mincaye cheerfully playing with the dogs, stroking the babies' heads, and smiling. How could it be that "he could have killed Jim?" she thought. "After all these months of living on tenterhooks, wondering, wondering—here I am. Here they are. And we live in peace."

A few weeks later, Betty and Val squatted in Mincaye's hut, eating with him, his wife, and a few others. After the "slurping and sucking" of tender bits, Betty noted that "It is quite impossible to bite monkey flesh—you simply clamp your incisors on it and tear." When the meal was over in about three minutes of enthusiastic consumption, everyone rose from their haunches and scattered into the growing darkness to relieve themselves and go to their own hammocks.

Mincaye's wife doused most of the fire. "Mincaye climbed into the hammock (naked, of course) and his pregnant wife lay down on top of him," Betty wrote later in her journal. "They murmured together in the dark—while the 'rest of the world went by.'" Dayuma, Akawo, and Rachel chattered "happily away on the other side of the house. It did something to me. I came to my leaf hut and fanned up my fire, thought what it would have been to get into this hammock with <u>my</u> husband. And it was <u>Mincaye</u> et al. who killed him. I still can't take it in. But Lord–you know it all, and why it has to be, and I thank Thee for the lot Thou hast chosen and dost maintain for me . . . It is strange—passing strange. I am happy here."

The airplane periodically dropped in mail, supplies, and news, and picked up correspondence from Rachel and Betty. Betty had shot reams of film as photographer Cornell Capa had taught her, capturing Val playing with her tribal friends, Rachel working on translation, and the mud, huts, monkeys, and every other aspect of daily life with the tribe. The resulting *Life* magazine story used her photos, as well as material she'd written, to create a story about Dayuma, Rachel, Betty, and Val living among the same tribal people who had killed the missionaries some twenty months earlier. "Glorify Thy name, Lord," Betty jotted in her journal.

In late November, Betty lay in her hammock one night, beside the fire, reading a *Time* magazine dropped from the missionary airplane. It included the story of a thirty-year-old Mennonite missionary named Kornelius Izaak who had been speared to death two months earlier by a tribe in Paraguay. Betty stared at the "sweet picture" of the murdered man's wife and three small children, empathizing, then jotted in her journal about her own strange surroundings: "the full moon, the river silver; a candle is my reading light, the coals of the fire glow softly, and on the other side of it, quite naked in the moonlight, lies a Waodani man, a killer very like those [who killed Izaak]. Beside the candle Valerie sleeps peacefully. How great Thou art, my God!"

Betty found much that she admired about the Waodani way of life. They were not burdened by possessions. Their palm-frond houses could be built in a few hours. They gathered enough food for each day; no storage, no dishes to wash, no property to keep up. She felt no "western superiority," but rather a deep sense of inferiority. The Waodani women could carry enormous loads that Betty could not begin to lift; they dealt with pain, childbirth, inconvenience, and hunger with great patience and fortitude.

In addition to the daily surrealism of living with her husband's killers, Betty found the jungle setting rife with other paradoxes. This was not the most natural habitat for our properly raised, mid-twentieth-century heroine. The woman who loved hygiene, order, and fine china dwelt in a hut in the mud, gnawing on a roasted monkey fist, tossing the bones into the jungle. The pensive introvert was surrounded by people day and night, people who had absolutely none of the cultural privacy courtesies that Americans tend to expect. The Indians watched her sleep, scoffed at her habits, put their fingers in her food, and asked constant questions about her every move. The writer, linguist, and intellectual was surrounded by people who had no written language and no need to read. They laughed at her dim inability to "hear" what they were saying and shook their heads at her tape recorder and piles of paper, wondering why any sane person would spend so much time scratching marks on such flimsy stuff. The woman who loved solitude lived in a leaf hut that had no walls. Neither did her toilet or shower, since they didn't actually exist. Couples enthusiastically had sex in their hammocks a few yards away from where she and Val were sleeping (or awake). Women's menstrual cycles and young girls' maturation were public info. Sexual matters dominated many conversations. And no question was off-limits.

Would Betty ever marry again? her friend Dabu asked her one day. Did her deceased husband have a penis? Then he answered his own question by deducing that Jim must have been so endowed since Betty had managed to produce a child.

Others brought mating animals to her attention, talked about the diameters of various women's private parts, and queried her about her own. Ever the linguist, she duly noted such questions in her journal, without comment.

Little Val also had questions for Betty, though not of a sexual nature.

"Mama, why don't people blow away?"

"Do spiders have tiny, tiny tongues?"

"Where do we get lots of spit?"

"Do chickens have foreheads?"

"Do baby ants cry?"

"Why do we have chins?"

"I keep asking Jesus not to let me do naughty things, but He lets me anyway!"

"Why?"

Such was life in the jungle. There were also budding tensions, but those did not originate with Val or the Waodani.

Betty noted sadly that Dayuma had already started to "civilize" the group by getting both men and women to wear clothes. After living in Ecuadorian culture for many years, Dayuma knew that the Waodani were considered the lowest caste among the Indian tribes. She was anxious for her own people to adopt "civilized" ways, so they would be better accepted, eventually, in mainstream society. She was hustling everyone into random shirts, pants, and dresses she had brought.

"This morning everyone has clothes on," Betty wrote dejectedly in her journal. "What a sad, motley-looking crew. Their beautiful red-brown bodies distorted and camouflaged in all manner of ill-fitting and wrinkled garments. Why, oh why this awful corruption of the supreme masterpiece of God's creation?

"Rachel is all for clothes—1) on Scriptural grounds 2) to protect them from gnats, 3) because she feels they are embarrassed without them!! I fear Dayuma, besides being a very great help, is also our greatest problem for reasons like this.

"I do not understand at all this clothing idea," Betty continued. "I am certainly not ashamed of my nakedness before either God or my husband. . . . Is this a valid reason for saying we are required to cover ourselves?" She felt that nudity among the Waodani was less provocative than North Americans' use of expensive or abbreviated clothing as status symbol or sexual tease. "It seems to me that these people, completely delivered from self-consciousness or the morbid curiosity characteristic of the 'civilized' man, have inestimable advantages. They are delivered from many sins, from the temptation of personal vanity, for the human body is a thing accepted *per se*, not compared, or pampered, or falsified, or hidden."

Not too long after the American women arrived in the clearing, food supply became a problem. Betty and Val would split an egg, or a tiny, roasted bird, for a meal. The hunters were generous with whatever they shot with their blow-guns, but the pickings were slim.

The Indians apparently expected the missionary plane to supply meat for the whole group. Rachel wanted to start ordering food regularly. Betty felt it unwise to set a precedent that the Waodani feel no responsibility for the white visitors. She noted in her journal how Dayuma had been fed and clothed by Rachel for years, and "now expects to be fed by her instead of taking her turn in her own environment and seeing to Rachel's needs." Concerned about creating tribal dependence on the Americans, Betty felt that Dayuma, now "at home," so to speak, should figure out a solution rather than demand that Rachel supply food dropped from a missionary plane. "I cannot but resent some of the ways D. runs things, runs Rachel, and hence me and all the rest around here," she wrote. "This, too, Lord, is not beyond You . . ."

In addition to concerns about fostering dependence on Americans,* Betty worried about Dayuma's Bible teaching, wondering what concepts of the gospel were actually getting across to the tribe.

She knew that Dayuma was the best person to recount Bible stories, and that stories themselves could have great power. This was not a time for expository preaching and footnoted references to theologians and commentaries. Dayuma's account of Jesus calming a great storm, for example, struck awe in the hearts of her Waodani listeners. They knew fierce storms; they could appreciate the power required to make one stop with just a command.

But later, when Dayuma told how God's plagues fell on Egypt in response to Pharaoh's disbelief, the lesson came across as if God will give us good things, materially, if we believe Him, and bad things if we

---

*In her concern about well-meaning Americans fostering dependence among indigenous people, Betty was ahead of her time. In her journal she reflected, "the desire to help ends in destroying—we come to bring them [unreached people] Christ, we teach them sins."

don't. Sensitive to propagating a subtle prosperity gospel, Betty worried that the tribe would focus on *what* God *gives*, rather than *who He is*. "Lord, teach her to lay the foundations for faith in Thee, not in what Thou [might] do. I see this as a terribly important thing for the tribe at this point—that they learn to love and obey and trust, not because they will thus be free of earthly ills . . . but because of who He is and what His claims are upon them."

What were the people learning, really? wondered Betty. "The message we had come to communicate went straight to the heart of things. It could not deal with the peripheral. Yet the language which was to be our medium seemed to be limited to the peripheral."[3]

As would become more and more apparent, Rachel Saint did not seem to have such questions.

One morning Dayuma told the story of Samson. Afterwards, without any explanatory bridge or spiritual "application" of the story, Dayuma turned to one of the teen-aged girls, and asked her about her own beliefs. The girl, uncomfortable about being in the spotlight, didn't know what to say. Maybe Samson's exotic life and death just hadn't persuaded her of her own need for salvation. But with some minutes of prodding and coaching from Dayuma, the teenager finally repeated the proper phrases about "wanting to believe and have her heart cleansed."

The next morning, during Rachel and Betty's daily prayer time, Rachel thanked God that the girl had made a "public confession of her faith." Betty believed that Rachel was "absolutely sincere and genuinely thankful . . . but I personally find it difficult to accept such 'signs' as the work of the Spirit of God." It seemed to Betty that the girl had been put on the spot, didn't want to make a public refusal, and so repeated the "required formulas."

Betty knew that the Holy Spirit *could*, of course, work through social coercion or repeated phrases or whatever He chose. But for her part, Betty shied away from the common missionary tendency to claim converts or exaggerate responses to the Sunday message. "[T]here is a need for caution in reporting 'results,'"[4] she wrote in a letter to her parents.

As always, though, God was working in, through, and in spite of His people. However odd, futile, glorious or untidy the story might have felt for those who were living it at the time, the invasion had come. In God's mysterious plan, where five men had been thwarted and killed, two American women and a child had been accepted by a murderous people who had been isolated for centuries. The wind of the Spirit was blowing gently through that muddy Waodani clearing.

God was drawing people to Himself there, and He would continue to do so for generations to come.

In December 1958, Betty mulled over the prior three months. She felt that Dayuma's stories *had* borne fruit. The Waodani did know something about God's Son, about living always in God's house, about following God's trail. The concepts were hazy, the language sometimes impenetrable. But Betty—not one given to grandiose or triumphal statements—wrote in her journal that "At any rate, the fact to be reckoned on now is that the gospel of Jesus Christ has come to the Waodani, and Paul says (Colossians 1) 'Wherever that gospel goes it produces Christian character, and develops it.'"

A day or two after Christmas, Betty sat with Mincaye. He told her about killing Jim and the other missionaries. "They didn't see us—we came upon them secretly. . . . We killed them, not knowing. We didn't live thoughtfully then—now we know. Now we think about God. We will not spear anymore."

Later that night, Betty lay in her hammock, pondering anew the irony of it all. Suddenly Mincaye* spoke to her in the darkness.

"Gikari?"

"Uh," Betty responded.

"You are my younger sister."

"Are you, then, my older brother?" she asked.

"I am your older brother," said Mincaye. "Your mother is my mother. I call her mother. Your father is my father. Your brothers and sisters are my own brothers and sisters. Will you tell them that? Will you tell them about me? Will you tell them I call them family?"

Mincaye knew, from having examined Betty's pen and thin stationery, that his foreign friend made squiggling marks on those fine pages and sent them away on the airplane so they could somehow get in the hands of her family far away.

Betty smiled into the dark. "Yes, Mincaye. I will write to them, and they, seeing, will know."

---

*Mincaye became a central figure in the Waodani community of Christ-followers. He would eventually travel all over the U.S., and the world, with Steve Saint, testifying about Jesus' power to transform human lives. He had a big, loving, funny, slightly goofy personality; I loved spending time with him in the jungle in the summer of 2019, when he was probably in his early nineties. He made me a spear. Watching him carefully shape and sharpen that weapon was like an experience of time travel. I thought of him sharpening spears in diabolical rage, so many decades earlier, as he and his fellow Waodani prepared to kill the missionaries. Now, here he was, a mellow brother in Christ, laughing and sharpening a spear as a gift. Mincaye died in late April 2020, a well-loved Christian leader, full of years.

CHAPTER 31

"Madness, Sheer Madness"

"I loved and respected these two women who were almost complete opposites. Betty was tall and thin. She was formal and cerebral. Rachel was shorter and plump. She wasted little energy on graces but was tenacious. What they shared in common was an unswerving, almost mystical devotion to obeying God."[1]
—Steve Saint

"When I heard that Betty and Rachel were going to the Waodani together, I just groaned. Each of them was so assertive, yet not seeming to have any feelings."
—Olive Fleming Liefeld

Betty began 1959 visiting with Jim's brother Bert and his wife, Colleen, at their mission station on the Huallaga River in Peru. The Bert Elliots—whose long, quiet heroic ministry in Peru was used by God to evangelize and disciple generations of Christ-followers—encouraged Betty immensely. This, plus the great camaraderie she always felt when she got to spend time with Marj Saint and Marilou McCully (in Quito), had the effect of making her return to Waodani territory in late February dismal, lonely, and difficult. Marilou made the arduous trip back to the clearing—now called Tiwaeno—with Betty, who loved her cheerful understanding and presence.

Betty found, to her horror, that her time away speaking Spanish had caused her to forget much of her Waodani language. Val missed playing with her cousins in Peru and other missionary kids in Quito. The usual conditions in the clearing—mud, flies, hunger, rain, thorns, infections, lack of privacy—now felt overwhelming. "The natural let-down of returning to this life after being with loved ones, in clean, bugless surroundings—coupled with Marilou's departure and Rachel's invectives as soon as [Marilou] had left made me wonder again if it was worth it all."

Betty was concerned, too, about Valerie, who had just turned four. "I would like to go back to Auntie Marilou's house, Mama." Betty watched her daughter's expanding mind, her new desire for books and more books. Was "this the best place for her?"

Was it the best place for Betty Elliot?

That question wasn't the type that Betty tended to ask. The issue for her wasn't what would cause her to thrive, or what she enjoyed, but obedience to the God who she believed had directed her to the Waodani. She was certainly willing to expend herself in His service. But what chafed in her gut was the sense that she was of no use in that calling.

"I don't remember ever feeling so useless in my life. I can do nothing it seems, which needs doing. Rachel teaches [Dayuma] faithfully—[Dayuma] in turn teaches the Waodani and possibly is the only one who will ever be needed to do so. . . . Were I running my own life, I'd quit now. Living conditions difficult. Val's growth and enlarging capabilities cause me serious concern as to the wisdom of staying here. No other course is open to me, however. I am as confident as ever that God put me here."

She was heartened by stories of faithful nineteenth-century missionaries who went to Africa, Nigeria, and the South Pacific. "Encouraged to read today that [David] Livingstone, Mary Slessor, and John G. Paton all expressed the thought that, were it not the consciousness of the presence of Christ, nothing on earth would keep them from losing their reason. I would echo this today here in Tiwaeno. Nothing but the knowledge that God is here with me, and will not forsake me, keeps me on the track."

Betty thought of T. S. Eliot's poem about the fictional J. Alfred Prufrock, who had measured out his daily life with coffee spoons. "Mine," she thought, "has been measured in quite another medium—here it is sticks of firewood, trips down the muddy bank to the river, file cards, etc. . . . My mind keeps turning over ways to get us out of this situation (when it was the one I had prayed so long to be gotten into)."

It was a relief to do something that actually made a difference.

On the night of April 12, Betty's buddy Dabu stumbled back into the camp. He'd been hunting in the jungle all day; a tree viper had struck and bitten him under his lower lip. There was no way to apply a tourniquet, and within an hour, the swelling had reached impossible proportions. Delirious, Dabu called Betty's name, over and over, asking if he would die.

He somehow survived the night. Betty wept at the sight of his unrecognizable face, his mouth protruding beyond his nose, his neck, cheeks, and nose swollen black and shiny. His gums bled constantly; he had no rest from constant spitting.

Wiba, his pregnant wife, was the only one from the tribe who showed compassion. "It was enough to break a heart of stone to see her helping [him] out into the drizzling morning rain to urinate—both of them naked and helpless, it seemed to me—she huge and heavy with child, his face huge and heavy, hanging forward in pain. But . . . the rest eat and whittle, shout, laugh, tease the babies, mold clay pots and exhibit general unconcern."

Betty used a syringe to constantly suction Dabu's mouth. She had no snake serum. Because of the constant rain, the missionary plane could not come. One eye was swollen shut, black and blue. His pulse was about 55, his skin sweaty. Still, Dabu was rational, and as Betty bathed the blood from his face, he said, "Gikari, leave me alone and let me die."

"Jesus carried all our sorrows," thought Betty. She knew God could heal Dabu. But she did "not know if He intends to." All she knew is that she had to "bring Dabu to Jesus," over and over, even as she worked desperately to save his life.

The rain cleared. The plane dropped supplies. Betty injected "20 cc of snake serum, 1 cc of vitamin K, and one cc each of penicillin and strep." She cleared blood from his gums and tenderly bathed his enormous, distended face. "God is your Father," she whispered. "He loves you. He sees you."

Dabu's voice was weak, thin, mumbling through bulging lips. "Gikari—I have loved you very much."

Oh! That face! "I would gladly give my life for his," Betty wished. "[But] . . . We are not given such choices."

The next day, Dabu's face was less swollen, but now his chest was puffy and sore. "Poor man," prayed Betty, "so patient and humble and subdued in his pain . . . O Lord—bring him into Thy fold."

Within another day or two, while still a mass of dark purple flesh, bloodshot eyes, and bulbous swellings, Dabu could speak clearly, eat, and even laugh. "Praise, praise to the Lord whose touch has still its ancient power!" exulted Betty. God had allowed horrific suffering . . . but He had healed her friend.

(Many decades later, when she was seventy, Betty would visit her Waodani friends in the Tiwaeno settlement. She and old Dabu reminisced about the awful time in 1959 when he nearly died from snakebite. But now he was a follower of Jesus, and told her, to her joy, "that it was the Lord who healed him"—not Betty—all those years earlier.)[2]

Tensions continued with Rachel. After Dabu's recovery, Betty offered to teach Rachel how to give injections, so Rachel could administer snakebite serum if Betty was not available.

No.

Any door of possible connection seemed locked. Rachel walked out on Betty during one discussion. Not one to give up, Betty followed her to her own house. No. No resolution, no common ground to even talk about differences. To Betty, it seemed that any question at all elicited contention.

"One of the great highways that leads into a human heart is that of need," Betty wrote. "I am constantly searching for roads into Rachel's, to learn to know her. I have as yet found no need which it is in my power to alleviate, no way whatever to help. This I hold before the Lord—asking for the . . . discernment of [Calvary love]. If she suffers, it is outside of my recognition completely. Lord, show me the way of Thy love."

Betty saw Rachel as "a strong, faithful type. She sticks at the business of language far better than I do; works even after dark by candlelight, or with tape recorder. She spends hours instructing [Dayuma]" . . . [She] seems to have no temptations, no difficulty in sticking at the language, no desire for any fellowship other than that of the Waodani (she has never once come to my house except to read and pray each morning). No longing for better living conditions . . . she's far better suited than I for this place. She's faithful, disciplined, unmoved, persistent, utterly confident and satisfied, so far as I can judge by appearance. I asked her if she ever got tired of listening to the Waodani language. Answer: No. She is superhuman."

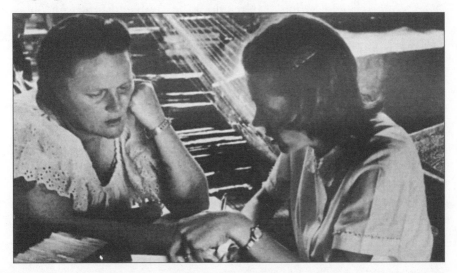

Rachel and Betty, 1958

Rachel had told Betty that she'd be with the Waodani for the rest of her life, and had plenty of time to learn their language. Meanwhile, Betty, yearning to make tangible progress toward an eventual Waodani New Testament translation, despaired over the time it took in the chatty Waodani community to get even one small nugget of language data.

The Waodani language—*Wao tededo*, or "the people's speech," was a linguistic isolate, unrelated to any other Latin American tribal tongues, or any other language on earth. Betty and Rachel were on their own, and the going was rough.

One day Betty recorded forty minutes of Mintaka talking. It took her five days to transcribe it. Then she met with Dayuma for the purpose of identifying words, meanings, and linguistic connections in the transcript.

They sat together in Betty's hammock, with M and M nearby. Betty was particularly curious about one word that Mintaka had said on her tape. *Owiyaki.* She played the word on the tape again, and asked Dayuma for its definition.

Dayuma's attention, however, was drawn to the fish that were smoking over the fire, then to the stable-fly that was biting Mintaka's derriere. "*Owiyaki, owiyaki,*" mused Dayuma. "Wait, Mintaka, there's a fly biting your ankle, get it, no, there it is, yes, oh, it got away!"

"Uh, Gikari, what did you say? Oh, what does *owiyaki* mean? Hmm, *Owiyaki, owiyaki,* Mangamu, what did you say about *owiyaki*?"

"No, no, it was Mintaka that said it," grumbled Mangamu.

"Mintaka," continued Dayuma amiably, "what did you say about *owiyaki*?"

"Ah," said Mintaka. "We were all in the yucca patch hiding from Moipa and his bunch. It was raining and my sister was lying in the hammock with a leaf over the baby, the water was dripping pitta pitta pitta pitta pitta [on] the hammock. Ounemi always said it was better to lie in a hammock even if you got wet. Snakes couldn't bite you there at night. So while we were there in the yucca patch Dabu lied, he said he had come over the hill and others came by way of the river."

Dayuma, nodding, translated the descriptions into Quichua for Betty She also included a few interpolations of her own, also in Quichua.

"Thank you," responded Betty in Quichua to Dayuma. "And just what did you say that *owiyaki* means?"

"*Owiyaki? Owiyaki?*" repeated Dayuma. She unleashed a flurry of *Wao tededo* at Mintaka. "Mintaka, did you say Dabu came over the hill, or went by the river?"

Mintaka responded, presumably, that it was others who went by the river.

"It was Dabu who came over the hill," Dayuma told Betty.

"*Owiyaki?*" pressed Betty, shredding her fingernails. "What does *owiyaki* mean?"

"Oh," said Dayuma. "It means up and around and through the forest and over the hill instead of through the river or by the beaches. That's what *owiyaki* means!"

Betty shifted, sighed, and duly noted this stunning progress. On to the next word on her list.[3]

Early in August, the dam broke, if not in Betty's waking life, in her subconscious. She dreamed, as she did so often, of Jim. He was warm, alive, real. She was desperate to do whatever she could to stay with him. She knew, even in her dream, that it was God's will that Jim was in fact actually dead. But still, the dreaming Betty cried out for Jim. "To hell, I said, with my role as a 'widow,' as a 'pioneer missionary,' as a 'testimony to the world.' Give me womanhood again, give me back my husband. I don't care about anything else."

Betty shook herself awake. Words from one of her favorite writers ran through her mind: "It is this terrible loneliness which opens the gates of my soul and lets the wild beasts stream howling through."[*]

"God alone knows whether the dream reflects the true state of my soul," she wrote later in her journal. "He knows that I do honestly try to accept what He has chosen for me—and He knows, too, the wild . . . aching loneliness for Jim. Well—may this hunger prove what is in my heart, and produce fruits of righteousness in the ultimate. I see little hopes of them now. Faith, faith."

By August, Betty was planning a writing furlough in the U.S. She and Cornell Capa had dreamed up a book about the Waodani, a volume unlike any missionary book yet produced. Betty's poignant photos and prose could tell the inside-the-tribe story for the same audiences that had eagerly consumed *Through Gates of Splendor* and Jim's biography, *Shadow of the Almighty*. She would call it *The Savage*

---

[*]Many years later, Betty would write more dispassionately about the process of grieving terrible loss. "[Jesus] carried our sorrows. He suffered . . . not that we might not suffer, but that our sufferings might be like His. To hell, then, with self-pity . . . Every stage on the pilgrimage is a chance to know Him, to be brought to Him. Loneliness is a stage (and, thank God, only a stage) when we are terribly aware of our own helplessness . . . We may accept this, thankful that it brings us to the Very Present Help."

My Kinsman, playing off the stereotypical 1950s view of indigenous people as "savages," versus the family bond that she knew to be true theologically and had also experienced in the tribe.

Like any writer, Betty was dubious about actually producing a worthwhile book. But she certainly felt more adept now in the writing life than the translation ministry—not because of her linguistic abilities, which were well-respected in the mission community, but because of the constant constraints created by Rachel Saint's strong personality.

Betty wrote in her journal on August 15, 1959, "Today was enough to convince me—as if I have not had the evidence presented to me repeatedly before—that I can be of no service to Rachel linguistically. Every suggestion was squelched, every piece of data doubted, every ancient term insisted upon, and the evidence I produced to support my theory was invariably doubted. I have hoped that experience, increased data, time together, etc. would produce some basis for working on the language profitably as a team. It has not done this.

"I am at peace about my personal relation to her. Never before have I been, but now, before God, I am clear."

At the time Betty was reading German psychiatrist and fellow believer Paul Tournier. She jotted a thought from *The Doctor's Case Book*: "There are two sorts of minds. The first is the superficial mind. For these people there is no mystery. They always know what to do. On the other hand there are those who possess the sense of mystery, who are conscious of the gaps in their knowledge and of its limits."

The next day, August 18, exploring some of this, Betty asked Rachel if she ever had occasion to question her own motives, if she ever wondered if her reasoning was real. "No," said Rachel. "I'm not very analytical, I guess. Don't have *time* to be really. That's the whole thing."

"It is madness, sheer madness," Betty would later write in her journal. "One is sure of everything, another not sure of even one thing. What a fellowship, what a joy divine."

CHAPTER 32

Home but Not Home

"Spoke at [church] women's meeting.
Seemed useless, tho' everyone wept."
—Betty Elliot

*I*n early September 1959, Betty and Val left the Waodani clearing
for a furlough in the U.S. They trekked with some of their Quichua
friends on the long journey out of the jungle, then boarded canoes on
the Añanga River under a glowering sky that grew darker and darker,
until the rain became a chilling, pelting storm. The river rose. The
Indians struggled to pole the slender canoe. Val and Betty sheltered
under big *lisan* leaves Betty had plucked to serve as umbrellas. She
made a tent over Val, who was sitting between her knees in the canoe,
and put another leaf on her own head.

They reached the deeper section of the river, where it narrowed
between overhanging cliffs. The water rushed furiously against the
canoe. The Indians slid it along the very edge of the river, under the
tree boughs, keeping out of the main current, which would have carried the canoe away like an eggshell.

Betty and Val shivered, hammered by the relentless rain. The men
leapt in and out of the canoe, hauling it by brute strength, sometimes
poling, sometimes clawing at the vines which hung from the trees near
the shore, pulling the canoe forward, pushing from the stern, always
taking great care that the bow did not inch outwards and catch in the
raging torrent.

Finally the river, roiling and boiling, rose to the level of the tree
branches, making it impossible to pass under them. They had no choice
but to tie up the canoe and strike out on foot through the untrodden
jungle. One man hacked a trail. Betty carried Val piggyback. They

crossed ravines flowing with swift streams. The Quichua man cutting the trail stopped abruptly, paralyzed, his machete in his hand. A huge fer-de-lance, one of the deadliest snakes of the Amazon, lay coiled at his bare feet.

Staring, he backed up and slowly, cautiously extracted Betty's long Waodani spear from their baggage. He hoisted it, and in a moment, pinned the fat snake to the ground, and beat it to death. The little group gathered around. The fangs were almost an inch long. "The Lord showed it to me," the porter told Betty. She nodded, grateful for God's protection.

The group hiked several more hours until they could see their destination, a Quichua settlement, across the river. They shouted and eventually their friend Dario poled across the river and took them to his house.

River travel, 1959

"Ah!" thought Betty. A fire! Roofs! Hammocks! A feast of fish, wild boar, plantains and manioc, after having eaten nothing all day.

The sonorous jungle night. Sleep. Dawn . . . and a mere nine-hour hike—four-year-old Val walked the entire way—through the jungle, heading with great joy toward Arajuno and the warm and loving hospitality of Marilou McCully.

From there Val and Betty traveled to Quito, and took a flight to Colombia for a visit with Betty's missionary brother Dave. Finally, they made their way to the United States, New Jersey, and the unbelievable comfort of Moorestown and Birdsong: home at last.

While Val stayed with her parents, Betty took a train to New York to meet with Cornell Capa and editor Mel Arnold about her new book about life with the Waodani. The woman who had just been trudging through the poisonous jungle in pelting rain, praying to stay alive, found herself at a Manhattan cocktail party full of staffers from *Life* magazine.

New Yorkers were as exotic a tribe as the Waodani. "Cocktails, smoke-green eyelids, seamless hose on thick ankles, beards, dyed hair, too many people."[1]

They could not understand just what Betty had been <u>doing</u> in the Amazonian jungle. (Sometimes Betty felt the same way.) She felt a pull toward this urban culture, one as secular as the untouched Waodani had been. She thought of Paul's words in Romans 1, where the apostle wrote that he had an obligation to "preach the gospel" to both "Greeks and to barbarians [the cultured and the uncultured]."[2] This was one reason, she decided, that she was writing another book. It was about "barbarians," or "uncultured" people, as it were . . . but she wanted to use the book to show people like these New Yorkers—"cultured Greeks"—the reality of Jesus' love.

By November 11, with Val staying with her grandparents, Betty secluded herself in an apartment in Ventnor, New Jersey. She there could dwell in glorious isolation in order to write her book. It was less than glorious—just the usual torture:

"Very little work done so far."

". . . and I am supposed to be writing a book. I am not writing one. I sit and look at the typewriter, read, shuffle papers, contemplate, and very nearly want to quit the whole thing. Why must it be so painful?"

"Not a word down on paper after an entire afternoon of quiet. If God doesn't do something there will be no book."

She wondered how much Scripture to include. "For every line I write, almost, there is a verse simply crying to be included. But I am checked—it must not be esoteric. It must be readable to all. It must flow. It must make sense."

"I feel utterly inarticulate, incapable of writing or speaking a single syllable which will convey my meaning. God! Father of Spirits! Give life."

Besides the usual burden of writing, there was the weight of reliving hard days. "I don't <u>want</u> to live the past over again. I don't want to experience those dark days in Shandia, on the Curaray, in Arajuno

. . . it makes me weary, depressed to go over them. Then I'm not sure this is relevant after all. Do people either need or want to know all that led to my going to the Waodani?"

Sometimes she got tangled up in her thoughts. Was all of this of any use to God?

". . . perhaps I am one of those who sit around, theorize, ask the questions, write the books. The simpler souls like Rachel pray and teach and please God."

"I think myself, as I have often said, two people—one with the Waodani, another with Americans. . . . I may not be analyzing it correctly at all. I know one thing: I shall not find joy at any time in the contemplating of what I am. It will be first in the contemplation of God, and then of those He has put around me."

She could not wait for "inspiration," whatever that was. She could not see the whole. Writing was like cutting a jungle path, one step at a time. By sheer discipline, she returned to the typewriter, day after day. She stared out the window, contemplated her fingernails, had another cup of tea . . . and wrote one sentence at a time.

By springtime, much of the book was—by some miracle—completed.

Betty and Val went for an extended visit to see Jim's parents in Oregon. Even though she was freed from the torture of writing, Betty's introspection and depression continued. As she "relaxed" with family and friends, she felt utterly alone.

"I just don't manage to tune in, somehow. Great longing for vital reality, truth, understanding. I don't want to do anything these days, but just sit and observe. No desire to participate . . . prefer to sleep! No one can 'make me out.' Can't myself."

She read D. H. Lawrence, *Lady Chatterley's Lover*. The 1928 British novel that had been banned for obscenity in the U.S. until 1959. It was not the usual reading of nice Christian women.

Betty resonated with some of its descriptions of human grief.

Lawrence had written, "And dimly she realized one of the great laws of the human soul: that when the emotional soul receives a wounding shock, which does not kill the body, the soul seems to recover as the body recovers. But this is only appearance. It is really only the mechanism of the reassumed habit. Slowly, slowly the wound to the soul begins to make itself felt, like a bruise, which only slowly deepens its terrible ache, till it fills all the psyche. And when we think we have recovered and forgotten, it is then that the terrible after-effects have to be encountered at their worst."[3]

Lawrence spoke to Betty's heart in ways the vague or timeworn reassurances of fellow Christians did not. All the odd letters and dim, clichéd condolences she had received over the past five years swirled in her mind. Too many people had asked if she "had victory" and was "over" Jim's death, since "all things work together for the good." She had heard too many admonitions regarding God's will for her life— proclaimed by people who knew neither Betty, nor God, very well. She had received too much advice about what she should do next, or what she shouldn't have done before.

It seemed to her that while Christians were quite comfortable talking about "missionary martyrs," they were uncomfortable with the suffering in those who were left behind. So they compulsively explained it away. She had heard too much from Job's chatty friends, so to speak. People weren't at ease with mystery, nor with silence, so they filled the awkward spaces with talk. She had not had a friend who had sat with her, empathetic and silent, at rest within the bruising reality of grief.

It was as if her fragile, egg-shell canoe had somehow survived murderous rapids. She was soaked, bruised, bloodied by jagged rocks. Others had shouted, from the shore all kinds of advice meant to be encouraging. But no one had waded into the roiling water and gotten into the boat with her.

In addition to the solitude of mourning, some of Betty's feelings of isolation had to do with questions about automatic concepts that had been part of her vocabulary all her life.

Now, in the familiar structure of Jim's home, in the familiar subculture of the Plymouth Brethren, she chafed at easy answers and pat phrases.

For example, what was "worldliness," after all? It was a phrase easily uttered in the Elliot home. Was it certain behaviors Christians deemed dangerous? Heart attitudes no one but God could see? Material things?

After a discussion of 1 John 3 with her father-in-law, Betty wrote, "I am tuned to an entirely different frequency from Dad E. and apparently all that we call Christians. It seems unequivocal, in this passage, that a man's deeds are sufficient test of his spiritual state. If he does bad, he is a child of Satan. If he does good, he is a child of God."

In Joshua 6:18–19, God commands His people to destroy some of the spoils of a captured, pagan city, but to retain its silver, gold, and bronze and iron vessels as "holy to the Lord," to be used in His service. Betty saw this tidbit as "a very significant lesson with regard to worldliness. If we are mature, we are able to discern between good and evil. All evil is devoted to destruction. All, that is, that is not God."

"But just because a thing may belong to the godless city, be associated with or possessed by those who do not love God, has nothing whatever to do with whether or not it is of true <u>value</u>. Obviously the [people of the] world have much that is good . . . [things] of practical use for the Kingdom—<u>sacred</u>, even, to the Lord. Let us grow up and recognize which are which, and learn to elect that which is pure and eschew that which is devoted to destruction."

Betty went on, "There is plenty in the average Sunday School which is of the world—it is going to have to be destroyed. . . . But we do not therefore quit Sunday School—we <u>try</u> at least to get the good and ignore the corruption.

"I find myself poles, poles, poles apart from those around me. I am bothered by this. I am tuned, it seems, to an entirely different wave length. I read Terstugen and MacDonald, and some utterly god-less writers, and my heart says a great YES to every word. I hear Dad [Elliot] preach and expound and I can only say NO. It simply does not appear to me as TRUTH. He has spent his whole life preaching and studying the Word. He comes out with an entirely different orientation than those who speak so clearly to me. My God, what *is* Truth?"

Many years later, when Betty read journals from her youth, she sometimes cringed. Perhaps the "honest inquiry" of her younger years seemed merely immature, or overly dramatic to the older, seasoned Betty. Perhaps she no longer asked such questions.

But her youthful questions weren't just philosophical poses. An eminently practical person, she knew, as C. S. Lewis once said, that as thirst was made for water, inquiry was made for truth. She would seek Him. And as frustrated as she was with automatic, "churchy" answers from others, her greatest criticism was against herself. She didn't want to be spiritually or intellectually lazy. If outside voices painted her as a strong model missionary icon, her inner voice still mourned over her lethargy and depression.

While she questioned the familiar answers of the Christians around her—as many do today—she never questioned Jesus Himself. If "Christian" culture had disguised or diminished the reality of Christ and the truth of the Scriptures, she wanted to strip away that cultural clutter.

And she wasn't angry at God because of pain and suffering. She expected it in this life. A mystic at heart, she was not daunted by our human inability to "explain" God's ways. Rather, she was irked with Christians who smoothed away the discomfort or the mystery of it all in favor of some easy platitude. She wanted to perceive the Truth and follow Him wherever He led, regardless of the pain, even if it meant messily hacking a new trail, leaving others wondering just what had happened to poor, dear Betty.

She had come a long way from the group-think mentality of her Christian schools or various missionary agencies. Now she could call a spade a spade—even if she didn't know quite what to do with that spade.

As Betty completed her year in America and her wrestling with secular writers that touched her heart and dear Christian people who did not, she rested in the simplest of comforts, and a two-line phrase from a simple song she learned as a child.

"Obviously, God has chosen to leave certain questions unanswered and certain problems without _any_ solution in this life, in order that in our very struggle to answer and solve we may be shoved back, and back, and eternally back to the contemplation of Himself, and to complete trust in Who He is. I'm glad He's my Father.

"'If heaven's not my home,
Then Lord, what will I do?'

CHAPTER 33

In the Pit

"As nothing is more easy than to think,
so nothing is more difficult than to think well."
—Thomas Traherne

After their year in the U.S., Betty and Val sailed back to Ecuador aboard a Grace Line passenger vessel called the S.S. *Santa Cecilia.* Dining with the captain one evening, Betty discovered that he and twenty-three other Grace Line captains had each solicited their crews to contribute $500 toward the fund set up for the widows and children after the five missionaries' deaths. She was indeed grateful, but the captain had had just a few too many cocktails to carry on much of a conversation afterwards.

But a passenger named Bill was listening, and sought Betty out over the next few days. What was in the Bible? he asked. Why did Christ do what He did? Later, after the ship arrived in Guayaquil, he visited Betty, very "thoughtful and kind, and so gentlemanly."

A few days later, in Quito: "Date with Bill Saturday." Dinner and a movie. "I enjoy his company. In fact, I enjoy men."

Bill's gentlemanly attentions were a brief encouragement for Betty—a taste, perhaps, of what life might be like if she stayed in "civilization." But she knew where God wanted her to go. She set her face like a flint, and plunged back into the jungle.

Betty's return to Tiwaeno was far easier than her trip out of the jungle a year earlier. The Waodani had completed their clearing of an airstrip, so missionary planes could land. The trip from Arajuno took ten minutes, rather than three days of fording rivers, trekking through the jungle, and dodging deadly snakes.

If the trip itself was easier, everything else was as hard as ever. A monkey pooped on Val's head while she slept. Bugs and flies buzzed in clouds. Mud everywhere. Smoke from the fire coiled over Betty's low "dining" table; chickens, dogs, cats, monkeys, and assorted tamed birds tried to share her plate. She just wasn't in the U.S. anymore.

However, cultural readjustment was soft and easy compared to the hard reality of the relationship, or lack thereof, with Rachel. When Betty arrived, Rachel was away from the clearing, attending a multi-day SIL language conference regarding Waodani translation with SIL president Ken Pike. Betty was not invited, and her exclusion made no sense to her—purely in terms of what was best for linguistic progress.

"Again I find myself in the position I've been in twice before—an independent missionary who nevertheless has had Wycliffe training and I believe I have some gift in language work—but Wycliffe carries on their program without the consultation or sharing of data which I had been led to expect by their pose in the U.S. as a servant to missions.

"I have repeatedly offered my materials to them—to Rachel many times . . . and they have not been needed. Quite apart from personal feelings of being 'ignored' or not appreciated—God save me from these—it appears unexplainable to me why they would not, as true scientists, seek all possible sources of data and consult with any who had had an interest in the language or work on it at all. But my position is a difficult one, for the very reason that other motives would unavoidably be attributed to any questioning I might do."

(Meditating on all this, Betty wrote in her journal about Matthew 11:28: "'Take my yoke upon you and learn of me, for I am meek and lowly in heart, and ye shall find rest unto your souls.'. . . The SIL problem is a good [yoke] through which to learn meekness and lowliness of heart, by leaving it entirely to Him. This is the only way to find rest.")

SIL anthropologist Dr. Jim Yost, who later lived among the Waodani for more than a decade, doing analytical research, believes that it was "a huge human-based error to exclude [Betty.] Rachel's linguistic skills paled in comparison with Betty's. The translation was impeded greatly by using only Rachel and [Dayuma]. Rachel once told me that God had called only her and [Dayuma] to translate. . . . NOT anyone else, not even Catherine Peeke [a gifted SIL linguist] who had immense translation skills and deep understanding of the Wao language."[1]

In the first week of November 1960, Betty noted two separate events in her journal. First, John F. Kennedy was elected president of the United States. Second, Rachel Saint returned to Tiwaeno after the language conference. The former had less bearing on Betty's life than the latter.

All the old stresses popped right up. Betty could do nothing right; Rachel saw her choices as culturally insensitive or self-indulgent. (For example, Betty wanted a house with walls, so she could homeschool Val without other people crowding in and distracting her daughter during lesson times. She asked Quichuas who were friendly with the Waodani to build it for her. Rachel was concerned about possible trouble, and humphed at Betty's softness: "It's a pretty sad state when you can't live in the kind of house the people you work with can build for you!"

Betty tumbled right into her familiar, circular pit of despair regarding Rachel. "So depressed," she wrote. "[T]otally lacking in any desire to do a single thing, longing only for death or escape of any kind." She prayed for a word of encouragement that would help her through her day, and opened her Bible to this one in Ezekiel 26:20: "'I will thrust you down with those who descend into the Pit'" [NRSV].

That was not exactly what Elisabeth Elliot had in mind in terms of divine encouragement. But at least depression had not robbed her of her sense of irony.

One night in early January 1961, Betty woke in the darkness. People were rolling out of their hammocks, running and shouting. A jaguar had slipped into the camp and killed a chicken. Unable to sleep after the excitement, Betty picked up a copy of her own book, *Shadow of the Almighty*. She thumbed through it, longing for Jim. Later, much later, she switched on HCJB, the missionary radio station based in Quito.

A choir was singing "We Rest on Thee," with its "gates of splendor" line, the hymn Jim, Ed, Nate, Pete, and Roger had sung so memorably before they were speared to death. Suddenly it struck Betty: it was January 8. Five years since Jim's death. Five long, long, lonely years.

One of the Waodani men, Nimonga, came in to Betty's hut, as he often did, to see what she was doing. He was wearing a pair of tattered white shorts. Betty caught a glimpse of a small, red-lettered name tape sewn in the waistband. It read, *James Elliot*.

She knew where Nimonga had gotten those shorts. Five years earlier, from the post-death pickings of a bloody, ravaged campsite on the Curaray River.

In March 1961, Betty jotted a few news items in her journal.

Marilou McCully, Ed's widow, was contemplating marriage, as was Marj Saint, after her kids were older.

A former American pupil of Betty's was in a mental hospital.

The United Nations appeared to be "on the verge of complete collapse."

The U.S. had announced that an American astronaut would be in outer space within two months.

Times were changing. Was she?

Feeling lonely, she listened as one of the men in the tribe prayed during a quiet moment in the camp. It was only the second time in his life, as far as Betty knew, that he had ever uttered a public word to God. "Father," he said, "I want very much to follow You. Help me!"

Missionary Betty Elliot nodded in the darkness. "I say the same," she thought.

In early April, Betty and Rachel had a long talk, from which Betty concluded that separation seemed the only solution. A day or two later, Rachel denied saying some of the things Betty had understood her to say . . . "One or both of us is blind <u>somewhere</u>. God have mercy on us. She tells me she avoids discussion with me because I make it so unpleasant."

Beyond specific questions, no conversation was plain enough for each to understand what the other was saying. Betty, noting her own sensitivities in her journal, wrote often about Rachel "flashing her ice-blue eyes" with disdain.

Rachel told Betty that "one reason she and I can never get together is that she always puts the good of the work first, and I always put peripheral things first (!)" A week or so later, while Rachel was away from the settlement, Betty noted that "Two radio messages from Rachel hurt me to the quick, and indicate again her attitude toward me." In another discussion, Rachel chided Betty for her concerns about the tribe's spiritual growth: "If you can't see [visible signs of repentance] I feel sorry. <u>Some</u> people can discern spiritual results."

Betty was baffled at every turn. "Rachel's father died last week. No visible reaction. I suggested she consider going to her mother . . . and inevitably, her reply was the old saw about loving father or mother more than God. How can this possibly apply in such a case, where the love of God ought to [be] manifested in the performance of filial duty? The sterility of her mind oppresses me."

Meanwhile Dayuma and Rachel often engaged in wild shouting matches, then continued on as if nothing had happened, which floored the emotionally-restrained Betty.

A friend wrote to Betty, reminding her that human beings don't usually consider a change when things are going smoothly. Perhaps this conflict was God's way of bringing Betty to a decision to leave the jungle.[2]

One day when Rachel was away, Betty jotted a translation[3] of the entire Waodani "worship service." Dayuma started with a dramatic retelling of the story of Jesus' death and resurrection. Then Kimu closed in prayer:

"'God—you live in Heaven . . .

"'You do well, You make us hear.

"'You are the only one.

"'Kuchi's foot is bad. You can make it well, You made his foot.

"'This is Your day. We won't sit here doing nothing. We'll think of You. All will hear of You. If they hear only once they don't remember.

"'Dabu doesn't hear. Make him hear and believe.

"'Long ago we used to live as black as night. Father God, You did well.

"'You made us all. We grew, but we didn't hear about You. Now You make us do well. We all hear well now. When Jesus comes back we'll go with Him.

"'You wash our hearts and clean off the blackness.

"'Who knows who will die next? Suddenly any one of us may die, but if he thinks about You, he'll go with You.

"'Tementa has diarrhea. Giii! He does it right on our trail. He grinds his teeth at night. He must have worms.

"'You made all the snakes. When we go in the forest, You throw them away. Then they won't bite us.

"'Jesus is our Ruler.

"'It is His trail.

(And then, in lieu of "Amen":)

"'That's all.'"

On June 26, 1961, Betty, Valerie, Kimu, Dayuma, Betty's Quichua friend Benito, and several others set off. Destination: Palm Beach, for a visit to the missionaries' grave. After a long trek, they piled into a big canoe, and glided downstream. Kimu was in the prow, Benito in the stern, poling as they scanned the forest, shoreline, and water for any signs of life. All was quiet. The dark, swirling water carried them toward the place where Jim had died.

They arrived at Palm Beach at about 2:30 in the afternoon, and pulled the canoe ashore at the upper end of the clearing. A huge tree had fallen right in the middle of the once-clear beach. As Betty looked at it, a huge jaguar sprang from its branches. Betty had never seen a live one before. She jumped, and could not for her life think of either the Quichua nor Waodani word for it, in order to alert the others. Finally Dayuma saw it, yelled, and it loped slowly along the beach, away from the group.

They walked in the sand toward where the men's camp had been. The tree house that Jim had built was long gone; Dabu had chopped the tree down not too long after the men's deaths, long before he ever met Betty. One of the Indians found a section of Nate Saint's airplane sticking out of the sand. Betty broke off a piece to bring back to Marj. The group walked to the missionaries' grave. There were some rotten boards and pieces of aluminum lying nearby, and the stump of the tree where the house had been.

Betty stared at the ground, the beach, and the trees. She marveled at Nate's skill in landing the plane there. She stared at the immense tree on its side in the sand. It was easily ten feet in diameter, a forest giant deposited here by the churning river during some springtime flood. She thought how easily God could have put a similar obstacle in the way back in 1956, obstructing any possible landing.

"I looked at the waters of the Curaray, flowing silently as ever, and the forest . . . apparently lifeless and impenetrable, and it seemed a dream that anything of any import could have happened there."[4]

But there was the piece of the plane, there was the grave, there was the aluminum that had roofed Jim's tree house. And there was Kimu. Kimu, who had killed so savagely that day back in 1956, now standing by Val, leaning on his long spear, smiling quietly. Betty took some pictures of her little daughter and her brother in Christ . . . and then the group climbed into the canoe and headed back upriver.

As Betty thought of Jim, a William Wordsworth poem floated into her mind, with its poignant lines that Jim used to quote about the loss of a loved one:

> "But [he] is in his grave, and, oh,
> The difference to me!"

That simple chord of lament, against the backdrop of Palm Beach, a place at once so ordinary and yet so calamitous. *Oh!*

At sunset the little group reached a place called Andia Yaku Pungu. They built a fire. Betty hung her hammock. The Indians gathered plantain leaves as sleeping mats. Kimu went fishing. Betty cooked his catch over the fire, and they ate their fresh fish with manioc and plantains. Val, whose whole life thus far had been an extended camping trip, giggled as she laid her little sleeping bag on the ground.

"Why can't we just live here?" she asked, as everyone settled in for the night. They slept until dawn, waking to the sound of a sloth chirping somewhere near. There were green plantains for breakfast, hours in the wooden canoe, and then the long, muddy trail "home."

CHAPTER 34

Two Women at the
End of the World

*"I sometimes wonder if she's quite sane. She wonders if I am.
I wonder if I am, too, when I hear her deny saying things I
could quote verbatim. . . . So we go on—two women, shut
up together at the end of the world, both convinced God
brought us here, both convinced we have nothing to confess,
both feeling the situation hopeless. Oh wretched woman that I
am. . . . Is it possible for two who love Him to be at odds, and
be right? These are questions I do not expect answers for."*
—Betty Elliot, letter to mother, April 8, 1961

*B*etty wrote an article for the *Sunday School Times* about her poignant trip to Palm Beach. When the well-known periodical made it to
the jungle along with the mail, Rachel Saint was beside herself. Betty
wrote in her journal: ". . . the question—and the ice-blue stare: 'Well,
were you <u>satisfied</u> with your trip to Palm Beach?' From anyone else I
would not have resented it. I am quite aware of my emotional block
now, and I'm sure it's mutual."

Betty wrote that Rachel told her, "I just <u>wept</u>! I wept for you,
I wept for Valerie, I wept for the Waodani. I wondered seriously if
you believed in the Resurrection. I doubt it. <u>Do</u> you believe in the
Resurrection?"[1]

She seemed to feel that Betty's reflections on the riverbank were
not what a genuine Christian would think—let alone write in an
article for public consumption. Perhaps Betty's quoting of Jim's
favorite Wordsworth poem, rather than solely quoting Scripture, was
suspicious. Perhaps Betty the widow's sorrow at Jim's grave did not

240

communicate an adequate sense of triumph and victory? Perhaps Betty the missionary should have made sure to preach the fact that though Jim's bones were there in the sandy soil, his soul was alive with Christ?

"Injustice. All . . . face it at some time in their lives. Rachel has levelled accusation after accusation at me for years without taking the trouble to discover whether she has understood me or the issue correctly. Today's charge of my not believing in the Resurrection is probably the most serious. I wonder if she realizes how serious it is, and what she does to me? Well—back to injustice. The question is simply how to meet it."

Betty wondered if part of Rachel's block against her had grown from feeling resentful of Betty's language skills. "It was clearer than ever that jealousy is the real root of R[achel's] trouble, and jealousy must kill its object . . . treating me as a heretic and an idiot. . . . She has no idea what she's doing. . . . I see, as I never saw before, why the expression 'insanely jealous' is used. It is a form of insanity. The jealous individual is totally incapable of exercising rational judgment or of logically evaluating the other's words or deeds.

"From the earliest days of our relationship, it is I who has made every approach, every attempt to close the breach. Ah, Rachel—if you could possibly know what I would give or do to reach an understanding! If you could know the ache to see even a glimmer of desire on your part for a solution, instead of this utter contempt and scorn."

From the beginnings of trying to decipher *Wao tededo*, however, "Saint had lived in Elliot's shadow."[2] Even after three years of living among the Waodani, Rachel Saint would write that "there seemed to be a general impression in Quito 'the Waodani linguistic work would fold up without her [Elliot's] help.'"[3]

Ken Pike, Rachel's boss, had this in mind when he decided to work with Rachel alone in the Waodani language project. "'It would have been much more difficult . . . to have tried to have helped Rachel if Betty had been at the table at the same time,'" he wrote. "'Rachel moves on these materials slowly—but I think solidly under guidance.'" Rachel would need to "stand on her own two feet 'without danger of accusation of having had the work done by someone else.'"[4]

As historian Kathryn Long concluded, "Despite Pike's support, however, Saint struggled with Bible translation, and her inability to collaborate with others would have long-term consequences."[5]

At one point Rachel said to Betty that she thought Betty was undoubtedly ahead of her in language.

"If that's the case," said Betty, "might I not be able to contribute something to the grammar and translation?"

"I have to answer for my own work," Rachel responded.

"Is this a matter of SIL policy?'" asked Betty.

"Purely personal," said Rachel.

During this conversation, Rachel "nervously twisted hands and hair," Betty wrote in her journal. "She acted very much as though my position was wholly reprehensible and she wanted to remain free of contamination."

Betty covered page after page in her journal on November 5, 1961, mentally processing the situation, "To this attitude I see no solution, except to withdraw. God knows my position of faith; He knows my utter willingness to work with Rachel; He knows as well my desire to know Him, to know His Truth and to DO it.

"R[achel] said she thought I had a strong desire to do God's will and this was her only hope for me. I guess this is my only hope for anyone—that those who know Him will be led on through obedience to know Him better; that those who do not yet know Him will one day be shown Christ in such a way that they, too, may want to obey.

"Clearly I cannot contribute to the work here as things stand. It is a kindness to Rachel to free her from what can only be a burden, in view of her attitude to me as a heretic.

"A thousand thoughts crowd in. <u>What</u> shall I tell 'the public'? <u>Where shall I go?</u> What shall I do? How will I bear leaving Indians whom I love? Thou art my Refuge."

The relationship difficulties with Rachel were not unique to Betty. As Dr. Jim Yost noted after his decade among the Waodani, "You don't work with Rachel. You either work under Rachel or against Rachel, but there's no such thing as working with Rachel."[6]

That tendency would surface again and again over the years, to the frustration of Wycliffe and SIL staff. There was no question that Rachel loved the Waodani and sought to do God's work, but her innate desire for control and her unwillingness to cooperate with other translators and missionaries created an environment that those trying to work with her called "stagnant," "oppressive," "devastating," and "condemning."[7]

Throughout the 1970s, after many attempts at discussion and discipline designed to resolve these issues, SIL leaders anguished: how do you disengage, after all, from your most famous missionary? After several attempts to put Rachel on probation, SIL and Rachel ceased their relationship in the early 1980s. Rachel remained in Ecuador as a retired missionary. About the same time SIL leaders John Lindskoog and Don Johnson visited Elisabeth Elliot at her home outside of Boston, humbly asking forgiveness for the ways they had wronged her so many years earlier.[8]

And Rachel Saint would live the rest of her days with the Waodani.[9]

But SIL's official acknowledgments of Rachel's propensities were far in the future on November 6, 1961. That afternoon Betty handed Rachel a typed one-page document declaring her departure from Tiwaeno and the end of her work on the Waodani language. She outlined brief points, one through four, citing Rachel's explanations that she could not work with Betty, and so "I feel that I should withdraw."[10] She asked Rachel to let her know if the statement was fair.

Eight days later, Rachel had still said nothing to Betty about this fairly significant development. Betty felt she now had no option but to send the document to others who were concerned with the matter: Missionary Aviation Fellowship, Dr. Tidmarsh, Marj Saint, and Marilou McCully—who had both been very encouraging to Betty— Don Johnson, Ecuador director of SIL, and her parents.

Don Johnson radioed Betty to ask if she was willing to come to Quito to discuss the matter with SIL's John Lindskoog, himself, Marilou, Marj, and Rachel. Betty agreed—at which point Rachel told her she was under orders to come to Quito too if Betty consented.

"Got nowhere," Betty wrote in her journal after the meeting. "Quite obviously the SIL crew had briefed one another quite thoroughly . . . before they came to talk with us. Their principal concern, it appeared, was how to defend SIL's reputation. The Truth was not what mattered. The issue was, what shall we say? What defense shall we offer our public?"

For her part, Rachel refused to say much at the conference, "'because anything I say will be held against me.' As Marj pointed out to her, that might be true of any of us! Well—God knows."[11]

Betty and Val returned to Tiwaeno to pack their things and make their sad farewells. Prior to their return, Betty had gotten Rachel to promise that she would not break Betty's news to the tribe. As soon as Betty arrived, however, her tribal friends were acting strange . . . it was clear Rachel had broken her promise.

"What did you tell them?" Betty asked, stunned. Rachel said that she had given the simplest explanation possible: Betty was leaving because she was "mad" at Rachel.

Betty had no words. "I felt weak and trembling and cried to God for the grace to forgive and forget," she wrote in her journal. "This was the lowest blow of all so far, but I don't feel that I can help the Waodani any by giving them the truth, other than to tell them that I am not 'mad' but that God says to go."[12]

As is clear from her constant mourning of this fact, Betty would be the first to say that she had no clue as to Rachel's true thoughts. Even her journals—a private place where most of us vent freely and passionately when we feel mistreated—show a remarkable, constant self-awareness on Betty's part that she was full of her own flaws. She recognized that she must seem as extraterrestrial to Rachel, as Rachel was an alien being to her. She wrote to her mother, "I have lost weight, sleep, and appetite agonizing over whether or not I was doing the right thing, praying to be shown if I am in the wrong, if I am sinning against Rachel and blinded to my own faults in this thing.[13]

"Once more I have had to face the lesson that He works in most inscrutable ways. . . . How can we see God's hand in such a terrible thing as the lack of unity and understanding and tolerance between two fellow missionaries?"[14]

A group of Betty's friends arrived in Tiwaeno on a SIL plane to help her pack up all her stuff: Marilou McCully, and Ed's dad, who was visiting, and Barb Youderian, who had, like fellow widows Marj and Marilou, been a great encouragement to Betty. Betty prepared a feast: beans, carrot sticks, Kool-Aid, hot oatmeal rolls and butter, coffee, and a custard pie. The SIL pilot and Dayuma joined them. Betty had invited Rachel as well, but Rachel chose to eat alone in her own house.

Betty's departure from Waodani territory was as inauspicious as her arrival. Few of the Waodani expressed anything about her going. The two Quichua men (Kuchi and Benito) wept. Kuchi came to Betty's house and asked her to teach him a bit more about the Bible, "so that I can think about it after you've gone." Benito brought her a rooster, a prized gift. It touched her deeply. "May God lead them all in His way," she thought. "That's the only hope for all of us."

She wrote to her mother, "I find that faith is more vigorously exercised when I can find no satisfying explanation for the way God does things. I have to <u>hope</u>, without any evidence seen, that things will come right in the end—not merely that we shall receive compensation, but that we and all creation will be <u>redeemed</u>. This means infinitely more than the good will eventually outweigh the evil."[15]

Steve Saint, Nate's oldest son, is genetically imprinted with the same inventiveness, tenacity, and entrepreneurial gifts that characterized his father.[16] He has lived among and loved the Waodani, relating his own experiences with them in *The End of the Spear*, a thoughtful book made into a Hollywood movie that could not begin to capture the spiritual realities of the story it adapted.

Steve has been honed by the awful realities of suffering and loss of all kinds. In personality, he is surely more like his strong, single-minded Aunt Rachel than his strong, reflective "Aunt Betty," which is what he grew up calling Elisabeth Elliot. He has written, "I could go on and on about the contrasts between Betty and Rachel. Suffice it to say, it is a wonder that there wasn't a huge explosion out there in the Ecuadorean Amazon. I know that both women were hurt by the other's lack of acceptance. But God works through hurt."[17] Steve goes on to say that each of these women carried on in faithful ministry—in different arenas—the rest of their lives.

God does work through hurt. God works in the midst of all things. And certainly Christian history is full of flawed characters and sad cases that might well have turned out differently if not for human failings.

Sometimes we can point to the outcomes of such rifts and say, "Aha! Look how God used it!" Right in the beginnings of the missionary movement, the apostle Paul and his colleague Barnabas "had such a sharp disagreement that they parted company."[18] Each took a new partner, and the gospel continued to spread.

Praise God.

But sometimes we look at outcomes in this life, seeking the reassurance of a happy ending, and it's just not there. What then? As Betty put it, His ways are "inscrutable." So we have to rest, not in the peace of a pretty story, but in the reality of faith in a Person we cannot see.

CHAPTER 35

The Bridges Burn

"One ought to be careful that he does not confuse
what he calls 'the will of God' with his own image
of the role he is playing, which is an obligation
to illusion only. Deliver me from this, Lord!"
—Betty Elliot journal, July 3, 1962

An SIL plane flew Betty, Val, and all their belongings to Shandia. Shandia—where she had lived with Jim, where she had brought baby Val home, where she had said goodbye to Jim that last, final day in January 1956 as he banged the screen door to go to the airstrip, anxious to get to the Waodani.

"Teach the believers, Darling!" he had said.

Now, a widow these long five, almost six years, Betty still dreamed of Jim constantly. Most dreams followed the typical pattern:

"We wept in one another's arms at the joy of being together once more, and spoke of the thousands of times we had <u>dreamed</u> it was so and then awakened.

"'<u>You</u>, too, wept on waking?' I asked him, incredulous that he had missed me.

"'Countless times, darling,' he said. 'But this time, ah, this time, at last, it was not a mere dream!'

"And then I woke."

After the constant stress in the jungle, however, Betty felt great relief living in Shandia. (The other missionaries to whom she'd earlier ceded her house were no longer there.) She wrote to her parents, "It is . . . refreshing, in a way I have hardly ever appreciated in just this way before, to be with those with whom I know a spiritual bond, with whom I need not feel under the constant pressure of, if not utter scorn, at least tacit disapproval, day after day, no matter what I did. The wide view of the big river from this bright, airy house; the chatter of Indians whose language I fully understand, this sense of being 'home' once more is invigorating, and I am deeply thankful to the Lord."[1]

During this season, Betty continued to homeschool Val and respond to her reams of correspondence. There was everything from fan mail to an exchange with one of her heroes, missionary Gladys Aylward, to scurrilous appraisals of her moral depravity in writing the unseemly *The Savage My Kinsman*, a book with actual pictures of naked people. There were the usual critiques of her life choices . . . some who had condemned her for taking her small child into the jungle to go to the Waodani now questioned why in the world she'd come out of the jungle. There were many who essentially wanted her to be their pen-pal. Others who sincerely congratulated her or berated her for things she'd never done. One dear woman mourned that Betty had not gotten the non-literate Kimu and Gikita's "autographs" for her.

Meanwhile Jim's final words about "teaching the believers" shaped Betty's days. She tutored other American workers in Quichua, and continued her Quichua translation projects—the book of 1 Corinthians, and a hymnal—with Venancio, the pastor Jim had discipled. She wrote articles for magazines that requested them. Being Betty, she also read material as eclectic as Gibbon's *Rise and Fall of the Roman Empire*, Oswald Chambers's devotionals, and Camus's *The Plague*.

In the midst of her philosophical musings, she was on call for medical help and to deliver babies, and did so frequently. She had a cool head in emergency situations. In one case, the baby had already died in the womb; the mother was now near death herself. After examining and calming the panicked mom, Betty arranged for her to be flown out to Shell for a caesarian section. Another family called her to their home to administer penicillin to their daughter. The father feared that this girl would die, as her small sister had the day before. He took Betty to the place where the corpse of the little girl lay in a crude wooden box, her face covered with rags. An Indian asked to see the face. Betty watched as the grandmother pulled off the rags. A long, pink worm was slowly writhing its way out of the child's mouth.

On another, briefly happy occasion, Betty delivered a little girl to a grateful mother, who named her tiny daughter "Elisabeth."

Little Elisabeth died just six days later, apparently from tetanus.

Rosa, a Quichua woman across the river gave birth to a healthy baby, but did not expel the placenta. A boy was sent to run get Betty Elliot. She arrived to find a horrific situation: "a huge hunk of red meat," still attached inside, protruding from the poor woman. Betty was sure Rosa would soon die of hemorrhage and shock.

Knowing there was little hope, she gave a shot of penicillin, a few sulfas, scrubbed her hands as well as possible, and with a prayer for wisdom, thrust the bloody mass back into the uterus. "I still don't know what it was," she wrote later, "for the uterus seemed intact and traceable to my hand. The woman was alive when I left."

The family managed to get Rosa to a doctor, who wrote to Betty a week later that "<u>without doubt</u>" she had saved the young mother's life.

Amateur obstetrics, however, was really not what Betty thought God was calling her to do. A number of other opportunities for the future presented themselves. A man from the American Bible Society talked with her about translating the New Testament into a Quichua dialect that would be usable throughout the sierra areas of Ecuador. A well-to-do patrona invited Betty to teach Bible classes to Quichuas who lived on and near her hacienda.

There were other options as well; Betty could stay in Ecuador for years to come if she chose to. She could enroll Val in a Christian and Missionary Alliance (CMA) school in Quito where she'd be surrounded by other missionary kids while Betty carved out an ongoing ministry of translation and discipleship work.

Was that what *God* wanted her to do?

Betty decided to meet with Señora Ester Sevilla, who had offered the hacienda teaching opportunity. The Señora became a friend, and Valerie stayed for a "sleepover" with the kind people at the hacienda. Betty went back to Shandia.

The next morning, the skies poured rain. It would be too hard for Val to make her way home. Val stayed another day and night at the hacienda. The rain continued. The river rose, a roaring torrent separating mother and daughter. One afternoon Val came all the way through the jungle to the bank opposite their home in Shandia. Betty, anxiously waiting on the other side, couldn't see her daughter's face, just a small girl in a pink dress, contemplating the roaring river. The little pink figure turned back into jungle to make the hour-and-a-half walk back to the hacienda.

Val—a sunny, independent, and jungle-savvy seven-year-old—finally made it home four days later.

Betty and Val, along with the heroic Bert and Colleen Elliot, flew to the U.S. in August 1962 for an Elliot family reunion in Oregon. Betty and Val proceeded to the East Coast for Betty's youngest brother Jim's wedding, and then a smaller group went on to Franconia, New Hampshire—one of Betty's favorite places on the planet. They returned to Shandia in late September.

"Sunday evening. The beauty of this home and its surroundings brings a sense of peace to my whole being, and an <u>ordered</u> quietness to each day. I was walking around outside after supper, inspecting my pineapples, some newly planted, some just turning yellow. The lemons hang heavy on the boughs of the trees, hibiscus bloom in profusion . . . the chonta palms drop their flowers with a pattering as of rain on the ground below. The sun has gone down now and the lawn is like the 'cricket-loud glade.'"[2]

"Val and Antuca are playing Old Maid in the living room. I finished reading *Tess of the d'Urbervilles* this afternoon." Betty contrasted this peaceful scene in the present with an unknown future. "Cannot help trying to picture the decay and eventual ruin of this house. Who will live in it after us? How long will it last? What will subsequent residents think about within these walls? How civilized will this section of the jungle become?"

These words, written in the smooth, energetic prose that characterizes Elisabeth Elliot's journals, are augmented by a late addendum, a shaky note added to the top of the page in 1996, when the seventy-year-old Elisabeth visited Shandia with Val and others to see if the house was still standing.

That journal page captures both the young woman in a golden, peaceful moment, looking ahead to the inevitable decay of the future . . . and then decades later, the older woman—herself already decaying with the early effects of an aging brain—laboriously scribbling on the same page that yes, the house had remained intact.

Today, the house Jim built still stands, serving as a makeshift museum honoring those who once lived there, and a gathering room for the surrounding Quichua community.[3]

As Betty Elliot considered different options for the future, it was not events in Ecuador or the U.S. that helped to shape her path, but chaotic developments 7,500 miles away, in Africa.

The new country then called Sudan had declared its independence from Egyptian interests in 1956. A coup upset that fledgling democracy in 1958, establishing a military government that soon compelled the country-wide use of Arabic, and the spread of Islam, throughout the country. Education thus shifted from the English curriculum of Sudan's many Christian missionaries, who provided the main means of education in the south. The government paid villagers as secret police, hustled some Christians off to prison, and eventually expelled foreign missionaries.[4]

One of those missionaries was a smart, iconoclastic young woman named Eleanor Vandervort. Eleanor—Van to her friends—had been a friend of Betty and Jim's at Wheaton. Like Betty, she graduated in

1949, majored in Greek, and longed to work as a pioneer mission-ary. At age twenty-four, she headed to south Sudan as a Presbyterian missionary. She worked among the Nuer, a primitive people living in the hard, dry land on the Sobat River. They had neither a written language nor any concept of—nor perceived need for—the gospel. Van found an informant who helped her painstakingly study their lan-guage, which had fourteen vowels and three levels of tone. She worked for thirteen years developing a written form of it, then translated the New Testament into the Nuer language.

Van struggled with some of the same issues that had so troubled Betty. She realized that the distinction between Christian culture and Western culture could be pretty blurry in mid-twentieth-century mis-sionary thinking. She saw that some tribal people wanted "our things" more than "our Gospel."[5]

In December 1962, Van received a stark notice from the comman-dant of police of the Upper Nile Province. She was informed that she, like other missionaries, must leave the Sudan within six weeks.

She tried to comfort herself with believing that "God would cer-tainly bless the translation work. This was His Word. He would see to its successful conclusion for His own sake and for the sake of the Nuer people." But she also knew that the new Muslim government was tran-sitioning the school systems to Arabic script. Her Roman script would soon be undecipherable for her intended readers."[6]

Van made her way from Khartoum, Cairo, Amsterdam, London, New York, Miami, Quito, and somehow arrived in Shandia in one piece to visit Betty. The kindred-spirit-starved Betty exulted in her journal, "This week has been the happiest I've had since Jim died. My God–how happy! Van arrived from the Sudan. Our time together has been an island in the sun. Peace. Complete understanding. Dialogue. I and Thou—the encounter of two individuals which alone makes union of spirit."[7]

Like Betty, Van had little desire to paint the developments of her missionary career in evangelical victory-speak. The two women spoke of the questions that they'd encountered, about what had strengthened them from Scripture, of the incongruities they'd seen. They laughed, reflected on the authors they loved, and bounced ideas off one another.

Betty wrote insights from Van in her journal, as if she was in school. "There is no pat formula for what it means to carry the gospel. If there were we might judge whether we're doing it." She asked Van, "Did you ever find yourself unable either to read or pray? [A.] Yes, and it didn't horrify me. I still knew the Rock was there!"

Betty: "What is the difference between discernment and judgment?"

Van: "Discernment is an unemotional act, judgment is more highly charged. Hence: judge not." (For her part, Van said, "'I love you for your honesty—for those torpedo questions you ask!'")

Jim's brother Bert and Colleen arrived to celebrate Valerie's eighth birthday in February. "Lovely to be together. Van still here, 'sitting still' till God shows some new steps. Surprised by joy. The revelation of God . . . the wideness in His mercy, the new vision of His love and the walk in the spirit/Spirit."

Betty felt, for the first time in a very long time, deeply understood. Someone had climbed into her boat with her. She was no longer emotionally alone.

Talking with Van one day, Betty considered, in a fresh way, the familiar story of Jesus raising a bound and buried Lazarus from the dead.

"Take away the stone!" Jesus had said. The astounded friends complied. The dead man came out.

Betty, for the first time, saw the big stone sealing Lazarus's tomb as "the cold weight of inert opinion." Jesus had told Lazarus's friends to take it away . . . and now, in Betty's case, in God's unlikely provision through events on the other side of the world, her friend Van was sitting in her living room, rolling the stone of others' cold opinions away for the emotionally wounded and half-dead Betty.

A few months before Van arrived, Betty had read *Escape from Loneliness*, by Paul Tournier. "He has encouraged my faith," wrote Betty. "He speaks of 'opening up,' or 'unburdening oneself' to another person. There is no one in Ecuador to whom I can do this. In attempting to discover why it occurred to me that I must really admire sincerely the one to whom I unburden myself. Since Jim, there have been very few whom I deeply esteem. This . . . may be the result of pride."

But now there *was* a person in Ecuador to whom Betty could unburden herself. She admired Van's discernment and courage to call things as she saw them. She no longer felt alone, poles apart from those around her.*

Around the same time, Betty's brother Tom (her soul mate among her siblings) wrote to her from Spain. He'd been struggling, like her, with questions about faith and the evangelical subculture. "I too have

---

*As C. S. Lewis wrote in *The Four Loves*, "Friendship arises out of mere Companionship when two or more of the companions discover that they have in common some insight or interest or even taste which the others do not share and which, till that moment, each believed to be his own unique treasure (or burden). The typical expression of opening Friendship would be something like, "What? You too? I thought I was the only one."

sort of a feebly renewed sense of hope or expectation," he wrote, with characteristic pessimism.

Betty smiled as she read her brother's letter. It seemed, during those April days, that a spiritual spring was coming. A renewed sense of hope, and renunciation of that which was dead, a face tilted toward heaven, and warmth.

On May 16, 1963, Van, Betty, and Val listened, on the radio to the "launching, space flight, and recovery of the Faith VII, carrying Major Gordon Cooper on 22 orbits around the earth. An utterly staggering fact—the technology defies imagination. Yet it is the MAN that really matters. The machinery, the statistics of speed, altitude, radio communication, etc., are all tributes to man's marvelous advance in science. But what we want to know, more than anything else is—how is the man? What does he do? How does he feel? What is his wife thinking? We want to hear his voice.

"We are human beings. We are bound in a common predicament, made by a Father-Creator. Hence ultimately we are concerned with our own kind—and with Him who is the Ground of all Being."

A week later a picture flashed into Betty's mind. Franconia, New Hampshire, the site of so many happy summers in her childhood. Thanks to her bestselling books, she had money to support herself. She could build a simple but beautiful house there. Put Val in school. Have a real home. Write more books.

This was it!

There would be a new beginning. In some ways, a new woman. Of course she was the same Betty Howard Elliot; this unique person God had created, cultivated, directed, loved, pruned, and refined by all that had blessed, bruised, and battered her. But now there was something new.

During happier times, Betty and Jim had climbed New Hampshire's Mount Washington together, relishing its beauty. She remembered her first hike. The summit had loomed high above them. A tantalizing goal. They struggled toward it, hour after hour. When at last they had reached it, they congratulated each other, then looked again—and there was another summit, far above. And another beyond that.

Ever since Betty arrived in Ecuador, she had walked the path God set out for her, keeping her eyes firmly fixed on the summit, then finding there were more and more peaks to climb. Language study in Quito. Waiting for Jim. Language, loss, and death among the Colorados. Learning Quichua. Marrying Jim. Ministry in Puyupungu and Shandia. Giving birth to Val. Dreaming about the Waodani. Jim's death. Being a widow with a baby. Betty's own opportunity to live among the Waodani. Then came the many thunderstorms on that particular peak, conflict with Rachel, exclusion, confusion, and departure. Back to Shandia.

She realized that on a subconscious level, perhaps she had thought that obedience to Christ would mean following Him to some destination—like a thatched hut in the jungle—and then staying there. Perhaps she'd assumed that obedience in ministry meant following Jesus to an endpoint where one would stay put, and all would flourish. Now she realized, yet again, that a life of obedience never really comes in for a landing, so to speak. "He leads us right on, right through, right up to the threshold of Heaven. He does not say to us, ever, 'Here it is.' He says only, 'Here am *I*. Fear not.'"

Now Betty didn't think of her life as a series of "summits" to be climbed, all the way to heaven, a steady, "triumphal" path toward victory, as it was sometimes presented in Christian circles. She thought more about Jesus than the particular outcomes or accomplishments He might have for her. It was all about walking with Jesus . . . and in a mystical way, *He* was both the journey and the destination.

"The bridges are burned," she wrote. Now she had a mysterious *peace*. "For once in my life I have had no question whatever, once the decision was made, that it was right."

She sold or gave away her pots, pans, furniture, and linens. As she and Val prepared to depart, the house that Jim built emptied, then filled again, as Indians who had come to say goodbye jammed the living room. Betty stole away to her bedroom for a few minutes. Several of her Quichua friends followed her. She grinned, ignored them, and opened her worn journal—the one she had started in the summer of 1959—one last time.

"June 15, 1963. Somehow I always imagined that my time in Ecuador might end with the pages of this book.

"It's very difficult to comprehend that I'm actually leaving this desk, this house, Shandia, the jungle, and Ecuador, for good.

> '*I the Lord have called thee,*
> *And will hold thine hand,*
> *And will keep thee . . .*
> *When thou passest through the waters*
> *I will be with thee.'*
> Lord, You have kept Your word."

PART THREE

Being

CHAPTER 36

What Happened Next

*"Thy eyes beheld my unformed substance; in thy book
were written, every one of them, the days that were
formed for me, when as yet there was none of them."*
—Psalm 139:16 RSV

Lord, You have kept Your Word." What would happen to Betty Elliot
after she closed her journal with that prayer on June 15, 1963?

First, Betty's journey to her new beginning in the United States
would not be the slow, scenic, solitary passage on a ship, as when she
sailed for Ecuador in 1952. Now her vessel was a spiffy "modern jet-
liner," the best 1963 had to offer. She flew from Quito to the U.S. with
her eight-year-old daughter by her side. As they came off the plane
in Miami, Val shouted to her mother, "Mama! Everyone is wearing
CLOTHES!"

There would be culture shock of many kinds. But Betty would
create a new life for herself and her daughter. She took the road less
traveled and built an airy home in the woods of New Hampshire,
next-door to the homestead of celebrated poet Robert Frost. Valerie
went to school. Betty spoke to groups anxious to hear her story. She
wrote the new books that had been burning within her in the jungle.
She saw Christian bookstores ban them and invitations to speak dry
up. In 1967 she traveled to the Middle East and wrote, in a way that
surprised many, about her experiences there. Back in the U.S., she
taught university students, addressed the growing women's movement
in the late '60s and '70s, and debated feminist icon Gloria Steinem
on college campuses. She was a tall, slender, strong, independent per-
sonage in the public arena. Then, to her shock, she fell passionately,
deeply in love with a fellow writer, much-admired seminary professor,

and former baseball player. She said he was like Jim Elliot might have been had he lived: Addison Leitch, her "best friend" and soul mate.

All would be well. For a while. Then Addison developed a growth on his lip. Betty bugged him to go to the doctor. Tests. And yes, her deepest fear came true: cancer. It was aggressive. Betty tenderly nursed her husband, cleaned up his vomit, and scribbled anguished prayers in her journal. Addison Leitch died as savagely as Jim Elliot had so many years before, but much more slowly.

As with Jim's death, Betty would face such pain without anesthesia. She walked through suffering, loneliness, and loss, step by step. She wrote books about it all, books that would give countless readers faith and courage to do the same, whatever form their own pain took.

She would eventually marry again. She would grow, and suffer, in new ways. In it all, God built on the foundation established in her early years in Ecuador, the years that caused her to become the woman the world knew as Elisabeth Elliot.

But I will tell those strong stories in another volume. For now, it is good to consider a few of the themes that emerge from Betty's early life.

CHAPTER 37

The Irrelevant Question

"God is infinite and incomprehensible,
and all that is comprehensible about Him
is His infinity and incomprehensibility."
—John of Damascus, eighth-century church father

Why did Jim, Nate, Ed, Pete, and Roger die, really? Was such a sacrifice made simply because of Nenkiwi's self-serving lie? Why would God leave nine children to grow up without their dads? Did God plan the tragedy, or allow it? What was the actual legacy of the martyr's deaths in terms of Waodani coming to faith in Jesus? What does their Christian community look like now?

For decades after her husband was killed, Elisabeth Elliot was constantly asked if the men's mission on Palm Beach was a "success." The word was like worthless currency. To her, the only measure of any human action came down to one thing: *obedience*. She'd look at an interviewer as if the "success" question was dull. Yes, yes, of course. After all, they knew God wanted them to go to the tribe, and they were obedient to His leading. Next question?

If "success" is defined not by obedience, but by measurable outcomes, then we've got to get into metrics. Perhaps we need to count up how many formerly lost people had been saved and calibrate that number against the five young missionaries' lives, presumably weighing in all the other people they might have reached if they'd just stayed alive for further ministry, then factor in all the young people who signed up for missions service, galvanized by the sacrifice of the five, and ascertain just how many *they* reached for the sake of the gospel . . . the calculations would never end.

Metrics are great, and a useful means of assessing stewardship of resources, but measuring eternal destinies by temporal formulas is a risky business. We just don't have enough transcendent dimensions in our brains to comprehend the mysterious, sovereign, quantum workings of God that emanate from eternity past for the purposes of His glory for eternity future. To opine about what God is up to in terms of results, can stray into the realm of hubris, or faithlessness. If we must *see* that there are worthy results in order to come to peace about what God has done or allowed, then we have no faith.

Elisabeth Elliot said it best in her classic response to those who would ask "why" in order to make sense of the tragedy. It's well worth quoting at length.

"There is always the urge to oversimplify, to weigh in at once with interpretations that cannot possibly cover all the data or stand up to close inspection. We know, for example, that time and time again in the history of the Christian church, the blood of martyrs has been its seed. So we are tempted to assume a simple equation here. Five men died. This will mean x-number of Waodani Christians.

"Perhaps so. Perhaps not. Cause and effect are in God's hands. Is it not the part of faith simply to let them rest there? God is God. I dethrone Him in my heart if I demand that He act in ways that satisfy my idea of justice. . . .

"For us widows the question as to why the men who had trusted God to be both shield and defender should be allowed to be speared to death was not one that could be smoothly or finally answered in 1956, nor yet silenced [later] . . . I believe with all my heart that God's Story has a happy ending. . . . But not yet, not necessarily yet. It takes faith to hold on to that in the face of the great burden of experience, which seems to prove otherwise. What God means by happiness and goodness is a far higher thing than we can conceive. . . .

"The massacre was a hard fact, widely reported at the time. . . . It was interpreted according to the measure of one's faith or faithlessness—full of meaning or empty. A triumph or a tragedy. An example of brave obedience or a case of fathomless foolishness. The beginning of a great work, and demonstration of the power of God, a sorrowful first act that would lead to a beautifully predictable third act in which all puzzles would be solved, God would vindicate Himself, Waodani would be converted, and we could all 'feel good' about our faith . . . But the danger lies in seizing upon the immediate and hoped-for, as though God's justice is thereby verified, and glossing over as neatly as possible certain other consequences, some of them inevitable, others simply the result of a botched job. In short, in the Waodani story as in other stories, we are consoled as long as we do not examine too closely the unpalatable data. By this evasion we are willing still to call the work 'ours, to arrogate to ourselves whatever there is of success, and to deny all failure.

"A healthier faith seeks a reference point outside all human experience, the Polestar which marks the course of all human events, not forgetting that impenetrable mystery of the interplay of God's will and man's. . . .

"It is not the level of our spirituality that we can depend on. It is God and nothing less than God, for the work is God's and the call is God's and everything is summoned by Him and to His purposes, our bravery and our cowardice, our love and our selfishness, our strengths and our weaknesses. The God who could take a murderer like Moses and adulterer like David and a traitor like Peter and make of them strong servants of His is a God who can also redeem savage Indians, using as the instruments of His peace a conglomeration of sinners who sometimes look like heroes and sometimes like villains, for 'we are no better than pots of earthenware to contain this treasure [the revelation of the glory of God in the face of Jesus Christ], and this proves that such transcendent power does not come from us, but is God's alone.' (2 Cor. 4:7 NEB)"[1]

After the theft of her Colorado language work, when Betty told her story—"for whom did you carry the stone?"—she wasn't suggesting that God is a Sisyphean sadist. There is always divine meaning and purpose in doing what He commands. It's just that most often we can't *see* that purpose; our human vision is not equipped with enough transcendent dimensions to access the loving purposes of eternity.

As we measure out our lives with coffee spoons, stuck in the "now," we must choose whether to trust God, or not. To follow Him, or not. Obey Him. Or not. And if we choose to trust, follow, and obey, then the measure of our success is not how things turn out in this life, nor in our understanding all the cogs and wheels and machinations of just what God is doing. "A close and fretful inquiry into how spiritual things 'work' is an exercise in futility," said Betty, having fretted her way through many a woe.

The only problem to be solved, really, is that of obedience. As Betty noted, futility—that spirit-numbing sense of despair—does not come from the thing itself, but from the demand to know "why." It is the question of the child, like little Valerie's endless "whys?" in the jungle. For Betty, the adult question is "what?" As in, *Lord, show me* _what_ *You want me to do. And I'll do it.*

And in that acceptance—"I'll obey, whatever it is"—there is peace.

CHAPTER 38

The Relevant Question

"God does not require that we be successful,
only that we be faithful."
—Mother Teresa

*D*uring her mutual difficulties with Rachel Saint, mourning over the seeming futility of her work among the Waodani, Betty plunged into a long study of Exodus. Sitting in the jungle, reading by the light of the lamp, she mined some nuggets that informed her thinking about God's strange ways.

She read the familiar story of Moses going to Pharaoh, over and over, warning the tan tyrant of plagues that would come if he did not let the Hebrew slaves leave Egypt. Perhaps you saw the movie. Moses, increasingly disheveled, would enter Pharaoh's throne room, his brother Aaron by his side. Moses faithfully proclaimed the Almighty's message: *God says "Let My people go!"*

The king had no interest in anyone's will except his own. "Who is the Lord that I should obey His voice to let Israel go?" he thundered. "I do not know the Lord, and besides, I will not let Israel go."[1]

God let Pharaoh know who He was. Each time Pharaoh refused to free the Hebrew slaves, God sent a plague. Then another. Ten times. Among other things, there were swarms of frogs, flies, locusts. Crops failed, water stank, livestock died. Blood, hail, and darkness. Egypt staggered the weight of God's judgments and the cost of Pharaoh's pride. Death: everywhere.

Rather than getting distracted by mental images of frogs populating the pyramids, Betty honed in on poor Moses. God kept sending him back to Pharaoh's throne room, and what *was* the use of his speaking to Pharaoh, over and over? From every human standpoint, his word carried no weight. But God insisted that Moses follow His commands to speak . . . even though the Bible says that *God* hardened Pharaoh's heart so as to render Moses' words ineffective.

What's up with that? wondered Betty. Except that's not how Betty talked.

The seemingly futile tasks went on. Once the Hebrews had finally and miraculously escaped Egypt, they set out for the new land God had promised. Betty knew the long and circuitous story well. At one point the huge throng of Israelites stumbled without water for three days in the desert. They came to a place called Marah, but the water there was "bitter"—unpotable. There was mutiny against Moses in the sweltering ranks, and Moses cried out to God, who showed him a tree and told him to throw it in the stinking pool. It purified the water, and the people drank. Then God led the people, through Moses, to a haven called Elim, brimming with palm trees and fresh springs of gushing water.[2]

"As Jim pointed out to me years ago," Betty journaled, "God led Israel to Marah. He could have led them directly to Elim, but He has chosen to lead His people into difficulties in order that they may know Him, and He may know them."

Further, she noted the detail in the story that the tree that made the water drinkable in Marah was right there, but God had to *show* it to Moses. Often the solution to our problem is right at hand, but we must be shown it. And the very cause of complaint can be made sweet.

It was a lesson for missionaries, Betty thought. "We might say, 'Well, if God is going to save them [unreached people groups] anyway, and my efforts will be useless, why on earth should I endure the hardships, frustration, and humiliation the missionary work means?' We are commanded. God will not fail to do His part, which is ultimately the only part that matters."

Elisabeth Elliot knew she was no Moses, though she was increasingly disheveled. But she was desperate to learn what God might teach her from the story of Scripture.

The question was not "why?" but "what?" *God, what would You have me do?* For Betty, whether God told her to go confront Pharaoh or to go live among the Waodani, she determined to do it, regardless of results.

Which is good, since Betty's obedience in such matters did not lead to stunning results that she could see.

CHAPTER 39

The Dust and Ashes

"Time is a kind friend, and he will make us old."
—Sara Teasdale

Betty's nine months among the Colorados in the early 1950s, "useless" due to the death of her language informant and the loss of her language notes, felt like an immense pile of ashes. Then, in late 1961, after the failed working relationship with Rachel and the seeming failure of her season among the Waodani—as well as her deep concerns about their future—the ashes were deeper yet.

But oddly enough, the very ashes of her Ecuador experience somehow became the platform by which the rest of the world looked up to her. The things that Betty saw as failures were, in the public mind, credentials. She was "the world-renowned missionary who brought the gospel to a savage tribe," the "gifted linguist," the brave and heroic widow, the wife of a martyr.

In Betty's eyes, these things were so much dust. By the end of her time in Ecuador, Betty had puzzled over what the word *missionary* even meant. In the jungle, Rachel had rejected her viable linguistic skills. The adulation heaped upon her and the other widows—they were the noble "wives of martyrs" and "our brave girls"—meant little. She preferred the farmer who named one of his cows after her.

Perhaps it's a pattern. The times of dust in our lives, their gray purposelessness, may well be God's building blocks. That which seems flimsy, lighter than air, immaterial, and weak—who would build on a "block" of ashes?—later can become our greatest strengths. It's an offshoot of what the apostle Paul meant when he wrote that God told him, "My grace is sufficient for you, for power is perfected in weakness." So, said Paul, I'll own my weakness, "so that the power of

Christ may dwell in me. Therefore I am well content with weaknesses, with insults, with distresses, with persecutions, with difficulties, for Christ's sake; for when I am weak, then I am strong."[1]

Betty resonated with Paul's perspective. The second that any of us starts to get preoccupied with our power, platform, image, or identity is the moment that we run into trouble.

"The search for recognition hinders faith. We cannot believe so long as we are concerned with the 'image' we present to others. When we think in terms of 'roles' for ourselves and others, instead of simply doing the task given us to do, we are thinking as the world thinks, not as God thinks. The thought of Jesus was always and only for the Father. He did what He saw the Father do. He spoke what He heard the Father say. His will was submitted to the Father's will."[2]

So Betty sought not to fixate on her own "identity." Again, she knew she was not any of the labeled assumptions others had put on her. Being a young widow, for example, was far more complex than the ways that outsiders liked to sum it up. They lauded her for things she did not believe to be true about herself. (Or, conversely, they vilified her for other things that weren't true: She was an alcoholic. She had borne a child by a Waodani man. She had lost her mind.)

The false assumptions, flattering or damning, weren't their fault; how could they know her? And, thought Betty, *How can I even know myself?*

As Betty wrote about the Waodani, "Many times I despaired of ever really knowing them, the secrets of their hearts. Then I realized that I did not know my own heart. In this we were one."[3]

In this question of identity, she would have agreed with Dietrich Bonhoeffer's summation of the matter. Bonhoeffer was the celebrated German pastor, writer, and martyr, executed by orders of Adolf Hitler while Betty was in college. One of his last poems came from his Nazi prison:

> Who am I? They often tell me,
> I come out of my cell
> Calmly, cheerfully, resolutely,
> Like a lord from his palace.
>
> . . . Who am I? They also tell me,
> I carried the days of misfortune
> Equably, smilingly, proudly,
> like one who is used to winning.
>
> Am I really then what others say of me?
> Or am I only what I know of myself?
> Restless, melancholic, and ill, like a caged bird,

Struggling for breath, as if hands clasped my throat,
Hungry for colors, for flowers, for the songs of birds,
Thirsty for friendly words and human kindness,
Shaking with anger at fate and at the smallest sickness,
Trembling for friends at an infinite distance,
Tired and empty at praying, at thinking, at doing,
Drained and ready to say goodbye to it all.

Who am I? This or the other?
Am I one person today and another tomorrow?
Am I both at once? In front of others, a hypocrite,
And to myself a contemptible, fretting weakling?

. . . Who am I? These lonely questions mock me.
Whoever I am, You know me, I am yours, O God.[4]

Like Bonhoeffer, *this* is where Elisabeth Elliot always came
home, no matter what.
I belong to God. He is faithful. His words are true.

CHAPTER 40

The Next Thing

*"The more you accept daily crosses as daily bread, in peace
and simplicity, the less they will injure your frail, delicate
health; but forebodings and frettings would soon kill you."*
—François de la Mothe-Fénelon

*B*etty was cerebral, mystical, reflective . . . but she was also a very
practical person. After Jim died, she didn't get through each day
by mourning, philosophizing, or getting in touch with her feelings,
though all those things flowed freely in her journal. Here she was, a
suddenly single parent, alone on the jungle station that she and Jim
had manned together. They'd had a tidy division of labor; she had no
clue how to do all the things he had done. She wanted to collapse into
a heap on the bedroom floor.

But she made it through each arduous day, one at a time, with a
simple mantra: *do the next thing.*

It came from an old Saxon poem Betty loved, transliterated in part
from the Middle English:

> Do it immediately, do it with prayer,
> do it reliantly, casting all care.
> Do it with reverence, tracing His hand
> who placed it before thee with earnest command.
> Stayed on omnipotence, safe 'neath His wing,
> leave all resultings, do the next thing.

Betty tried to take each new and confusing duty as the will of God
for each moment. What was she going to do about the diesel genera-
tor? How was she going to keep the airstrip clear for small planes?
She found herself the foreman for dozens of Indians, managing and

paying them as they swung their machetes on the airstrip, cleared the pineapple bed and jungle trails, and maintained the buildings. This was not a familiar or comfortable role.

Then there was the hydroelectric system that Jim had just begun to put in before he died. Hydroelectrics were not Betty's strong suit: should she hire men to finish it, or forget it?

She was also teaching a women's literacy class, managing the Ecuadorian teacher running the boys' school, and delivering babies. Then there was the translation of the Gospel of Luke, which she and Jim had finished only in rough draft form before he was killed. She had to carry on with that; there were no Scriptures in Quichua. If the church was to grow, they had to have spiritual food.

And what in the world *was* she going to do about the Quichua church? There were fifty newly baptized believers who a year before had not been Christians. Jim had been teaching them daily and on Sundays. Jim Elliot was not there anymore. There was no other male missionary.

Betty knew that she was not going to run that church. But she was the only person around who knew the Scriptures. And one of the last things Jim had said to her before he left for the Waodani was that she must continue to disciple the believers.

So she took two of the young men that Jim had picked out as potential leaders. She told them it was not her role to be head of their indigenous church; it was their job to take responsibility. But she was there to help them.

So every Saturday afternoon, Betty and one of the other of these men would meet. They sat down, and she would translate a few verses from Spanish and Greek and English into Quichua. They would discuss the Scriptures, outline a sermon, think of illustrations from jungle life, and pray. And on Sundays the men would preach to the congregation.

"I could have done a better job," Betty wrote without pride. "But I felt that it was not my job to take over the church simply because I was competent to do it. It was my job to encourage these men so that they would become competent."[1]

They did.

Even though Betty's to-do list after Jim's death was daunting, she somehow chipped through each day. "You can imagine how tempted I was to just plunk myself down and say, 'There is no way I can do this,'" she said later. "I wanted to sink into despair and helplessness." But doing the next thing, no matter how small, somehow created an impetus that carried her through each long day, one hard hour at a time.

CHAPTER 41

The Problem of Pain

"My life is like a faded leaf,
My harvest dwindled to a husk;
Truly my life is void and brief
And tedious in the barren dusk;
My life is like a frozen thing
No bud nor greenness can I see:
Yet rise it shall—the sap of Spring;
O Jesus, rise in me."
—from "A Better Resurrection," by Christina Rossetti

*B*etty Elliot's young adult years were not overwhelmingly cheerful.

That's not to say there weren't joyful seasons, Betty would laugh until she cried with her siblings. She loved her friends. She felt deeply content when she was at home, wherever home was, if it was a space of order and beauty. A flower in a tin cup, set on a jungle "table," made her smile. She loved swimming, walking, and hiking; she exulted in the wonders of nature. She knew deep, real joy during those rare times she was actually *with* Jim Elliot before their marriage, rather than living a correspondence relationship. She took great joy in Valerie, marveling over her daughter's development, funny personality, and creative use of language. She loved the Waodani, and knew joy as she swung in her hammock, listening to the night sounds of the camp.

But still, if we were to pass an emotional Geiger counter over her journals, setting it to register the hard times, it would click away madly over her entries evoking sadness, confusion, frustration, loneliness, and rejection. (Like many of us, she probably wrote more when she was sad, and often skipped journaling on the full, happy days.)

For Betty, the sad days weren't times to be denied, suppressed, or avoided. Betty's medical training, and her theology, did not allow her to deny the existence of pain. It was a symptom. It showed God was at work. If she walked the path of obedience, He would in fact use her very pain for His good purposes.

But the problem with pain is that it hurts.

Many of us, particularly if we live in North America, are culturally programmed to avoid pain at all costs. We're subliminally taught to think that our lives will be like a trip down a long, peaceful river of productivity, peace, and purpose. We expect occasional rapids, rocks, and other perils, but for the most part, the assumption is that the river will be smooth.

Shaped by her jungle experience, Betty Elliot knew that any river is full of rapids and studded with dangerous rocks. Pelting storms break out more often than not. Poisonous snakes lurk on the riverbanks; anacondas lie in the shallows. Betty didn't *expect* seasons of tranquil flotation, tanning on her sun-warmed inner tube.

She often called herself a pessimist, saying it was a gift that ran in her family. I prefer to call her a realist. Life *is* hard. It's a lie to project that God's will on this earth is for us to be safe, pain-free, and prosperous. Ask any hardy Christian suffering persecution at the hands of hostile governments or majority-religion extremists today. God keeps our *souls* safe, secure for eternity. He may give riches in this world, yes, to some. But to all His children who hide in Him, He gives security and riches to the soul. Suffering in this world somehow refines our character and marvels in the next world; the one that lasts forever, the one with joys beyond human conception. And suffering is one of God's sanctifying tools. God is not a cosmic plumber who shows up to make things run smoothly for us. When He doesn't fix broken situations in our lives, it's usually because He is fixing us through them.

Living with the promise of heaven enhances earth. The "not yet" gives us a rich freedom: we can hold this life lightly, as did Jim Elliot and his friends.

Many of the mature Elisabeth Elliot's later books would organically return to this theme. Those who know her writings well can't imagine her life and body of work without this trademark theme of suffering. In an increasingly pain-averse North American culture, Betty and a few others, like Joni Eareckson Tada, served as the authoritative voices on the topic for the second half of the twentieth century (and beyond).

Though some of us may think of Elisabeth Elliot as the authority on suffering, it's important to remember that she wasn't actually born middle-aged and twice widowed. In her early years, she had no idea of the bereaved direction her narrative would take.

During college, Betty's relationship with Jim brought her out of the emotional refrigerator. But their courtship consigned her to five years of exhausting self-control, when she could not express her love for him. Already introspective, this caused her to spend even more time "in her own head," . . . and poor Betty Elliot didn't have the internet or its thousands of cheery self-help websites to tell her "how to get out of your head." All she had was the Bible.

Once married to Jim, once she was a mother to Val, for all Betty knew, she would live out her days in jungle ministry with Jim. They looked forward to having more children—the next baby, if a girl, would be named "Evangeline"—equipping Quichua believers, and raising a tribe of strapping young Elliots. Happy plans. All lost.

Then, a bruised Betty made new plans. She yearned to live with the Waodani and eventually make a Bible in their language. To add insult to her earlier injury, though God led her to the Waodani, the thorny difficulties with Rachel Saint forced her out.

Licking her wounds, all Betty could think about were *Jesus'* thorns. A derisive crown had pierced His head; He had gone to the cross. He had prayed fervently, with tears, to the One who could save Him from death. God heard Him. And Son of God though He was, Jesus learned obedience from what He suffered.[1]

Yes, some of us might say. But Jesus was saving the world. And He is God.

But God's designs are woven into the fabric of the universe, true for His own Son and true for the human beings He died to save. Obedience.

We "must look clearly and unflinchingly at what happens and seek to understand it through the revelation of God in Christ," Betty wrote. ". . . There was the scandal of the virgin birth, the humiliation of the stable, the announcement not to village officials but to uncouth shepherds. A baby was born—a Savior and King—but hundreds of babies were murdered because of Him. His public ministry, surely no tour of triumph, no thundering success story, led not to stardom but to crucifixion. Multitudes followed Him, but most of them wanted what they could get out of Him, and in the end all His disciples fled. Yet out of this seeming weakness and failure, out of His very humbling to death came the power that transforms everything.

So it is no surprise that, as Betty put it, "To be a follower of the Crucified means, sooner or later, a personal encounter with the cross. And the cross always entails <u>loss</u>. The great symbol of Christianity means sacrifice and no one who calls himself a Christian can evade this stark fact."[2]

In her own encounter with the cross, Betty determinedly sought the path of obedience, regardless of how she felt. Thus in her jungle madness with Rachel Saint, she didn't act according to her emotions. She tried—not always successfully—to confine most of her anguish, anger, confusion, and hurt feelings to her journal, rather than spewing all of the above onto Rachel. She sought God's will, even as her biographer and others might be yelling to her from the sidelines of time, "Sister, get out of there!"

Betty knew that it was "always hard to look at things spiritually, especially when they look a mess." One could easily fall into one of two extremes analyzing the work among the Waodani. One is cheery triumphalism, which shines up the story, glosses over any inconvenient failures, quote amazing "results," and pass the plate. The other is to focus solely on human flaws, magnify any weaknesses, and bitterly discredit the entire work as a failure. The hard road is to see both the good and bad, know that God works in all kinds of ways through all kinds of people, and praise Him that He is sovereign over it all.

One of Betty's favorite poems about this "hard road" came from the iconoclastic Amy Carmichael.

> Hast thou no scar?
> No hidden scar on foot, or side, or hand?
> I hear thee sung as mighty in the land,
> I hear them hail thy bright ascendant star,
> Hast thou no scar?
>
> Hast thou no wound?
> Yet, I was wounded by the archers, spent.
> Leaned me against the tree to die, and rent
> By ravening beasts that compassed me, I swooned:
> Hast thou no wound?
>
> No wound? No scar?
> Yet as the Master shall the servant be,
> And pierced are the feet that follow Me;
> But thine are whole. Can he have followed far
> Who has no wound nor scar?[3]

Our twenty-first-century minds have to slow down to absorb this hard poem. It can seem a bit morbid and guilt-producing. What about those who, by God's grace, have led pretty unscarred lives? Was Amy Carmichael shaming them into self-flagellation?

But there is a rich sweetness in Carmichael's poem. It's almost a Rosetta Stone to understand Betty Elliot, as well as Jim, who quoted it often. Or perhaps the Elliots are the translation device that unlocks the poem for us.

Whether you agree or disagree with their choices, whether you resonate or not with their particular personalities, the takeaway from their lives is a reckless abandon for God. A willingness to cast off any illusions of self-protection, in order to burn for Christ. An absolutely liberating, astonishing radical freedom that comes only when you have, in fact, spiritually died to your own wants, ambitions, will, desires, reputation, and everything else.

When Jim or Elisabeth Elliot wrote about "dying to self," it was familiar Christian jargon. Easy to gloss over, easy to sing in a rousing chorus and then go out to lunch after church. The Elliots, as well as the other missionaries, meant it literally. For the men, physical death was the gateway to Life at the height of their youth. The widows' dying may have looked less dramatic, but was slower and harder: years of a resolute, determined obedience to the dangerous, unpredictable God who had taken away their young husbands.

Betty Elliot would never have chosen the suffering God had for her. But when she quoted Amy Carmichael, she wasn't just indulging in poetry appreciation day. The thorns and scars God allowed in her own life—or, to change the metaphor, the extinguishing deaths that snuffed her comfort and joy—were not surprising strangers but friends to be welcomed. When pain, disappointment, lack of fulfillment, derision, suffering and death came, she did not flee the dark waves, sucked backwards by their relentless undertow. She met them straight on, diving toward the cresting surge, sparing herself nothing, considering the bracing, salty shock of the cold waters just part of the big Story. Nothing new. Nothing original. Just basic Christianity, from its paradoxical beginnings.

Betty wrote, ". . . the will of God is not a quantitative thing, static and measurable. The Sovereign God moves in mysterious relation to the freedom of man's will. We can demand no instant reversals. Things must be worked out according to a divine design and timetable. Sometimes the light rises excruciatingly slowly. The kingdom of God is like leaven and seed, things which work silently, secretly, slowly, but there is in them an incalculable transforming power. Even in the plain soil, even in the dull dough, lies the possibility of transformation."[4]

Perhaps the end of Elisabeth Elliot's time in Ecuador was, as she felt in Shandia in 1963, the beginning of spring. Over her years there, she had thawed from a refrigerated rose to a passionate wife and mother. But still, the losses of her lover and soul mate, and the loss of any sense of accomplishment in her linguistic or missionary work, had almost killed her hope. She wouldn't have minded dying at the hands of the Waodani.

There was another death as well, the passing of a triumphal religiosity that responded to both life's tragedies and life's deep questions with platitudes. And if Betty felt stark grief at Jim's loss, grief was almost easier to bear than the anger she felt about the pious postures of performance-based religious agencies concerned more with image and PR rather than the state of one's heart.

Many who feel such anger or disillusionment about the cultural Christianity of their youth check out of faith altogether, or create a vague spirituality that likes Jesus as long as He is self-defined. Betty pressed on. At one point in her literal and metaphorical jungle journey, she wrote, "it is unsettling . . . to think how much even our moral consciousness is conditioned by what is currently and/or locally accepted. . . . Cultural adaption that we unconsciously adopt as part of our faith outlook. . . . Right now, I am sure of a few things: The Inexorability of Resurrection/Redemption; the Love of God; the power of Faith (but it is a gift)."

Betty wrote in her journal, purposing that when she returned to the States, she would try to write books about this gift of faith. "But how, how, to put this on paper so as to disarm people into contemplating it for once, seriously? I have not any great creative imagination or ability, but I do believe that if I worked hard I might produce a little which would set forth a moment of truth now and then. How well I know my limitations, but let it not be an excuse for throwing in the sponge."

After all, she now had something to say. She had been a Christian for many years. But now the focus was not Christianity, but Christ. "I suppose the general opinion of missionary work says that it is intended to bring [people] to Christ. Only God knows if anything in my 'missionary career' has ever contributed anything at all to this end. But much in that 'career' has brought me to Christ."

A Note from the Author

As I mentioned at the beginning of this volume, the earnest biographer's task is hopeless. This is not only because readers may have preconceived notions about one's subject, and prefer that image to what the biographer might discover. It is also because the biographer can be tempted to think that her job is to chronologically report a series of life events, and the subject's image will then neatly project onto the page. Or just gather enough precise facts, get enough descriptions, and the puzzle pieces will snap together. No. Consider a video that actually records a person sleeping, minute by tedious minute throughout the night. It might correctly chronicle the sleeper's actions. But it cannot reveal her dreams. (And any viewer would die of boredom.)

Michelangelo said that every block of stone has a statue within; the task of the sculptor is to discover it.

My stone was the body of Betty's writings and the testimonies of those who knew her. An immense monolith. I wasn't chipping with a chisel. I was shaving away millions of words. (Be glad that I discarded most of them.) As I did so, the shape of the woman began to emerge.

To change the image, I'd gaze at the tiny, faded handwriting filling the thin pages of Betty's old journals, steeping in her thoughts as if I was water and she was a tea bag. As I absorbed her essence, I found I wasn't just carrying around my own life, which was heavy enough at the time. In the strangest way, I was carrying around Elisabeth Elliot's life, every day. I was not a biographer, but a steward, with a mundane but sacred task. *Write the story.*

Turning the thin pages of her journals, I knew the end of that story. The young Elisabeth, writing, did not. I wanted to warn her, to shout across the decades to prepare for the storm. *Get ready! The hurricane is coming!*

It's a mercy that none of us knows what is coming.

This was reinforced by my own experiences as I wrote this book. My own husband's rare brain cancer had been quiet for years. Then, even as I worked away, peering with a magnifying glass, as if I were an archeologist, at Betty's closely written journals, Lee developed new, small tumors. He had Gamma Knife surgery. Several times. Months later, he began acting strangely. Pressure in his brain. Necrosis, from the proton radiation that had saved his life years earlier. Then a raging infection surged, promising to kill him. Massive emergency brain surgery, guarded condition. He almost died three times. (I guess we "almost die" often, but we aren't usually aware of it.)

At any rate, I then found myself reading Betty Elliot's journals and jotting notes about her life while in operating room waiting areas, intensive care units, rehab facilities, and by any number of hospital beds. I carried Betty's loss of Jim even as my own loss of Lee was not only theoretical, but seemingly imminent.

Yet it was good.

By this I mean that the truths that carried Betty Elliot through her particular storms carried me through mine. *I belong to God. He is faithful. His words are true. And transformation—the ultimate Springtime—already planted, is coming.*

So, in spite of our very different personalities, habits, or preferences, this sister's story strengthened my own. And that is my hope for any reader, whatever your situation may be.

With Gratitude

Thank You, God. Every heartbeat comes by Your grace. Or, as EE would say, by *Thy* grace.

Valerie Shepard, for entrusting me with the story of your mother's life; I am so grateful for our friendship, and to you and Walt for generously sharing your lives and all things EE; similarly, thank you, Arlita Winston, for trusting me to steward this project of your dearest friend! Thank you to Arlita and Joe for hours and hours of conversation, memories, prayer, and beautiful meals and cups of tea in Betty's favorite china;

Lars Gren, for giving me access to closed archives at Wheaton, for sharing photos and memories, and for cooking and feeding me a VERY fresh fish one New England afternoon;

Dave and Janet Howard, Tom and Lovelace Howard, Jane Elliot Hawthorne, Olive Fleming Liefeld, for sharing your thoughts and memories of your loved ones, and thank you to Beverly Hancock, for putting me in touch with your mom;

Joni Eareckson Tada, for writing the foreword and for your wonderful, unanticipated prayer support from the beginning of this project;

Robert Wolgemuth, Erik Wolgemuth, as always, for your long friendship and abiding representation, particularly in negotiating the changing waters of this particular book, and Nancy DeMoss Wolgemuth, for your encouragement and support;

B&H's incomparable Devin Maddox, Clarissa Dufresne, Susan Browne, Jenaye White, and Mary Wiley, for your wonderful expertise in your various fields and your gracious help in getting this here book out the door;

Jennifer Lyell, for your original vision for this book, and for being a champion for EE;

Dr. Kathryn Long, thank you for so meticulously going through this manuscript, for your uniquely nuanced historical insights, and for your friendship; Dr. Jim Yost, thank you for your wry expertise regarding the Waodani and the challenges of working with indigenous groups, issues that laypeople like me know little about;

Anthony Solis, for graciously sharing tons of research, as well as for your input on the manuscript; Sue Moye, for enthusiastic research help, and for dropping off TP and masks when COVID hit—you're an all-purpose friend;

Steve and Ginny Saint, for so many thoughtful reflections and for your hospitality in the midst of your tribe of dozens of grandchildren;

Phil Saint, for so kindly translating my interviews in Ecuador and for so many thoughtful insights, Jim Tingler, I-TEC USA; Jaime Saint, Galo Ortiz, and the amazing I-TEC guys in Ecuador, for keeping me alive in the Amazonian jungle, as I was quite pleased about that;

Miriam Gebb, who went to Ecuador for a short-term medical mission about forty years ago, and still faithfully serves there today, for your insights and stories; Chet and Katie Williams, for your hospitality in Shell and your "ministry of presence" among the Waodani;

Jon and Jeanne Lindskoog, for your friendship in the jungle and memories of long-ago events in Ecuador, and for your copies of photographs of the 1956 recovery expedition;

Gary Tennant, missionary near Tena, Ecuador, for info on the Elliot house in Shandia;

Bob Shuster and colleagues at the Wheaton archives, for your expertise and gracious help;

Kevin and Jan Engel, for your cozy hospitality in Wheaton;

Cynthia Fantasia, Lisa Steigerwalt, Sarah Christmyer, for your memories of EE; Paul and Jeannie Edwards, thank you for housing me in the China Room of your Gordon College manor;

Lois Bechtel, for your sunny insights about your mom, Katherine Morgan, and her story, and thanks to Hyatt and Anne Moore, for putting me in touch with Lois—I love the tapestry of connections in God's family;

Margaret Ashmore, Kathy Gilbert, Cathy Sheetz, Marion Redding, Jan Wismer, Kathy Reeg, thank you for your particular insights into EE, and for your prayer support;

Fellow ICM Board members and friends, and ICM CEO Janice Allen, for prayer support and for connecting ICM with Elisabeth Elliot's adventures in Ecuador; the Waponi Women, for your prayer support; Albert Allen of ICM, for your creativity and patience in herding a group of twenty opinionated Waponi Women to Shell, Ecuador;

Patti Bryce, for life-long friendship and prayer and manuscript review; Lisa and Scott Lampman, Babs and Rob Bickhart, Mary Ann Bell, Ellen and David Leitch, for your enthusiasm and prayer support;

My sisters Gloria Hawley and Gail Harwood, for your prayers;

Jamie Longo and Carey Keefe, literary visionaries and strange-event magnets;

Wendy Fotopolous and Sheila McGee and Sheila's small group, for commenting on early drafts of the book's first few chapters;

Supper Club, Medium Group, HMS, CHEEKS, T-Time, Joanne Kemp's Friday Group, for such kind prayer solidarity through many rough waters;

Rachael Mitchell, for your funny comments and excellent review of the manuscript draft;

Jim and Andie Young, for your loving hospitality and cheering me on in all things EE during Lee's long hospitalization; UPMC surgeons Dr. Paul Gardner, Dr. Carl Snyderman, Dr. Dade Lundsford, Dr. Mario Solari, and all on their teams for your creative expertise in addressing Lee's significant medical challenges;

Lee, Emily, Brielle and Daniel, Haley, and Walker: thank you, as always, for your support, curiosity, care, and prayer as I slogged through yet another book. I love you forever!

Ellen Vaughn
Reston, Virginia
June 11, 2020

Notes

CHAPTER 1

1. Jim Elliot, letter to parents as quoted in *Shadow of the Almighty*, 55.
2. It can also be spelled "Waorani."
3. Were I to reference every single one of Elisabeth's journal entries throughout this book, the hundreds of footnotes would litter the reader's experience. For that reason, I've elected not to note journal entries throughout. Also, for what it's worth, wherever Elisabeth used "+" in her dozens of journals, I've replaced it with "and" for smoother reading.

CHAPTER 2

1. "'Go Ye and Preach the Gospel': Five Do and Die," *Life* magazine (January 30, 1956), 10. [Vol. 40 No. 5].
2. Elisabeth Elliot, *Who Shall Ascend: The Life of R. Kenneth Strachan of Costa Rica* (New York, NY: Harper & Row, 1958), xi.
3. Ibid., xii.
4. Ibid., xii, emphasis added.

CHAPTER 3

1. Interview of Elisabeth Howard Gren by Robert Shuster, March 26, 1985, Collection 278, Tape T2, Wheaton College Archives, https://www2.wheaton.edu/bgc/archives/transcripts/cn278t02.pdf.
2. Tom Howard interview with Kathryn Long, February 14, 2002.
3. Tom Howard interview with Ellen Vaughn, June 19, 2018.

CHAPTER 5

1. Hampden Coit DuBose and his wife arrived in China in 1872, settled in Suzhou (Soochow), and served there thirty-eight years until his death. He is remembered not only as a preacher and evangelist, but as founder of the Anti-Opium League, which informed and mobilized public opinion against its nefarious trade. Dubose enlisted the support of President Theodore Roosevelt, the U.S. Congress, and the International Opium Commission, and in 1906 the British Parliament declared the trade "morally indefensible." A petition signed by more than one thousand missionaries was presented to the emperor. An imperial edict (following verbatim the petition Dubose had drafted) prohibited its trade and use. He was honored in Suzhou with a stone monument and in the United States by being elected moderator of the General Assembly of the Presbyterian Church, U.S. (Southern) in 1891, http://bdcconline.net/en/stories/dubose-hampden-coit.

2. EH to "Dearest Folks," May 5, 1946.

3. Elisabeth Elliot Newsletter, May/June 2002 and Elisabeth Elliot interview with Bob Schuster, March 26, 1985, Collection 278 Papers of Elisabeth Elliot, CN 278. Billy Graham Center Archives, https://archives.wheaton.edu/repositories/4/resources/484; accessed February 27, 2020.

4. Elisabeth Elliot, *A Chance to Die: The Life and Legacy of Amy Carmichael* (Old Tappan, NJ: Revel, 1987), 15.

5. http://www.elisabethelliot.org/newsletters/2002-05-06.pdf

6. http://dohnavurfellowship.org/amycarmichael/

CHAPTER 6

1. EH to "Dearest Mother," September 12, 1944.

2. Wheaton President V. Raymond Edman letter to incoming freshmen, August 1944.

3. EH to "Dearest Mother," September 12, 1944.

4. Ibid.

5. https://www2.wheaton.edu/bgc/archives/transcript/cn278t02.pdf

6. EH to "Dearest Folks," September 24, 1944.

7. https://www.bartleby.com/39/36.html

8. EH letter to family, February 4, 1945.

9. EH letter to "Mother," February 1945.

10. EH letter to "Mother," January 26, 1945.

11. EH letter to "Mother," October 9, 1945.

12. Ibid.

13. Anthony Solis, of Wheaton, Illinois, is a patient and meticulous researcher who was of immeasurable help with research details on this project.

14. Phil Howard to "Dear Betty," October 1, 1943.
15. Phil Howard to "Dear Betty," October 1, 1943.
16. EH to "Dearest Mother," March 12, 1945.
17. Quotes in this section are from EE letters of September 10, 12, 14, 1944. Phil's letter is October 1, 1943.
18. EH to "Dearest Folks," May 5, 1946.

CHAPTER 7

1. Pvt. Albert, in Australia, to Betty Howard, January 26, 1945.
2. Pvt. Albert, in Australia, to Betty Howard, January 26, 1945.
3. Ibid.
4. EH to parents, April 15, 1945.
5. EH to parents, April 20, 1945.
6. https://www2.wheaton.edu/bgc/archives/transcripts/cn278t02.pdf
7. EH to parents, October 21, 1945.
8. EH to "Dearest Folks," February 2, 1945.
9. EH to parents, October 14, 1945.
10. Ibid.
11. EH to "Dearest Mother," October 6, 1946.
12. EH to "Dearest Folks," January 18, 1946.
13. EH letter to "Dearest Folks," May 5, 1946.

CHAPTER 8

1. EH to "Dearest Mother," September 14, 1946.
2. EH to "Dearest Mother," September 20, 1946.
3. EH to "Dearest Mother," October 6, 1946.
4. EH to "Dearest Mother," October 6, 1946.
5. EH to "Dearest Mother," October 6, 1946.
6. Interview of Elisabeth Howard Gren by Robert Shuster, March 26, 1985, Collection 278, Tape T2, Wheaton College Archives.
7. EH to "Dearest Folks," November 11, 1946: "Mother, please stop being concerned for 'poor George.'"
8. EH to "Dearest Folks," December 1, 1946.
9. EE letter to "Mother," February 10, 1946.
10. Interview of Elisabeth Howard Gren by Robert Shuster, March 26, 1985, Collection 278, Tape T2, Wheaton College Archives, https://www2.wheaton.edu/bgc/archives/transcripts/cn278t02.pdf.

CHAPTER 9

1. Dave Howard, https://urbana.org/blog/my-roommate-jim-elliot.

2. Ibid.

3. Elisabeth Elliot, *Shadow of the Almighty* (New York: Harper, 1958), 117, journal entry from January 4, 1950.

4. Ibid., 39.

5. Ibid., 50.

6. David Howard, interview with Kathryn Long, May 31, 2000, as well as similar comments in interview with Ellen Vaughn, February 7, 2018.

7. From *Shadow of the Almighty*, 56–57.

8. *Journals of Jim Elliot*, edited by Elisabeth Elliot, entry for June 10, 1948 (Old Tappan, NJ: Revell, 1978), 65.

CHAPTER 10

1. Elisabeth Elliot, *Let Me Be a Woman* (Carol Stream, IL: Tyndale, 1976), 30–31.

2. Elisabeth Elliot, *Shadow of the Almighty* (New York: Harper, 1958), 98.

3. Dave Howard, https://urbana.org/blog/my-roommate-jim-elliot.

4. Ibid.

5. Ibid.

6. The Elisabeth Elliot Newsletter, September/October 1989, "A Call to Older Women."

7. Ibid.

8. EH to "My own dearest Mother," Feb. 9, 1949.

9. Ibid.

10. Ibid.

11. Ibid.

CHAPTER 11

1. Elisabeth Elliot, *Shadow of the Almighty* (New York: Harper, 1958), 55.

2. Ibid., 108.

3. Ibid., 73.

4. Ibid., 117, citing Jim's journal of January 4, 1950; also Elisabeth Elliot, editor, *The Journals of Jim Elliot* (Old Tappan, NJ: Fleming H. Revell Company, 1978), 205.

5. Elisabeth Elliot, *Through Gates of Splendor* (Carol Stream, IL: Tyndale, 2005), 253.

6. https://www2.wheaton.edu/bgc/archives/faq/20.htm

7. From Jim's journal, Oct. 28, 1949, see photo on https://www2. wheaton.edu/bgc/archives/faq/20.htm.

8. Elisabeth Elliot, *Let Me Be a Woman* (Carol Stream, IL: Tyndale, 1976), 26.

9. Elisabeth Elliot, *Passion and Purity: Learning to Bring Your Love Life Under Christ's Control* (1984; repr., Grand Rapids, MI: Revell, 2002), 61–62.

10. All these gems are from Jim Elliot to EH, September 19, 1949.

11. Jim Elliot to Betty Howard, September 22, 1949.

12. EH to JE, September 27, 1949.

13. Ibid.

14. JE to EH, October 7, 1949.

15. Ibid.

16. EH to JE, October 14, 1949.

17. Kathryn Long, "Jim Elliot and Nate Saint: Missionary Biography and Evangelical Spirituality," unpublished typescript of chapter 3, Narrative [draft] 2, 114, God in the Rainforest (New York: Oxford University Press, 2019). Unpublished chapter copyright 2015, Kathryn T. Long, used by permission.

CHAPTER 12

1. Jonathan Edwards, "A Treatise Concerning Religious Affections, 1746," quotes from online edition by International Outreach, Inc., PO Box 1286, Ames, Iowa, 50014, 79.

2. See Ellen Vaughn, *Radical Gratitude* (Grand Rapids: Zondervan, 2005). I wasn't immersed, as I am now, in Elisabeth Elliot's writings when I wrote this book fifteen years ago, but smiled when I found such congruency in our conclusions about the power of radical gratitude.

3. JE to EH, November 28, 1950.

4. Elisabeth Elliot, ed., *The Journals of Jim Elliot* (Old Tappan, NJ: Fleming H. Revell Company, 1978), 349.

5. Ibid.

CHAPTER 13

1. Interview of Elisabeth Howard Gren by Robert Shuster, March 26, 1985, Collection 278, Tape T2, Wheaton College Archives, https://www2.wheaton.edu/bgc/archives/transcripts/cn278t02.pdf.

2. Carl E. Armerding, *Brethren Historical Review*, Vol. 11, 2014, obituaries, "Elisabeth Elliot (1926–2015): Accidental Brethren Missionary?" 115–16, quoting Elisabeth Howard Carol Smith Graham, October 17, 1952.

3. http://ourlifecelebrations.com/2015/05/hospice-pioneer-traces -family-line-faith/

4. Email correspondence with Lois Bechtel on February 28, 2020.

5. Ibid.

6. Armerding, "Elisabeth Elliot (1926–2015: Accidental Brethren Missionary?" 118.

7. Elisabeth Elliot interview with Bob Schuster, March 26, 1985, Collection 278 Papers of Elisabeth Elliot, CN 278; Billy Graham Center Archives, https://archives.wheaton.edu/repositories/4/resources/484; Accessed February 27, 2020.

8. EE letter home, September 24, 1955.

9. Elisabeth Elliot Gren, *Discipline, the Glad Surrender* (Old Tappan, NJ: Fleming H. Revell, 1982), 141.

CHAPTER 14

1. Elisabeth Elliot, *These Strange Ashes: Is God Still in Charge?* (Ann Arbor, MI: Servant Publications, 1998), 16.

2. Ibid.

3. Elisabeth Elliot, *Shadow of the Almighty* (New York: Harper, 1958), 173.

4. Elisabeth Elliot, ed., *The Journals of Jim Elliot* (Old Tappan, NJ: Fleming H. Revell Company, 1978), 400.

5. Betty Howard to "Mother, dearest," August 6, 1952.

6. *The Journals of Jim Elliot*, 406.

7. Betty Howard to "Mother, dearest," August 6, 1952.

8. Olive Fleming Liefeld, *Unfolding Destinies* (Grand Rapids, MI: Discovery House, 1998), 122.

9. Liefeld, *Unfolding Destinies*, 129.

10. Betty Howard to "Mother dearest," August 15, 1952.

CHAPTER 15

1. Elisabeth Elliot, *These Strange Ashes: Is God Still in Charge?* (Ann Arbor, MI: Servant Publications, 1998), 24–26.

2. Ibid.

3. Ibid., 35.

4. Ibid., 39.

5. Ibid., 51.

6. Ibid.

CHAPTER 16

1. Elisabeth Elliot, *These Strange Ashes: Is God Still in Charge?* (Ann Arbor, MI: Servant Publications, 1998), 94–95.

2. Ibid., 60.

3. Ibid., 62.

4. Ibid., 63.

5. Ibid., 127.

6. EH letter to "Dearest Folks," February 1, 1953.

7. JE letter to his parents, February 2, 1953.

8. JE letter to "My dear Mr. and Mrs. Howard," February 1, 1953.

9. These adjusted and annotated quotations are from Betty's journal of February 1953.

10. EH July 1953 letter to "Dear Friends."

11. Ibid.

12. Elliot, *These Strange Ashes*, 125–26.

13. Ibid., 127.

14. Quoted in *These Strange Ashes*, 127.

15. *These Strange Ashes*, 127, emphasis added.

CHAPTER 17

1. EE to "Dearest Mother," March 17, 1953.

2. Elisabeth Elliot, *Shadow of the Almighty* (New York: Harper, 1958), 212.

3. Ibid., 212.

4. EE to "Dearest Family," November 19, 1953.

5. Elliot, *Shadow of the Almighty*, 214.

6. EE to "Dearest Family," November 19, 1953.

7. EE to "Dearest Folks," Dec. 5, 1953.

8. EE to "Dearest Family," Dec. 17, 1953.

9. EE to "Dearest Folks," Dec. 5, 1953.

10. EE to "Dear Folks," March 13, 1954.

11. EE to "Dearest Family," December 17, 1953.

12. Ibid.

13. Ibid.

14. Russell Hitt, *Jungle Pilot* (Grand Rapids, MI: Discovery House, 1959), 160.

15. Ibid., caption in photo section.

16. EE to "Dearest Folks," December 5, 1953.

17. Quoted in EE to "Dearest Folks," April 15, 1954.

18. Elliot, *Shadow of the Almighty*, 218.

19. EE to "Dearest Folks," May 8, 1954.

20. EE to "Dearest Folks," May 30, 1954.

21. Elliot, *Shadow of the Almighty*, 220.

22. EE to "Dearest Family," November 29, 1954.

23. JE to "Dear Folks," October 8, 1954.

24. EE to "Mother," November 19, 1954.

25. EE to "Dearest Mother," December 11, 1954.

26. EE to "Dearest Family," October 28, 1954.

27. EE letter to family, November 8, 1954.

CHAPTER 18

1. Elisabeth Elliot, *Shadow of the Almighty* (New York: Harper, 1958), 223.

2. Ibid.

3. Elisabeth Elliot, *Through Gates of Splendor* (Carol Stream, IL: Tyndale, 2005), 59.

4. Russell Hitt, *Jungle Pilot* (Grand Rapids, MI: Discovery House, 1959), 160.

5. This is according to Phil Saint, with whom I visited the Nate Saint house in Shell—and the Waodani in the jungle—in July 2019.

CHAPTER 19

1. Elisabeth Elliot, *Shadow of the Almighty* (New York: Harper, 1958), 225.

2. EE letter to "Dearest Family," May 25, 1955.

3. Ibid.

4. These events from 1955, not necessarily in chronological order, are designed to give a sense of the Elliots' lives and ministry in the jungle.

5. EE to "Dear Family," October 28, 1955.

6. EE to "Dearest Family," June 5, 1955.

7. "Excerpts from Peter Fleming's Letter, November 26, 1955," *The Fields*, February 1956, the magazine of Christian Missions in Many Lands, New York, NY.

CHAPTER 20

1. Kathryn Long, "Jim Elliot and Nate Saint: Missionary Biography and Evangelical Spirituality," unpublished typescript of chapter 3, Narrative [draft] 2, 114, *God in the Rainforest* (New York: Oxford University Press, 2019) Unpublished chapter copyright 2015, Kathryn T. Long. Used by permission.

2. Ibid.

3. Elisabeth Elliot Gren, interviewed by Kathryn T. Long, June 27, 2001, Magnolia, MA, Accession 19–15, Papers of Kathryn Long, 1949–2018, Billy Graham Center Archives, Wheaton, IL. Used by permission.

4. EE letter to "Dearest Folks," May 15, 1961.

5. Elisabeth Elliot Gren, interviewed by Kathryn T. Long.

6. Elisabeth Elliot, ed., *Journals of Jim Elliot* (Old Tappan, NJ: Fleming H. Revell Company, 1978), 451.

7. Now called Cairn University.

8. Rachel often told her nephew, Steve Saint, about her call to work with the Waodani. Interviews with Steve Saint, Dunnellon, Florida, April 22–26, 2019.

9. R. Saint, "Unreached . . . and Unreachable?" February 9, 1955, unpublished typescript to friends and financial supporters, Edman Records, Wheaton College Archives, Wheaton, IL, quoted by Long, *God in the Rainforest*, 49.

10. Wade Davis, *One River* (New York, NY: Touchstone, 1996), 250.

CHAPTER 21

1. Nate's letter to Rachel, and the account of the men's plans, are drawn in part from *Jungle Pilot*, by Russell T. Hitt, 1959, published at the time by the Auca Foundation, updated edition released in 1997, Discovery House Publishers.

2. Hitt, *Jungle Pilot*, 262.

3. EE to "Dear Mother and Dad and family, and Mom and Dad Elliot and family," January 27, 1956.

4. Hitt, *Jungle Pilot*, 232.

5. As quoted by Elisabeth Elliot in *Through Gates of Splendor* (Old Tappan NJ: Fleming H. Revell Co., 1978), 152–54.

6. Olive Fleming Liefeld, *Unfolding Destinies* (Grand Rapids, MI: Discovery House, 1998), 192.

7. Elliot, *Through Gates of Splendor*, 145–46ish.

8. "Rescue or Search?" unpublished paper released by Frank Drown in January 2010, 8.

9. Hitt, *Jungle Pilot*, 266.

10. Jim Elliot journal selections from *The Journals of Jim Elliot*, ed. Elisabeth Elliot (Old Tappan: NJ: Fleming H. Revell, 1978), 470–75.

11. Liefeld, *Unfolding Destinies*, 198.

12. Nate's quotes are from *Jungle Pilot*, 272.

13. Ibid.

14. JE journal, December 31, 1955, Billy Graham Center archives, Wheaton, IL.

CHAPTER 22

1. Quoted in EE to "Dear Mother and Dad and family, and Mom and Dad Elliot and family," January 27, 1956.

2. Like the account of the killings, descriptions of Nenkiwi's deception and the displacement of the tribe's rage toward the North Americans vary on some points, but accounts agree on the major thrust and development of the angry discussion. Some who were part of the recovery effort concluded that the Waodani did not throw the bodies into the river, but that the missionaries backed into the water, showing that they would not fight, but firing their guns in the air in an effort to frighten the Waodani. The beach was torn up with deep heel marks and signs of struggle; the recovery party found spent shell casings. This account draws on information available years later from translated accounts from Mincaye and Gikita, Kathryn Long's *God in the Rainforest*, and Steve Saint's discussions with the Waodani regarding what transpired that day, as relayed in my interview with Steve in April 2019. Nenkiwi was speared, and buried alive, by other Waodani in unrelated events about a year or two after the missionaries' deaths.

CHAPTER 23

1. EE to "Dear Mother and Dad and family, and Mom and Dad Elliot and family," January 29, 1956.
2. Frank's descriptions are from Frank Drown, *Rescue or Search?* an unpublished article about the missionaries and the search party's expedition on the Curaray, circulated in January 2010 from his home in Kansas City, MO.
3. All this is from Frank Drown's memoir of the recovery efforts.
4. EE to "Dearest Mother and Mom," February 8, 1956.

CHAPTER 24

1. EE to "Dear Betty and Joe," January 29, 1956.
2. EE to "Dearest Family," April 2, 1956.

CHAPTER 25

1. Jeremiah 6:2, 12 (emphasis added)
2. As quoted from Cornell Capa and Richard Whelan, eds. *Cornell Capa Photographs* (Boston: Little, Brown, 1992), 152, in Kathryn Long, "Cameras 'Never Lie': The Role of Photography in Telling the Story of American Evangelical Missions," Kathryn T. Long, *Church History* magazine, December 2003.
3. EE to "Dear Mother and Dad and family, and Mom and Dad Elliot and family," January 27, 1956.
4. Long, "Cameras 'Never Lie.'"

5. *The New York Times*, Philip Gefter, May 24, 2008, https://www.nytimes.com/2008/05/24/arts/design/23cnd-capa.html.

6. Capa wrote in 1963, "It took me some time to realize that the camera is a mere tool, capable of many uses, and at last I understood that, for me, its role, its power, and its duty are to comment, describe, provoke discussion, awaken conscience, evoke sympathy, spotlight human misery and joy which otherwise would pass unseen, un-understood and unnoticed. I have been interested in photographing the everyday life of my fellow humans and the commonplace spectacle of the world around me, and in trying to distill out of these their beauty and whatever is of permanent interest," https://www.nytimes.com/2008/05/24/arts/design/24capa.html.

7. http://artdaily.com/news/24409/Cornell-Capa--Founder-of-International-Center-of-Photography--Died-at-90#.XWflql2JI_4

8. http://artdaily.com/news/24409/Cornell-Capa--Founder-of-International-Center-of-Photography--Died-at-90#.XXZ3zF2JI_4

9. EE to "Dearest Folks," May 15, 1961.

CHAPTER 26

1. Wade Davis, *One River* (New York: Simon & Schuster, 1996), 264. "When the news of her brother's death reached Rachel Saint, her first reaction, by all accounts, was not grief but anger at the thought that he had dared to contact the [Waodani] without her."

2. Kathryn T. Long, *God in the Rainforest* (New York: Oxford University Press, 2019), 65.

3. Ibid.

4. EE to "Dearest Folks," January 9, 1955.

5. Long, *God in the Rainforest*, 51.

6. *Time*'s article observed, "Having run through every faded actress still able to cry on cue. Ralph Edwards' This Is Your Life, probably the most sickeningly sentimental show on the air, lately turned to ordinary people as subjects for its weekly, treacly 'true-to-life' biographies." "Television: This Is Your Wife?" *Time*, October 17, 1960.

7. Review of *Through Gates of Splendor*, by Elisabeth Elliot, *Evangelical Christian*, February 1958, Folder 5, Box 1 EHE Papers, Billy Graham Center Archives, Wheaton College.

8. Letter from H. E. Lowrance to J. G. Parrott, August 30, 1956, MAF Records.

9. Ibid.

10. Long, *God in the Rainforest*, 69.

11. See Kathryn Long, *God in the Rainforest*, pages 69–70, for a fuller picture of these tensions between mission agencies in the context of evangelization among the Waodani.

12. Hobey Lowrance to Grady Parrott and Jim Truxton, November 15, 1957, Folder 23, Box 5, MAF Records, italics in the original.

CHAPTER 27

1. EE letter to Elliots and Howards, May 13, 1957.
2. Betty Elliot notes, November 13, 1957, Curaray River.
3. EE notes from the Curaray, November 23, 1957.

CHAPTER 28

1. EE to parents, June 6, 1958.
2. Kathryn T. Long, *God in the Rainforest* (New York: Oxford University Press, 2019), 86.
3. Biola, mentioned in EE correspondence to family February 5, 1958.

CHAPTER 29

1. Elisabeth Elliot, *The Savage My Kinsman* (Ann Arbor, MI: Servant Publishers, 1961), 41.
2. EE to parents, May 15, 1958.
3. Account used in correspondence, 4/14/58, journal, and *The Savage My Kinsman*, 42.
4. Rachel Saint journal, undated entry, June 1958.
5. Rachel Saint journal, June 10, 1958.
6. Rachel Saint journal, July 17, 1958.
7. Ibid.
8. EE letter to family, June 28, 1958.
9. EE letter to family, July 15, 1958.
10. Kathryn T. Long, *God in the Rainforest* (New York: Oxford University Press, 2019), 87.
11. The aftermath of Dr. Tremblay's demise shows the cruelty, which, along with great charm, was a central characteristic of Waodani culture. Dr. Jim Yost, who lived with the Waodani for many years, says that, "They love this story." This account of Dr. Tremblay's death is a composite taken from several sources: Long, *God in the Rainforest*, 86–87; letter from Mary quoting Betty to Dr. and Mrs. Howard, Sam and Jeanne, November 6, 1958; John Man and Jim Yost, transcript of "Oral History Interview with Waodani," April 1987, Ecuador, 92–95, Yost Papers;

Mincaye et al., as told to Tim Paulson, *Gentle Savage Still Seeking the End of the Spear* (Maitland, FL: Xulon Press, 2013), 203–8.

12. EE prayer letter, July 23, 1958.

CHAPTER 30

1. "They just said they speared them. So then I talked to them about the nice foreigners. They said, 'Now we understand. Now we see that we did this for nothing. It was only because [Nenkiwi] lied.'" Translation of tape made by Betty Elliot interviewing Dayuma, conversation in Quichua, September 25, 1958.

2. Betty spelled Mincaye's name differently in her journal entries, but I've elected to use this more common spelling of his name that is used today. Many Waodani names can be spelled a number of different ways when they're rendered into English.

3. Elisabeth Elliot, *The Savage My Kinsman* (Ann Arbor, MI: Servant Publishers, 1961), 135.

4. EE to "Dear Folks," February 6, 1961.

CHAPTER 31

1. https://www.itecusa.org/2015/07/16/do-the-next-thing-elisabeth -elliot-rachel-saint/

2. Emphasis added, Elisabeth Elliot, *The Savage My Kinsman*, originally published 1961, Harper, revised edition, Servant Publications, 1996, Epilogue II, 151.

3. EE's description to Kathryn Long, interview transcript from 2001, though the spelling in the transcript—*owiyaki*—was corrected by Jim Yost to what is used here.

CHAPTER 32

1. This description, typical of Betty's wry observations of New Yorkers, is from the February 2, 1960 opening of Cornell Capa's exhibit of his brother Robert Capa's famous photographs.

2. Romans 1:14 AMP

3. From D. H. Lawrence, *Lady Chatterley's Lover*, 1928, as copied in Betty's journal, May 10, 1960.

CHAPTER 33

1. Email from Dr. Yost to ESV, February 16, 2020.

2. Mentioned in letter to "Mother" April 8, 1961.

3. We should note that Betty's translation reflects her best under-standing of the Waodani language at that time. Dr. Yost notes that her jottings are interesting "since 'to think,' 'to believe,' 'to remember' are all the same word. Only a greater context can tell which rendering to use in English, although maybe our distinguishing/contrasting them may not even be appropriate. To a Waodani speaker it's all the same semanti-cally. A mental activity. The Waorani I know who have no contact with Christian beliefs and practices are confused by the Christian distinc-tions." Email from Dr. Yost to ESV, February 16, 2020.

4. EE to "Dearest Folks," June 28, 1961.

CHAPTER 34

1. EE to "Dearest Folks," November 13, 1961.

2. Kathryn T. Long, *God in the Rainforest* (New York: Oxford University Press, 2019), 130.

3. Rachel Saint to Cameron Townsend, January 1, 1962, Townsend Archives #21126, quoted by Long, *God in the Rainforest*, 130.

4. Kenneth Pike to Cameron Townsend, December 14, 1961, Townsend Archives #20052, quoted by Long, *God in the Rainforest*, 130–31.

5. Long, *God in the Rainforest*, 131.

6. Dr. Jim Yost, interview with Kathryn Long, March 15, 2001, Wheaton, IL, quoted in *God in the Rainforest*, 213; confirmed by Dr. Yost in a phone interview with Ellen Vaughn, February 12, 2020.

7. "Stagnant," Catherine Peeke to Rachel Saint, March 20, 1975, Long, *God in the Rainforest*, 208; "Oppressive," Dr. Jim Yost, per-sonal notes, February 22, 1974, Long, *God in the Rainforest*, 205; "Devastating," Patricia Kelley, quoting an anonymous SIL official, in Pat Kelley to Catherine Peeke, n.d. [probably 1977], Peeke Papers, Long, *God in the Rainforest*, 392, n. 59; "Condemning," Peeke to Saint, March 20, 1975, Long, *God in the Rainforest*, 208.

8. Ellen Vaughn phone interview with Dr. Jim Yost, February 13, 2020.

9. For a carefully researched account of Rachel Saint and SIL, see Kathryn Long's *God in the Rainforest*. Dr. Long painstakingly combed through letters, archives, Rachel's own writings, and conducted many interviews to create a dispassionate, historical account of Rachel's rela-tionship with the Waodani and her departure from SIL. See particularly Chapter 12, "Breaking a Pattern of Dependence."

10. Elisabeth Elliot, "To a few who are intimately concerned," November 6, 1961, typed, one-page document enclosed in Dan Derr to

Grady Parrott, November 16, 1961, Folder 69, Box 6, MAF Records, Billy Graham Center Archives, Wheaton College.

11. EE to "Dearest Folks," November 15, 1961.

12. EE to "Dearest Folks," November 29, 1961.

13. EE to "Dearest Mother and Dad," November 13, 1961.

14. Ibid.

15. EE to "Dearest Mother," November 30, 1961.

16. Steve and Ginny Saint were wonderfully hospitable and helpful to me in this project. It was through I-TEC—the ministry Steve started to help indigenous people not just in Ecuador, but around the world—that I traveled to Ecuador, lived in the jungle with some of the Waodani for a few days, and met Mincaye and Kimu, two of the "Palm Beach killers," my brothers in Christ. (Also on this trip I found myself in a wonderful family gathering of sorts. Phil Saint, Nate's youngest son, had brought his wife, Karla, their sons Dan and Ben, their wives, and their kids. Jaime Saint, Steve's son, led the trip. I loved being in the fellowship of the Saints.) Back at home, Steve shared one slim diary written by Rachel Saint in 1958 with me, but did not pass on Rachel's journals from her difficult jungle relationship with Betty Elliot.

17. Steve Saint and Ginny Saint, *Walking His Trail* (Carol Stream, IL: Tyndale, 2007), 34–35.

18. Acts 15:39 NIV

CHAPTER 35

1. EE to "Dearest Family," December 3, 1961.

2. Betty was referencing a William Butler Yeats poem.

3. According to Gary Tennant, a missionary who lives and works not far from current-day Shandia.

4. https://www.britannica.com/place/South-Sudan/Sudanese-independence-and-civil

5. https://michelemorin.net/2018/06/04/the-missionary-faith-paradox/

6. https://hendricksonpublishers.blog/2018/02/21/a-leopard-tamed-a-book-fifty-years-too-early/

7. EE journal, February 14, 1963. "I and Thou" refers to Austrian philosopher Martin Buber's book about the essence of human relationships and the centrality of the ultimate relationship with God.

CHAPTER 37

1. Elisabeth Elliot, *Through Gates of Splendor* (Carol Stream, IL: Tyndale, 2005), 267–72.

CHAPTER 38

1. See Exodus 5:2 NASB.
2. See Exodus 15:22–27.

CHAPTER 39

1. 2 Corinthians 12:9–10 NASB
2. Elisabeth Elliot, *A Lamp Unto My Feet* (Ann Arbor, MI: Servant Publications, 1985), Day 28, Identity.
3. Elisabeth Elliot, *The Savage My Kinsman*, 140.
4. "*Wer bin ich?*" translated from the German by Thomas Albert Howard, https://www.patheos.com/blogs/anxiousbench/2014/09 /bonhoeffers-who-am-i/, emphasis added.

CHAPTER 40

1. Elisabeth Elliot as quoted in https://carolinerosekraft.com/do-the -next-thing-by-elisabeth-elliot/.

CHAPTER 41

1. See Hebrews 5:8.
2. Elisabeth Elliot, *These Strange Ashes: Is God Still in Charge?* (Ann Arbor, MI: Servant Publications, 1998), 145.
3. https://womenofchristianity.com/hast-thou-no-scar-by-amy -carmichael/
4. Elisabeth Elliot, *The Savage My Kinsman* (Ann Arbor, MI: Servant Publishers, 1961), 147.

Photo Credits

Images used with permission from the Capa Archives of the International Center of Photography/Magnum Photos:

Cover image, p. 23, p. 130, p. 161, p. 167 (and front flap), p. 223

Images used with permission from Mission Aviation Fellowship and the Saint family:

p. 4, p. 115, p. 145, p. 153, p. 156, p. 179, p. 212, p. 213, p. 228

Images used with permission from Elisabeth Elliot's daughter, Valerie Shepard:

p. 20, p. 24, p. 63, p. 92, p. 94, p. 109, p. 118, p. 124, p. 171, p. 194, p. 203

Photo used on dedication page taken by Joe Summers.

Author head shot used on inside cover flap taken by Jonathan Whitten.

Photo on page 160 by U.S. Department of Defense. The appearance of U.S. Department of Defense (DoD) visual information does not imply or constitute DoD endorsement.

ELISABETH
&
JIM ELLIOT

WERE MARKED BY THEIR LOVE *for* EACH OTHER & THEIR LOVE *for* THE LORD.

Jim's life was cut short when he attempted to bring the gospel to the Waodani people of Ecuador. Elisabeth lived a life of faith, but also a life of great suffering. Her final message reveals that her suffering was actually the greatest gateway for joy. That never-before-published message is available now, along with a book by Elisabeth and Jim's daughter Valerie about the love of her parents.

ELISABETHELLIOTBOOKS.COM

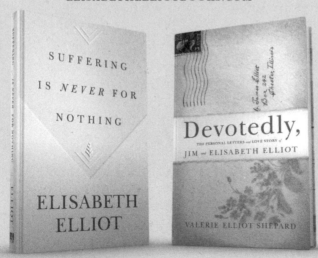

Available wherever books are sold